THE FILMS OF CARLOS SAURA

THE FILMS OF CARLOS SAURA

THE PRACTICE OF SEEING

Marvin D'Lugo

PRINCETON UNIVERSITY PRESS   PRINCETON, NEW JERSEY

Library of Congress Cataloging-in-Publication Data
D'Lugo, Marvin, 1943–
The films of Carlos Saura : the practice of seeing / Marvin
D'Lugo.
p.   cm.
Includes bibliographical references.
Includes index.
ISBN 0-691-03142-8—ISBN 0-691-00855-8 (pbk.)
1. Saura, Carlos, 1932–   —Criticism and interpretation.
2. National characteristics, Spanish, in motion pictures.
I. Title.
PN1998.3.S28D57   1991
791.43′0233′092—dc20   90–19244

Publication of this book has been aided by The Program for
Cultural Cooperation Between Spain's Ministry of Culture
and United States' Universities
This book has been composed in Linotron Galliard

A version of the discussions of *Los golfos*, *Peppermint Frappé*, *La prima Angélica*, and *Elisa, vida mía* originally appeared in *Magill's Survey of Cinema: Foreign Language Films*. Reprinted by permission of the publisher, Salem Press, Inc. Copyright Frank N. Magill, 1985. A version of the discussion of *Carmen* appeared in *Wide-Angle* 9.3 (Fall, 1986). Reprinted by permission of The Johns Hopkins University Press.

For Nena and Myque

Contents

Illustrations _____

Stills from *Hooligans* and *Lament for a Bandit* are courtesy of the Filmoteca Española, Madrid. Stills from *Carmen, Love, the Magician,* and *Stilts* are courtesy of Emiliano Piedra. Stills from *El Dorado* and *The Dark Night* are courtesy of Andrés Vicente Gómez. All other stills are courtesy of Elías Querejeta.

Acknowledgments ————————————————————

I AM INDEBTED to a number of individuals in Spain and the United States who have supported the development of this book:

In Spain, the U.S.-Spanish Joint Committee for Educational and Cultural Exchange awarded me two year-long grants which enabled me to explore Saura's work in depth. Special thanks go to Thomas Middleton of the Joint Committee who provided me with the benefit of his knowledge and experience of Spain throughout my work. The Filmoteca Española and the Ministerio de Cultura allowed me access to a large number of films related to this book. In particular, Dolores Devesa and the staff of the Filmoteca Española Library gave me invaluable assistance in locating a critical corpus of journals, stills, and shooting scripts of Saura's films.

I thank Josep María Forn for sharing with me his painful experiences of film censorship. My conversations with Elías Querejeta, Emilio Sanz de Soto, Rafael Azcona, and Antonio Saura Medrano yielded valuable insights that have helped me better understand the critical contexts that shaped Saura's development. My gratitude goes, as well, to José Luis Borau, for both his encouragement in this project and the wealth of information he shared through many lively conversations on Spanish cinema. Finally, of course, my sincere thanks to Carlos Saura, who gave generously of his time during two extended interviews, providing me with both factual information and important perspectives on his films.

In the United States, there are a number of friends and colleagues who have helped me develop my ideas through their discussion and sensitive reading of various portions of the manuscript. My sincere thanks to John Conron who labored with me over early drafts of the book and who provided sage advice about making Saura "readable" for an American audience. The late Katherine Kovacs encouraged this work in its early stages and offered important critical perspectives that have altered my way of looking at Saura. My special thanks to Marsha Kinder for her supportive reading of the manuscript, her invaluable advice for ways to improve it, and her stimulating conversations on Saura and countless other aspects of Spanish film that have inevitably crept into the pages of this book.

I have been fortunate to have found at Clark University the intellectual nourishment from colleagues—Marcia Butzel, Phil Rosen, and Michael Spingler—whose lively discussions of film and culture did much to shape my outlook on Spanish cinema. I give special thanks to William Ferguson for his sensitive and moving translation of verses from Garcilaso de la Vega. Finally, my most profound appreciation goes to Carol D'Lugo whose critical eye in matters of substance as well as style has greatly enriched my own practice of seeing.

THE FILMS OF CARLOS SAURA

Introduction _____

The Practice of Seeing

THE OPENING SEQUENCE of Carlos Saura's twenty-first film, *El Dorado*, returns to the problematic question of sight and belief that has been the conceptual signature of the Spanish film director's style for three decades. The filmic narrative begins with the haunting images of an exotic golden land that first fired the imagination of Spaniards over four hundred years ago. It is a brief re-creation of one of the Indian versions of the tale of the fabled El Dorado in which we see a ritual painting of an Indian's body with shimmering gold dust. At this early point it is too soon to have suffi-cient bearing within the filmic space to recognize that the alluring vision of El Dorado is not a direct representation of events but the efforts of an impressionable young girl, Elvira, the daughter of the fierce Lope de Aguirre, to conjure up the image of the storybook paradise she has so often

1. *El Dorado* (1988)

heard described. Like so much in Saura's films, this scene is the visual representation of the beliefs of other Spaniards.

The year of the film's action is 1560. A royal expedition in the name of his Catholic majesty, Philip II, has gathered in a jungle outpost somewhere along the Peruvian inlets of the Amazon River, preparing to embark on a voyage they are assured will bring them to the mythical golden land. The new world lies open for Spaniards to seize, to discover if not to invent. Yet precisely because they are Spaniards, because self-consciously they define themselves with the cloak of national identity, they are bound by a way of seeing, a spiritual and mental confinement that leads them to impose upon the openness of this unchartered new land the old mental maps of a closed world that was stabilized for them before they left Spain. One of Saura's implicit messages in *El Dorado* is that sight for the Spaniard, even at this early moment, has become institutionalized in what Michel Foucault has called a "discursive practice." Interested in unmasking the rules and dynamics that govern social constructions of knowledge, Foucault defines discursive practice as a "delimitation of a field of objects, the definition of a legitimate perspective for the agent of knowledge, and the fixing of norms for the elaboration of concepts and theories" (Foucault 1977, 199). The importance of the concept of discursive practice lies in its shifting of emphasis away from the impression of historical and cultural homogeneity in a given social or cultural milieu and toward an interrogation of the manner in which this impression of homogeneity becomes embodied "in institutions, in patterns for general behavior, in forms for transmission and diffusion and in pedagogical forms which impose and maintain them" (Foucault 1977, 200).[1]

It is precisely in this light that Saura focuses on the enterprise of "discovery" and "conquest" as symptomatic discursive practices that form and sustain a notion of Spanishness, thereby leading his audience to consider

---

[1] Foucault's discussion of discursive practices arises out of his effort to develop a conceptual framework within which to analyze forms of knowledge. In *The Archeology of Knowledge* (1969: *L'Archéologie du Savoir*) he establishes the notion of "discursive formations," the clusters of rules presumed to govern entities of knowledge and their dispersion. In that discussion, Foucault describes the situation of nineteenth-century medical science out of which he sees emerge particular discursive regularities: "nineteenth century medical science was characterized not so much by its objects or concepts as by a certain *style*, a certain constant manner of statement. For the first time, medicine no longer consisted of a group of traditions, observations, and heterogeneous practices, but of a corpus of knowledge that presupposed the same way of looking at things, the same division of the perceptual field, the same analysis of the pathological fact in accordance with the visible space of the body, the same system of transcribing what one perceived in what one said" (Foucault 1972, 33).

Saura's interrogation of Spanishness suggests the existence of a similar type of discursive regularity which serves as the theoretical matrix within which the Spaniard's sense of identity is shaped and through which his actions are mediated.

the ideological architecture within which the very foundational myth of Spanish cultural identity is situated. The search for El Dorado is seen as the occasion of the massive suppression of the heterogeneity of the New World and its reordering, at least mentally, within the framework of a social and political system that has already assigned fixed meanings to individual and collective experience.

Saura's protagonists are men of the Counterreformation for whom the experience of America has been predetermined by the religious and social biases of a notion of Spanishness emblemized by their ascetic monarch. No longer seeing with the empirical force of their own powers of observation, the Spaniards see only what they have been positioned to see by the political, religious, and economic structures of the cultural ideology of the empire they have been enlisted to explore. Even their notion of individuality has become confused with the idea of the nation, as each Spaniard unconsciously speaks, thinks, and sees himself in the world through a mediation of that collective identity. He conveniently ignores the historical fact that the Spanish nation as he knows it is merely a political fiction that conflates Catholicism with the Spanish state. The nation he calls Spain, once a plural society of different peoples, has only recently been hammered into the "straitjacket of unity by Castilians" (Carr and Fusi 1981, 11). Saura views the extravagant adventure of these Spaniards in search of El Dorado as part of the discursive formation of Spanishness, of a way of seeing oneself in the world, that is still with Spaniards four centuries later.

In his telling of the most famous of the ill-fated expeditions in search of the golden land, Saura frames his narration through the eyes of a character for whom sight and belief have not yet become so fixed, the adolescent Elvira. The action of the film begins as the bright beams of the morning sun awaken Elvira as she lies in her hammock, visualizing that dream of El Dorado as it has been described to her by many of the Indians who are about to serve as guides on this expedition. Juana Torralba, the maid and female guardian to the girl, hurriedly enters the room and is startled to see her young ward still undressed. "Do you believe that El Dorado exists?"[2] Elvira asks the older woman, distancing herself from her dream to now interrogate it. "Of course it does," Juana replies. "Why else would your father get involved in this expedition if it didn't?" Elvira's question defines the young girl's attitude of inquiry toward the received knowledge that is intended to shape her way of seeing the world. Similarly, her maid's answer crystalizes the certitude of beliefs against which Elvira's questions will have to struggle.

Elvira gets out of her hammock and washes herself. As she dries her face, Juana Torralba speaks again: "She arrived last night," alluding now to

---

[2] All dialogue quoted from Saura's films is my own translation.

Dona Inés, the mistress to Pedro de Ursúa, the leader of the expedition. "Did you see her?" Elvira asks. "Is she as beautiful as they say?" "She was all covered up with a shawl," Juana Torralba replies. But Elvira perseveres: "You didn't see her hands? her ankles?" "Her hands, yes," the old woman acknowledges. "Very fine ones, very delicate and white." Elvira looks at her own dark-skinned hands and retorts: "They can't be white because she is a mestiza, the same as I."

From the very beginning of the film, Elvira is identified with the power of specular inquiry: She sees, and, through her gaze, she reasons. But she is a curiously ambivalent character, embodying both narrational norm and deviance. On the one hand, she appears to function as a somewhat conventionalized enunciative figure through whose eyes much of the story of *El Dorado* will be told. In this, Elvira serves as the agency of classical cinematic narration, metaphorically constructing for the spectator a position of coherence in "reading" the fiction of the film. Yet curiously, even as she embodies classical practices of cinematic telling, her questions speak against the regime of dominant cultural meanings, continually exposing its contradictions and gaps, disturbing the conceptual if not always the visual coherence she otherwise appears to embody.

In the enterprise of the conquest, of course, Elvira is a marginal figure. Like certain other Saurian characters, she is an inexperienced child in a world populated by cynical adults. It is not only her age that distinguishes her from other Spaniards; Elvira is also of mixed race in a community that boasts its own *limpieza de sangre*, its "purity of blood." Her skin color, though relegating her to an inferior social place, has given her an awareness of the world around her, forcing her to stand apart from others and, from that distanced position, to begin to practice a different way of seeing. In effect, Saura has transformed Elvira's marginality into a critical subjectivity through which to interrogate the world that has shaped and misshaped her experiences. Through her obstinate practice of seeing, she moves toward a sense of lucidity that everything in this social world has contrived to mask.

By equating Elvira's way of seeing with the film's way of telling its own story, Saura is able to enact a "discursive resistance" (Silverman 1988, 212) to the dominant forms of cultural intelligibility. Her practice of seeing, we quickly come to realize, constitutes a counter-discourse, opposing the textual and cultural unity defined by the Spaniards' manner of imaging themselves in the world. Gravitating toward the symptomatic marks of a troublesome heterogeneity, she continually documents the signs of disruption and discontinuity around her.

Clearly, Elvira's position in *El Dorado* transcends the mere function of enunciation and redefines the narrative as a field of disruptions that address the contemporary audience and begin to engage them in precisely the kind of social, political, and historical inquiry that is dramatized by her place within the fiction. Through this process of specular interrogation, Elvira, in effect, "reauthors" the dominant discourse of Spanish history by reframing it from the perspective of social, cultural, and gender marginalization. In so doing she exposes the underlying assumptions of conceptual and perceptual coherence, the discursive formations that have stabilized a skewed notion of Spanishness.

Within the grand scale of Saura's historical epic, Elvira may appear to many as only a secondary character, but I purposely linger on her cinematic and dramatic function because in her development we find a reflection of and response to the problematic situation that underlies individual perception and belief within Spanish culture: constant themes in the director's development over thirty years. The restaging of spectatorship within the filmic narrative expresses in its most basic form the filmmaker's distrust of the simple visual dictation of social reality that many of his contemporaries during the Franco years were clamoring for in the name of social realism. Almost from the start of his professional career, Saura preferred to use the cinematic medium to map the emotional and spiritual relation of Spaniards to the dubious projections of a mythologized Spain that had "Francoized" Spanish culture. Central to his development, therefore, was the intense scrutiny of the socially determined ways of seeing that the characters in any given film had absorbed as part of their formation as Spaniards. Against the normative patterns of institutionalized social sight, Saura depicted characters who "mirrored" the position of the real spectator of the film, but who, unlike that spectator, paused to gaze and interrogate the social *mise-en-scène* in which they found themselves. Through this interrogative practice of seeing, Saura was able to question the discursive practices that had naturalized the various myths of Spanishness that had formed and deformed the contemporary Spaniard.

To repeat the forms of intelligibility of a repressive and backward society was, to his thinking, a futile task. His intuitive response to this circumstance of constraint was to look outside the illusionist frame of the cinematic project to the place of the spectator, and, from there, to conceptualize his films within an intertextual mode—that is, the folding back upon itself of the discourse of Spanishness, postulating the narrative and its telling as a ". . . rewriting or restructuration of a prior historical or ideological *subtext*" (Jameson 1981, 81). The result of that outward-looking approach is a character such as Elvira, an on-screen spectator whose placement within the fictional space of cinematic action provides a position of coherent reading for the real spectator, but whose destiny within the film's action is to practice a way of seeing that puts those received forms of cultural representation into question.

Though developed as a necessary response to the constraints of state censorship during the final fifteen years of the Franco dictatorship, Saura's hermeneutic "practice of seeing" has remained a critical axis of narration in all his subsequent films. In both periods, what is decisive is Saura's effort to forge a subtle but clear equation between cinematic praxis and social praxis: the pairing of the ways fictional characters look at the world and the way the cinematic apparatus appropriates a spectatorial view of representation. Saura perceives Spain and the historical condition of Spanishness it implies as what Stephen Heath calls ". . . a form of social seeing, a form like other social forms, to be learned, repeated, consumed" (Heath 1972, 21). In dramatizing in his characters this socially determined way of seeing and then juxtaposing it against the defiant practice of seeing of his protagonists, Saura seeks to effect a radical shift in the perspective of his audience as they view the distorted images that not only have constructed their way of seeing, but also have made them the accomplices to their own victimization.

To speak of such conceptual coherence across a body of nearly two dozen films over a period of three decades as the result of a single directorial consciousness naturally begs the polemical question of auteurism. That polemic, however, does not remain on the margins of Saura's films. Rather, it surfaces insistently within a variety of filmic narratives as interrogations of the possibility of individual creativity and, consequently, authorship, in a social milieu that nurtures the cult of false individualism while thwarting legitimate self-expression. From the beginning of his professional career in film in the late 1950s, Saura's aim was not simply to make movies, but, as he would insist, to be the "author" of his films. Motivated to some degree by the examples of European and American *auteurs*—Rossellini, Hitchcock, Buñuel, and the young European directors of the New Wave, particularly Godard and Truffaut—his attraction to cinematic authorship was also a response to the political and cultural environment of Francoist Spain. Early in his career, he established as a goal the control of the means of cinematic expression in choice of subjectmatter, scale of production, script, and direction, which he hoped would enable him to circumvent the censorial constraints that had hampered Spanish filmmakers during the 1950s.

His initiation into commercial filmmaking coincided with the general acceptance in film circles in France, England, and the United States of the idea of the film director as the cinematic auteur. Profoundly influenced by these currents from abroad, many young Spanish filmmakers identified passionately with the notion of cinematic authorship. The handful of liberal film journals in Spain during the fifties and sixties further nurtured this mystique by promoting certain younger Spanish filmmakers as auteurs: Berlanga and Bardem at first, and then Saura, Eceiza, Patino among others (Tubau 1983, 42–43). The aura of authorship was not placed lightly around just any director. The Spanish auteur was mythologized as the heroic opponent of the regime, his very individuality having been shaped by his resistance to the implacable forces of censorship.

Ironically, with the rise to prominence of young auteurs as resistance fighters on the battlefield of cultural politics, the government appropriated for its own advantage the promotion of the cult of authorship. The underlying premise of their packaging of "New Spanish cinema" (the generation of young filmmakers, many of whom had recently emerged from the National Film School in the early sixties, among them Mario Camus, Victor Erice, Angelino Fons, Basilio Martín Patino, Miguel Picazo, and Francisco Regueiro) was to show the outside world that Franco's Spain repudiated its belligerent origins and was opening itself up to new ideas, even to internal political opposition. So strong were the inducements toward auteurism, in fact, that even a decade after French and British film theorists had largely discarded the cult of the auteur for more theoretic readings of cinematic textuality, Spanish filmmakers continued to see themselves as auteurs, fighting a battle against the political forces of Francoist conservative orthodoxy.

Saura is, to a degree, a product of that peculiarly politicized cultural environment. Yet ironically, while actively pursuing such authorial control over the material aspects of filmic production, he reveals within his films clear evidence that the notion of authorship remains for him a problematic issue. Running parallel to nearly every one of his films, and intimately related to the hermeneutics of sight, multiple allegories of authorship can be discerned. These symbolic representations place under a mark of suspicion the very presumption of the characters' individuality that, outside the fictionality of the film, Saura himself appears to pursue.

His filmography, in effect, evolves as a double-tiered configuration of dramatized authors "inside" the text and the biographical author "outside" the text," as described by Kaja Silverman (193–212), each in apparent conflict with the other. As he achieves progressively more authorial control, his protagonists seem more emphatically locked in the trap of discovering the social and historical constraints that negate their ideal of autonomy. Not more than a half dozen of his characters are literal authors-in-the-text. Yet, throughout his other films the paradigm evolves of individuals who strive to achieve a figurative authorship, that is, as the external author has done, to become the originator of discourse.

That authorial discourse is most often expressed within Saura's films through a scopic register the underlying energy of which, as in the case of Elvira, is narrativized as the ability to question the world through the agency of one's own gaze and thereby to uncover the possibilities of an individuality that the ideological apparatus of Spanish culture has denied. What is clearly at the root of this development is the strategy of equating cinematic sight with social sight and, through that equation, exploring the constructions of individuality within the space of Spanish culture.

In *The Imaginary Signifier*, Christian Metz argues that "the cinematic institution is not just the cinema industry . . . it is also the mental machinery—another industry—which spectators 'accustomed to the cinema' have internalized historically and which has adapted them to the consumption of films. The institution is outside us and inside us, indistinctly collective and intimate, sociological and psychoanalytic . . ." (Metz 1982, 19). The function of Saura's specularized authors-in-the-text is to place in question the larger relation of cinema to the dominant forms of cultural and political imaging that spectators have internalized. Such patterns of figuration within the cinematic text are aimed at exposing for the audience the discursive practices that shape their own sight and, consequently, their knowledge and understanding of the world. With Saura, therefore, it is less an issue of authorship per se than of the "allegories of authorship" through which the filmmaker explores the problematic dimensions of individuality within repressive Spanish society, though, obviously, those allegories allude to a real author.

As Stephen Heath contends, the basic argument of film theorists against the auteurist approach has been that the figure of the author represents a denial of the heterogeneity of the textual enterprise: "The function of the author (the effect of the idea of authorship) is a function of unity; the use of the notion of the author involves the organization of the film (as 'work') and, in so doing, it avoids—that is indeed its function—the thinking of the articulation of the film text in relation to ideology" (Heath 1981, 217). Yet precisely because of their troubled sense of autonomy, Saura's on-screen authors unmask the cinematic text as a site of that heterogeneity. Unlike the Romantic notion of the author as hero and originator of discourse, Saura's allegories of authorship are posed as problems, not solutions: the tension between the creative agency of the individual as author of his acts and the contrary figuration of the individual as a socially constructed subject in ideology.

Finally, if the question of the author is to have any meaning in relation to Saura's films, it is not in terms of any mystically construed, oracular author as Heath rightly notes, but rather as what Foucault called the author-function, ". . . not defined by the spontaneous attribution of a text to its creator, but through a series of precise and complex procedures; it does not refer, purely and simply, to an actual individual insofar as it simultaneously gives rise to a variety of egos and to a series of subjective positions that individuals of any class may come to occupy" (Foucault 1977, 130–31).

Throughout Saura's work the polemic of authorship continuously shifts ground to the empowerment of the spectator, displacing notions of textual unity from the mystique of authorial origins to the locus of spectatorial reading. In those cinematic texts designated by Saura's name, the author and the spectator increasingly merge into a single figure defined against the constraining norms of a social order by a defiant and, at times, renegade practice of seeing.

I   ———————————————————————

The Burden of Spanishness

The Formative Years

SHORTLY after the completion of Carlos Saura's first feature-length film, *Los golfos* (1959: Hooligans), an article appeared in a Spanish film magazine in which the young director reflected on the cultural underdevelopment that he had to endure given his country's social, intellectual, and artistic backwardness. "To make films in Spain," Saura wrote, "is a thankless task. There is no doubt that we have begun to make films prematurely. We haven't had the opportunity of knowing the films that were made elsewhere, nor even the chance to familiarize ourselves with our own classics. Then all at once, we hear about a film that a friend, better informed than we, has seen. Someone who had the chance to run off to France returned to tell us about what he had seen. Those of my generation are self-taught, abandoned to intuition, and only with a great effort are we bringing ourselves up-to-date" (Saura 1960, 8).

In the hostile political environment of Francoist Spain, where writers had long since mastered the symbolic codes of expression to circumvent the censors, Saura's personal lament was easily read as a coded denunciation of the restrictive cultural policies of the dictatorship that had marginalized Spain and Spaniards in the world. For centuries, of course, Spain's intellectuals, artists, and writers had struggled against that repressive cultural climate, and even if the Franco dictatorship had, in a sense, formalized the style and dogma of backwardness into a state ideology, Saura's plight was not qualitatively different from the predicament that creative artists before him had confronted. What was distinctive about his situation, however, and what perhaps has given his work a special status both in Spain and abroad, is the deliberate way in which he was able to channel the burdens of being Spanish into a creative impulse, transforming the very obstacles to creative expression into the substance of his cinema.

Saura was born in the Aragonese city of Huesca on January 4, 1932. His mother was a concert pianist and his father held a post in the Republican government: "My father worked in the Ministry of Interior and followed the fortunes of the government; because of that we lived in Madrid, Valencia and Barcelona. Politically speaking, I consider my parents more liberal than anything else. They have always been tolerant and understanding"

2. Carlos Saura during the filming of *El Dorado*

(Harguindey 1975, 123). Saura was younger than five when the Civil War began, but owing to his father's position in the government, he found himself an ingenuous witness to the violent images that would inspire his later film work:

> I remember my childhood very well and in a certain fashion I think the war marked me even more than I know. It is possibly the period of my life I remember with most detail. Remembrances of the day the war started, basically visual memories like flashes: the abandoned building next to my house in Madrid; a parade of soldiers with their arms lifted in salute; and everyone closing windows. From that point on I remember an infinity of things with incredible vividness: the war songs, the children's games, the bombings, the lights being turned off, the hunger, the death. Because these years were so extraordinary for a small child, with the passage of time, these memories acquire even greater force. Let's say, and it's a rather banal example, that for Proust, his childhood was a series of more or less poetic details built around his family life; for me those memories are much more violent: a bomb that fell on my school and one of the girls in class all bloody with pieces of glass having cut her face. And this is not some literary invention; it's a fact. For that reason I think that the atmosphere of the war weighs upon me . . . and weighs upon the things I do. (Brasó 1974, 23)

At the war's end Saura was separated from his parents and sent back to live with his maternal grandmother and aunts in Huesca. He describes these relatives as "right-wing and very religious" (Harguindey 1975, 123), who imposed upon the young Carlos the very antithesis of the kind of education he had begun to receive in the Republican zone. Removed from his brother and sisters, he felt himself the outsider in his own family—a stigma that is perhaps the most indelible of his memories of this period. Years later, in *La prima Angélica* (1973: *Cousin Angelica*), Saura would depict a character who, long after the war's end, relives childhood memories of a similar kind of estrangement in his grandparents' home.

With the war finally over, the Saura family was eventually reunited in Madrid where Carlos and his older brother, Antonio, began their high school studies in a religious school. Carlos finished his secondary education in a secular school where he showed special aptitude for mathematics. Following the pattern of many middle-class youths of this period with similar academic skills, he entered the University of Madrid, choosing engineering from among the various professional schools. The choice proved not to his liking and, through his brother, Antonio's, prompting, he switched to the fledgling National Film School (Instituto de Investigaciones y Experiencias Cinematográficas: IIEC), which he formally entered in the 1952–1953 course. This interest in film was, in a certain way, an outgrowth of and complement to an avid interest in photography which he had displayed since the age of ten.

Between 1950 and 1953, when he entered IIEC, he worked as a professional photographer with favorably reviewed public exhibitions of his work in Madrid and Santander. At one point he even started working on a book-length photographic study of Spain, traveling the peninsula for representative images. It was as a consequence of that trip that he felt the necessity to move on to film and so made the decision to apply for entrance to the National Film School (Castro 1974, 383).

Founded in 1947, the National Film School was a response by the government to the perceived need to provide professional training for aspiring filmmakers. But, ironically, within a few years of its establishment, IIEC had become known as the hotbed of dissent against the government's official policies on control of the film industry, largely as a result of the activism of the school's two most precocious and outspoken students, Juan Antonio Bardem and Luis García Berlanga. IIEC clearly served as a focal point for film culture, a place where young Spaniards attracted to filmmaking could come together, discuss the abysmal state of film production in Spain, and theorize ways to move beyond the official status-quo cinema that the regime had cultivated for over a decade through its intricate system of censorship, production subsidies, and shooting licenses. By all accounts, the school's curriculum was negligible. Saura's early education in film culture was, in fact, a series of revisions by his peers of the official program of the National Film School.

> Because of the influence of the Film School, we thought what we had to do was Eisenstein, epic cinema . . . . The question never existed as to why you had to make a film, or what kind of film you could make in Spain, or what relation should exist between Spanish literature or art and film. Buñuel didn't exist. In effect, there was nothing. You studied Russian films at a certain distance . . . because there wasn't any opportunity to see *Potemkin*. You talked about these films but you didn't see them. We only saw German Expressionist films, *Caligari*, etc.
>
> For me, therefore, Neorealism came as a shock. The Italian Cultural Institute brought a "Week of Italian Neorealist Cinema" . . . and they invited members of the Film School to screenings. It was a fantastic experience. I will never be able to thank them enough for that. We saw Antonioni's *Croniche d'Amore*, Fellini and Lattuade's *Luce di Varietá*, De Sica's *Bicycle Thief* and *Miracle in Milan*, *Roma*, *Cittá Aperta*, *Paisá*. And it was then that we started to formulate the problem for ourselves, Bardem and Berlanga, naturally, before the rest of us: a cinema within the terms of Spanish underdevelopment, that is to say, with more of a basis in realism and a cinema of a very modest production scale. (Brasó 1974, 31)

Looking back upon these years, Saura would often emphasize to interviewers his sense of frustration at having been formed as a filmmaker within a marginal, underdeveloped culture, forced to improvise and invent the cinematic traditions that are taken for granted in the rest of Europe and America.

Utopian Spain

The cultural underdevelopment of Spain and the Spanish film industry was the legacy of the first fifteen years of Francoism. Even before the war's conclusion, the Nationalists had begun to develop a cultural apparatus to promote the ideology of traditionalist values which had been invoked to justify their military insurrection in 1936. Through speeches and press reporting, but also through a systematic development of press and film censorship in the Nationalist zone, the process had begun of inculcating in the Spanish populace the values and ideals of the "new" order. Of those values, perhaps the most central was the exaltation of a Hispanic race, clearly inspired by German and Italian fascism. Stressing the spiritual superiority of this vaguely defined racial stock, Francoist apologists emphasized the religious unity of the nation in traditional Catholic values. *Hispanidad*, Spanishness, as the new order insisted, was a crusading mission to which all true Spaniards were tied: the recuperation of the historical greatness of the long-lost Spanish empire.

The ideological project of Francoism, from the very start, was the resurrection of a hypothetical utopian past in which the true Spain, heroic and religious, was distinguished against the background of a heathen and heretical Europe. In November of 1940, the first issue of a new literary magazine, *Escorial*, appeared, heralding the spirit of the new order which was anything but new. It was a publication whose collaborators would find their inspiration in the religious and imperial values of a Spain that had ceased to exist three centuries earlier (Mangini 1987, 21). The magazine's name evoked the pristine virtues of Philip II's sixteenth-century palace pantheon, the building that, perhaps more than any other, embodied the austere and narrow-minded vision of Spain that was to be the hallmark of the Franco dictatorship for the next two decades.

The ideological activity of Francoism was two pronged. On the one hand, the government cultivated its imperial style, replete with the extravagant anachronisms suggested by *Escorial*. On the other, it developed a system of suppression of all forms of dissent through the expansion of the censorship boards that had ordered cultural life in the Nationalist zone since 1937. Film was one of the areas of popular culture most profoundly influenced by the government's policies, but the effects of the war had had a devastating effect on the film industry. Producers were in desperate need of capital, which the government readily provided. Artists, directors, and screenwriters sympathetic to the Republican cause had fled the country, leaving those whose allegiance to the new regime was greatest to occupy prominent positions in the new order. Understandably, the result of this situation was the emergence of a cinema that was both acquiescent to the will of the regime and willingly complicit in the task of inventing the images and narratives to coincide with the rhetoric of the new era.

The practice of film censorship involved the establishment of local boards to review and pass judgment on films. There were, however, no explicit guidelines set forth reflecting the criteria of the boards whose judgment was often arbitrary and always infallible, leaving no recourse to the filmmaker to question a decision. The vagueness of a censorship code that was only implied, but never formally articulated, inevitably led to the "transfer" mechanism of the censorial activity from the official boards to the scriptwriters and directors who effectively became "self-censors." In this way the film industry in the early forties passively assumed the authorship of new variations of the mythology of Francoism, elaborating the favorite heroic Spanish legends suggested by the regime, or inventing the stereotypes and resurrecting the sanitized clichés of Spaniards and Spanishness that would coincide with the cues provided by Franco and his underlings. Though relatively few of the films made in the decade following the Nationalist victory dealt explicitly with the war theme or the Francoist credo, the vision of the historical tradition and values of the Spanish people that informed most films made in this period appeared to connect logically to the mentality identified with Franco.[1]

Much of post–Civil War cinema was understandably escapist: folkloric comedies and romantic genre films. Yet from the very beginning of the government's coercion of the film industry there was a perceived need for the cultivation of a heroic cinema that would reinforce the mythic ideals of the Spanish race. Efforts to capitalize on the recent events of the war were largely failures, such as Enrique del Campo's *El crucero Baleares* (1940: The Cruiser Baleares), a film of notably poor quality that angered a number of admirals. After a brief public screening, the film was withdrawn from distribution and all copies destroyed. What was needed, it was believed, was a film that could serve as a reinforcement to audiences of the heroic Spanish ideals for which the recent struggle and current sacrifices were being made, and also as a model for a genre of films of the Francoist crusade. That model was found in the 1941 film *Raza* (Race, or The People), directed

---

[1] This situation leads Diego Galán to group as political cinema in the decade following the end of the Civil War most films that appeared either to defend the established order or to justify the narrow and skewed vision of Spaniards in the world so closely identified with Nationalist ideology. Such a wide-sweeping revision of the concept of political cinema thus leads him, understandably, to classify among the complicit genres of Francoist cultural politics most examples of seemingly innocuous evasionist cinema, namely historical, religious, and folkloric films of the forties. See Galán, *Cine político* (89–107).

by José Luis Sáenz de Heredia and based on a film script actually penned by Franco under a pseudonym.

As Manuel Vázquez Montalbán asserts, *Raza* captured the historical project of Francoism: Spain regenerating itself by returning to the greatness of its imperial past, resurrecting the models of individual and collective values and action linked implicitly to the hegemony of Castilian, centralist culture over the rest of the peninsula (Vázquez Montalbán 1987, 33–37). More than merely an illustration of the thesis, Franco's script, in its crude and unsubtle way, offered a theory of Spanish history to explain the periods of greatness and mediocrity of the nation (Vernon 1986, 30–31). The *Caudillo*'s mouthpiece in the film is the brave sea captain who dies in defense of the Spanish empire in the misbegotten war with the United States: don Pedro Churruca, patriarch of what Franco makes clear is the paradigmatic Spanish family, a microcosm of Spain itself.

Pedro's two young sons, Pedrito and José, represent the opposing mentalities and interests that will, in time, become the antagonists of the insurrection of 1936. Pedrito is selfish and sadistic; he doesn't understand why it is beautiful to die for one's country and seems to have little respect for the values his family attempts to teach him. José, on the other hand, is the good and obedient son who respects his father's teachings and dreams of someday being able to fight for family and country. Early in the film, before don Pedro is sent off to fight the Americans in Cuba, he gives his two sons a lesson in the history of Spanish valor, describing the courage of one of their forebears, Cosme Damián Churruca, who died courageously defending Spain in the sea battle of Trafalgar against the British. By invoking national history in the name of the family, the film effectively collapses the distinction between history and personal memory, crystalizing as plot a process that was to be one of the ideological constants of Francoist domestic propaganda for decades.

Preceding the elaborate flashback of the battle, the patriarch tells his sons that the courage of the warrior is the courage of the *almogávares*. "Who were the *almogávares*?" José asks. "The chosen warriors," his father explains. "They were the flower of the Spanish race, firm in battle, agile and determined in every maneuver. Their valor has not been equaled in the history of any other nation." "How beautiful it is to be an *almogávar*," the child says. "How come there aren't any *almogávares* now?" "There will be," don Pedro responds, "when they are needed"—an obvious prefiguration of José's patriotic actions during the Civil War.

The narrative process of *Raza* is an unsubtle rewriting of recent Spanish history, the period from the loss of Spain's last overseas possessions in 1898 to the Civil War, in terms of the past glories of the empire. Periods of decadence, such as the nineteenth century and the years of the Second Republic, are viewed as periods in which Spanish politicians betrayed the country to foreign interests. Conversely, the periods of greatness, and the

THE BURDEN OF SPANISHNESS 19

film insistently underscores the Civil War as such a period, are years of crusade when true patriots followed the model of their heroic ancestors. In this the film is a true X ray of Francoism, with its xenophobic attitudes, its gross distortions of recent national history, and finally, its projection backwards to an ill-defined, bogus sense of a utopian Spanish golden age when national greatness was synonymous with struggle and sacrifice.

The paralleling of the destinies of the family and the nation was in no way an original narrative strategy, nor was the joining of individual memory with history. *Raza* clearly partook of the devices of historical fiction. The real value of the film, it has been argued (Gubern 1977, 113), lay in its function as a model text in both narrative and ideological spheres: its reduction of a variety of political positions into a simplistic Manichaean structure; finally, its implicit establishment of a code of "safe" or tolerated social representations to be used as a guide by the directors of other, seemingly nonpolitical films of the period. In something as simple as the chaste kiss that Alfredo Mayo, the adult José, plants on the forehead of his fiancée, Ana Mariscal, at the film's end, other directors read the model of a code of sexuality that would guide film production for the next two decades.

With the Axis defeat in the Second World War, the cultural style dictated by Francoism only seemed to widen the gulf that separated Spaniards from the outside world. Quite unself-consciously and surely unintentionally, Spanish cinema of the forties reflected that backward slide into an antique culture by resuscitating older theatrical forms such as the comic *zarzuela* that had been popular in the thirties, the folkloric comedy, films of religious thematics, and, finally, the costumed historical epic. The most popular of these latter films was Juan de Orduña's *Locura de amor* (1948: Madness of Love), a historical recreation of the life of the mad Spanish queen known as Juana, "*la loca*," that seemed to breathe new life into the historical-epic genre that had been dormant for a number of years. If such a cinema did not or could not reflect the actual social and political reality of the country, the film genres of the forties clearly reflected, as Diego Galán argues, the mentality of those who were directing film culture and the country in general (Galán 1974, *Cine*, 91). And it was the persistence of that "mentality" of an imaginary Spain populated by theatrical characters who moved through stage sets that was to plague Saura and other young filmmakers in the fifties as they set out to shape their own careers in the film industry.

Oppositions

After a decade of "deculturalization," the fifties seemed a period of relative artistic and intellectual reawakening.[2] Though the state censorship appa-

[2] The term is used by Shirley Mangini to describe the combined effects of the war's devas-

ratus was still in place, as it would be for another two decades, the rise to prominence of Joaquín Ruiz-Giménez in 1951 as minister of national education and his significant liberalization of the Spanish university system gave a breath of fresh air to the otherwise-dormant intellectual and cultural life of the country. The effect was certainly minor when compared to culture under the Second Republic. But the founding of a number of university magazines out of which would come the first voices of dissent against the triumphalist style and consensus of the forties was a significant, if only symbolic, sign of a change in the Spanish cultural landscape.

The admission of Spain to the United Nations in 1955 marked the end of her ten-year isolation from Europe. Ironically, while returning to normal diplomatic relations with other nations and boasting of her status as a democratic nation, the country experienced increasing popular resistance to the regime in a series of strikes and other actions that revealed publicly the repressive force of Francoism. By the mid-1950s a number of the students from the National Film School, for instance, had become involved in "counterculture" activities that went well beyond their work as fledgling filmmakers. Some were members of the clandestine Communist party, while others were involved in the recently founded film journal, *Objetivo*, a publication of pronounced liberal sympathies.

By all accounts, the influence of *Objetivo* was much greater than either its circulation or its publication life might suggest. The magazine only ran from May of 1953 to the spring of 1955, when it was closed down by the government. Its principal editors, Juan Antonio Bardem, Eduardo Ducay, Ricardo Muñoz Suay, and Paulino Garagorri, produced a magazine that tried to open up previously ignored avenues of film and cultural criticism. The magazine inserted itself into an already established current of realist and neorealist cinema so recently brought to Spain by the Italian embassy. Its immediate inspiration was the Italian journal *Cinema Nuovo* and the positions held by its founder, Guido Aristarco. Thus it rejected American commercial cinema but defended American independent films, especially those with a social or testimonial dimension. It advocated social realism as the highest ideal of cinema. In turn, members of the *Objetivo* editorial board became aggressive spokesmen for the renovation of Spanish society through a cinema of social demystification which sought to expose the contradictions and tensions of the structure of contemporary Spanish society. Bardem and Muñoz Suay were, of course, militants of the Spanish Communist party, and their positions regarding film were part of a much

tation on Spanish artistic and intellectual life and the Francoist approach to culture which might best be characterized by the stabilization of the state censorship apparatus. See Mangini, Chapter I: "*La desculturalización de España.*"

broader political project.[3] In 1955, the editors of *Objetivo*, in collaboration with the outspoken leader of the University of Salamanca Film Club, Basilio Martín Patino, organized a first-of-its-kind colloquium on the state of film culture in Spain: *Conversaciones sobre el cine nacional* (Conversations on National Cinema). The Salamanca Conversations were to prove the most permanent legacy of *Objetivo*'s activities, crystalizing the liberal spirit that would reshape Spanish cinema in the next decade (Pozo 1984, 141). Ironically, the conference had received financial support from the government's office of film education. Though the activity was spearheaded by individuals of obvious leftist sympathies, the gathering included filmmakers and critics of all political persuasions. Yet it was the firebrand Juan Antonio Bardem who was to set the audience astir with his vituperative denunciation of national cinema under Franco. In an often-quoted pentagram, he called the Spanish cinema " . . . politically futile, socially false, intellectually vapid, aesthetically void and industrially paralytic" (Larraz 1973, 46). Taking aim at the contradictory nature of the government's coercion of the film industry, Bardem laid bare one of the essential indictments of official cinema in Spain: its progressive distancing from social or cultural reality:

> Living with its back to Spanish reality, our cinema has not been able to show us the true face of the problems, the land, or the people of Spain. This atemporal hermetic and false creation of a supposedly Spanish reality, such as it appears in our films, totally distances itself from the rich realist tradition of the Spanish novel. Right here and now, the spectator of Spanish cinema is unable to learn from a Spanish film about the Spanish style of living, how Spaniards revel or how they suffer, or what are man's conflicts, or Spanish society's. The Spanish spectator is not informed by Spanish film about his own reality. The vision of the world, of this Spanish world, portrayed in Spanish film is false! (Larraz 1973, 47)

The privileging of social realism that Bardem's words implied coincided with a more general tendency among Spanish artists and intellectuals of the period and was the natural consequence of the rigidity of the censorship system that had proscribed a vast range of social and political topics from discussion or even allusion in literature and the arts. The regime's policy regarding film censorship, derived from the broader fabric of Francoist cultural politics of the immediate post–Civil War era, was the product of the biases and attitudes of Gabriel Arias Salgado, Franco's Minister of Information from 1951 to 1962, whose office supervised film licensing, shooting, and final censorship of domestic film productions. Anything that was less than the idealized utopian vision of the Spanish people was viewed

---

[3] For a more detailed discussion of the film debates of the fifties and the position of *Objetivo*, see Tubau (14–18).

by his administration as either unpatriotic or subversive. Frustrated by the power of intimidation that the censorship policy had created, as well as by the results of that policy which Bardem's words so accurately described, many young filmmakers saw the occasion of the Salamanca meeting as a forum for venting their frustration at the government's handling of the film industry. At the same time, many protested the absence of explicit criteria upon which films were judged by the censors. Such an absence, it was correctly argued, forced each scriptwriter to invent and internalize the patterns that appeared to him to be "safe" cinematic representation.

Bardem's defiant tone in his five-point denunciation was itself contradicted by his closing remarks at the meeting, when he pleaded with the government to establish explicit norms of censorship that would allow film to assume a more creative, less confining relation to Spanish culture: "We need for censorship to show us its face, to show us the way out of this labyrinth, to codify its taboos" (Larraz 1973, 50). But rather than achieving either the independence implied by Bardem's defiant opening statement, or the conciliation suggested by his closing remarks, the Salamanca meeting only succeeded in making it easier for the government to identify the dissident intellectuals. As the most immediate result of the Salamanca Conference, publication of *Objetivo* was suspended, and people like Berlanga and Bardem were now pariahs in the film industry. It would be nearly seven years before José María García Escudero, one of the prominent voices of Catholic liberalism at Salamanca, would become the director of the government's film office and establish some of the policies advocated by the conference speakers.

From Salamanca to Cuenca

Saura was still a student at the National Film School when he attended the Salamanca Conversations. He recalls his reactions to the speakers this way: "At Salamanca I was really a spectator, although totally fascinated by something which had never crossed my mind before: the formulation of Spanish cinema in political terms; the possibility of making films rooted in reality; the return of realism" (Brasó 1974, 34).

Realism, however, would prove to be more of a catalyst than a concrete model for Saura's own aspirations as a filmmaker, as the next two years were to show. During his time at IIEC he worked on the crew of Eduardo Ducay's never-completed documentary, *Carta de Sanabria* (Letter from Sanabria) and his own film project, a short work called *La tarde de domingo* (1957: Sunday Afternoon), which earned him his diploma from the film school, the only student to be approved for graduation in the 1956–1957 class. *La tarde de domingo* shows the striking influence of De Sica's *Umberto*

D. and is perhaps most notable for its technical qualities: the use of hand-held cameras, street locales, and, for the first time, an IIEC student film shot entirely in 35mm.

This short, in turn, was followed by Saura's first independent film after graduation, *Cuenca*, a documentary commissioned by the government of the Castilian province of Cuenca. Shot in Eastmancolor and marked by some of the first use of zoom lens in Spanish film, *Cuenca* suggested Saura's own self-defined distance from the more doctrinaire realism of social protest—though by no means was it a rejection of the defiant politics that underlay the critical realism of his more vocal contemporaries. Commissioned simply as a publicity film for local industry and tourism, the film, when finally completed after a year's work, turned out to be a cynical look at the contrived cultural images of a storybook Spain that had formed and deformed Spaniards' notion of their place in their own culture.

Like Buñuel's *Tierra sin pan* (1932: Land without Bread), which it resembles in its treatment of peasant customs and certain scenes of rural village life, *Cuenca* takes an almost parodic stance toward the genre of documentary. The film focuses on the mythology of traditional Castile: its land, its history, and its monumentality. These Castilian themes had been one of the conceptual links that united the writers of the Generation of 1898—Unamuno, Azorín, Machado—but it was eventually picked up and exploited to political advantage by Francoist ideologues who sought to embellish the notion of a unified and centralized Spanish nation.

Though hardly a political film, *Cuenca* is conceptually linked to the spirit of the Francoist opposition movement as it aims to demystify the rhetoric of Spanishness by uncovering the historical baggage that immobilizes and dwarfs the Spaniard. There is, for instance, a thematic affinity in the coincidence between Saura's subject matter and Bardem's most recent film, *Calle Mayor* (1956: Main Street), also shot in the city of Cuenca, which helps the contemporary spectator of the period situate *Cuenca* within a political framework. In *Main Street* Bardem focused on the plight of an individual character who was a victim of the oppressive social structures of conservative and repressive provincial society. Saura's film uses that same cultural landscape to deflate the bombastic rhetoric of Spanishness that historically has extolled the uniqueness of the Spanish character as emanating from the severe Castilian landscape. *Cuenca* is further linked with Bardem's film by a common note of condemnation of the Francoist ideal of Spanish provincial life which has alienated and imprisoned the modern Spaniard.

Saura situates *Cuenca* intertextually as part of a chain of subversive, countercultural readings of the dominant Francoist ideology that came into vogue in the mid-fifties under the literary rubric of "objectivist" fiction, an apparent borrowing of the French *nouveau roman*. In his landmark essay, *La hora del lector* (1957: The Hour of the Reader), José María Castellet describes the hermeneutics of reading the objectivist novel in ways that suggestively align the reading process of objectivist fiction with a broader, more politically oriented kind of reception theory in which artists and audiences are invited to circumvent the omnipresent reality of censorship. In a world where all public forms of discourse are insistently circumscribed by the fact of censorship, the construction of a seemingly nonpolitical, aesthetic discourse begins to awaken the interest of socially engaged artists. Castellet writes: "The writer creates for his reader a work which the latter accepts as a personal task to complete. Concretely, in the case of the novel, the author will reveal a world which the reader is obliged actively to populate, on his own part, putting in everything the author has either omitted or forgotten. . . . In the act of writing, the novelist begins with a dissatisfaction in his own life, or in the life he sees around him. And he pushes the reader to read that same dissatisfaction. The objective of improving oneself or of improving our life lies with both of them and the literary work offers them a unique opportunity in each case" (Castellet 1957, 51).

Like Rafael Sánchez Ferlosio in *El Jarama* (1955), the most heralded of the Spanish objectivist novels, Saura attempts in *Cuenca* to develop a provocative form of discursive "restraint" in the face of external coercion. He plays off the documentary rhetoric of an extensive and quite literary voice-over commentary against a series of images and scenes that, while not exactly contradicting the spoken commentary, invite the spectator's reflection on the anachronistic and archaic culture of Castile. The effect is intended to be self-consciously "aesthetic," that is to say, to make the spectator aware of the repetition as text of a certain way of social seeing that is readily identified with the historical project of official culture. This overstated readability thus works as a meta-commentary on the imposed burden of history that is an otherwise "unspeakable" theme in films of the day.

Cuenca is divided into three sections: the geographical, lyrical, and folkloric surfaces of Cuenca, as Enrique Brasó has described it (Brasó 1974, 44). The first section details the physical images of the region, its mountains, rivers, forests, and finally, its villages. Saura's strategy is to move his spectator gradually from a natural scenario of the provincial landscape of Cuenca to the artificial mise-en-scène of the regional capital. Only after a considerable scrutiny of the physical terrain does he introduce the human geography of Cuenca; and again, following his design of a progressive distancing from the natural, the camera moves from images of isolated individuals to more and more elaborate configurations of social groupings.

To the chagrin of the Cuenca government, who believed they had hired Saura to produce images of tractors and modern farming techniques, the first view of a human figure in the film is of a farmer plowing a field with a primitive instrument pulled by a horse. Francisco Rabal's commentary tells us that farmers use the same kind of implements for farming that their forebears have used for centuries. Gradually, the human presence gains prominence, especially as Saura details the harvest as performed by groups of peasants. With almost no verbal commentary at this point, the camera captures the movement of peasants and their families as they harvest wheat to the background sounds of traditional folk songs. This highly stylized scene will be repeated with only minor variations in the *siega*, or harvest scene, from Saura's second feature-length film, *Llanto por un bandido* (1963: Lament for a Bandit). Similarly, the siesta pause, a montage of striking close-ups of immobilized human figures as they sleep in the mid-day sun, prefigures the pictorial style of a similar scene in Saura's third film, *La caza* (1965: The Hunt). The idealized images of peasants in a lush, natural setting contrast with the later shots of the Holy Week ceremonies in the city of Cuenca, where individuals are seen as constrained by the environment of social ritual.

The second part of the film depicts what Saura calls "historical" Cuenca (Brasó 1974, 44), centering on the cultural monuments of the community: castles and cemeteries. With a silhouette of the classic touristic image of Castile, a windmill, Rabal speaks of the symbols of all Manchegan towns— "churches, graveyards, and, in a few instances, castles." The historical Cuenca is conspicuously devoid of human figures for the most part; there are only the cold images of abandoned buildings and churchyards, as Rabal reads lines from the medieval lyrical poetry of Jorge Manrique. The recitation of Manrique's "Coplas por la muerte de su padre" (Verses on the Death of His Father) combined with the images of the barren landscape of monumental Castile serve to remind us that the only remains of the once-great lords who built these castles are abandoned graves in an all-but-forgotten cemetery. For Saura, the timelessness of Castile has a dark and somber side as well.

The images of the *Ciudad encantada*, or Enchanted City, provide an appropriate segue into the third section of the film: a biting presentation of the contemporary city of Cuenca, characterized as another "enchanted city" by means of Saura's reduction of the whole of urban life to three social festivals: the September feast of St. Matthew with its running of the young bulls through the streets; a pre-Lenten carnival; and finally, Holy Week processions. During the first of the city images in *Cuenca*, the running of the bulls, the camera lingers on the scene of youths taunting a young bull on the steps of the cathedral in the center of the city. A similar image will, in fact, provide the credit sequence for Saura's first feature-length film, *Hooligans*. During the carnival scene, groups of revelers, some on stilts, others wearing huge masks, parade around the city. The camera follows them as they cross the famed hanging bridge which spans the

Cuenca gorge and enter the medieval city proper. This final section of the film is almost entirely devoid of voice-over commentary.

The medievalism of the Holy Week processions of the cofraternities, viewed at various points during the twenty-four-hour ritual, perfectly captures the obsessional religious fervor that will be one of the key features of provincial life depicted in Saura's fourth film, *Peppermint Frappé* (1967). The rapid montage of eccentric camera angles from which the procession is viewed underscores the hallucinatory effect that the Holy Week ceremony has on both its participants and its spectators. The implicit critique of provincial traditionalist Spain couched in what Saura's camera chooses to include and omit gives us a first clear sign of the dominant theme of a distorted Spanishness that engulfs the individual. The procession is the longest and, cinematically, the most elaborate sequence of the film. It is especially noteworthy in terms of Saura's montage and framing techniques, the first explicit indication of the young director's efforts to approximate his thematic impression of the deforming social ritual through camera positioning and angles.

The initial logic of Saura's filming schedule was to shoot images of the province during a cycle of four seasons. The resulting film, however, reveals a much more expansive vision of the Francoist dream of traditional Spain: a timeless community steeped in rituals that have isolated it from the outside world; a Spain trapped in a constrained mise-en-scène of its own design in which natural and man-made fantasies blend together and harmonize with the isolating religious rituals of the film's final section.

The picturesque landscape, costumes, and ceremony all become marks of indictment within Saura's critical structure. Finally, the historical Castilian community is revealed in the last sequence as having been trapped in its own self-induced anachronism. The film ends with a picture-postcard view of the city and the gorge, as Rabal reminds the audience: "Cuenca es distinta y siempre la misma" (Cuenca changes and is always the same), the force of Saura's critical vision again ironically couched in the ambiguity of the touristic cliché.

Though *Cuenca* was destined not to please the government officials who had commissioned the film, there were other audiences who recognized its merits. The film went on to receive Honorable Mention at the 1958 San Sebastián Film Festival and the Silver Medallion at the 1959 Bilbao Festival. Yet, Saura would minimize the value of *Cuenca*, claiming later that its only merit was "that it's the first thing I made that was my own on all levels" (Brasó 1974, 45). Nonetheless, from the retrospective vantage point of a quarter of a century later, one can view *Cuenca* as suggestively rehearsing some of the principal ideas and images that would shape Saura's films over the coming decade. It is, as well, a young filmmaker's first sustained reflection on the cultural and discursive practices that have contributed to the static and deformed image of traditionalist Spain, told through a narrative cinematic language that actively engages its spectator in the interrogation of that deforming process.

Discovery and Reencounter

Cuenca was largely a work of intuition based on a long period of reflection on the ideology of Francoist cultural representation. Yet, other than the neorealist movement with its political agenda, there were few avenues through which an aspiring student of film could really grow in Spain: "In the fifties and sixties what they spoke about most was the need for a realist cinema, one that posed social problems. . . . But most of the time they confused things and when they talked of "social" films they meant films about workers' grievances, social injustice, films about the proletariat, and rarely did they consider the possibility of an incursion into the intimacy of the individual, to probe his contradictions and his sense of abandonment" (Harguindey 1975, 119).

After he had completed work on *Cuenca*, a short-term solution to this sense of cultural isolation came—in the form of an invitation from José Francisco Aranda for him to attend an international conference on Hispanic cinema at Montpellier in France. Here he met Georges Sadoul and Edgar Morin, and he began to explore, perhaps for the first time in a conscious way, the meaning of his own cultural isolation. It was at Montpellier where Saura first viewed films by his fellow Aragonese, Luis Buñuel. *Tierra sin pan* (1932); *Subida al cielo* (1950); and *El* (1952) were films that sparked his imagination, not only because they were "connections with an earlier historical and cultural process" (Brasó 1974, 40), but also because at least two of these films posed what he quickly identified as alternative strategies of cinematic narration which embodied devastating critiques of Hispanic cultural order: "There was never truly a possibility of confronting a Spanish problem head-on. And then I discovered Buñuel's films. It was a fantastic solution: on the one hand the encounter with a whole prior cultural and historical process; on the other, because he [Buñuel] was a man who worked on reality in his own films, and Spanish reality, and to all of that he had a personal world to express, a critical, even a moral way of seeing things" (Brasó 1974, 40).

With time Saura would meet Buñuel personally and maintain a long and rich friendship. Inevitably, his name would be linked with Buñuel's in a series of associations, cinematic and political, placing the young filmmaker in the aura of Spain's most internationally renowned film director, but also creating the impression that Saura was a more political filmmaker than indeed he was during those years. But just as he had resisted the temptation merely to imitate the style of Italian neorealism, he would limit his admiration for the work and aesthetic of his fellow Arangonese, Buñuel, to a profound respect and admiration that fell well short of what some critics would imagine to be imitation. The definitive orientation that Buñuel seems to have provided Saura appears to have been in the way of a style of cultural questioning through cinema that had long been one of Buñuel's signatures and would, in time, become Saura's. More than any tradition, model, or external influence, it is, finally, this self-definition as an autodidact that accounts for the emergence of Saura as a distinctive filmmaker. A strong sense of empiricism, of observing, reflecting on, and questioning the terms of Spanishness—these are the dominant features of his cinematic as well as his intellectual style during his years of apprenticeship. They are, not surprisingly, the same features that are insistently transposed to his characters who, like the author-outside-the-text, must grapple with the burdens of a constraining Spanishness.

II

Spectators

THOUGH *Cuenca* received critical attention and awards, Saura was keenly aware, as he said, that nobody in Spain was really interested in documentary as a genre (Brasó 1974, 45). So by the end of 1958 he began in earnest to work on what would be his first feature-length film. The six-year period from 1959 through 1965 marks his formal apprenticeship in commercial filmmaking. During these years, he charted a risky itinerary across the troubled landscape of Spanish cultural politics, completing three films: *Los golfos* (1959: Hooligans), *Llanto por un bandido* (1963: Lament for a Bandit), and *La caza* (1965: The Hunt). The intricate narrative structures that highlight these early films appear shaped by a common conceptual aim: the implicit desire to demystify aspects of the cultural mythology of Francoism.

Each of the three films, for instance, is ordered by a pattern of narrative duplications—not just stories within stories, but dramatizations of what might be called the consumption of cultural narratives. An acquiescent film industry had appropriated a number of popular myths, icons, and stereotypes and tailored them for mass consumption: the image of chaste, Catholic Spain, isolated in heretical Europe; the redeeming force of the family; and the cult of the individual. The Francoist "culture industry," to borrow Adorno's and Horkheimer's phrase, determined the nature of these myths and also the terms of their consumption. By dramatizing the stories of the consumption of such myths, Saura's early films construct a diagnostic position toward this cultural mythology. Picking up from *Cuenca* the idea of an unrecognized burden of culture that deformed individuals, Saura now sought to shape his narrative films around a truly ambitious deconstructive project: to mirror through cinematic plotting the patterns of cultural practice that implicated and confined the spectator within social snares; further, to emphasize these narratives of ensnarement so that the filmic plot might serve as the catalyst for the audience's revision of their understanding of that social practice.

Los golfos (1959: Hooligans)

The conventional wisdom is that Saura's first feature-length film, *Hooligans*, represents the apotheosis of Spanish neorealist cinema. The use of authentic street locales in Madrid as the principal space of action and the appearance of a nonprofessional cast of actors connect in a seemingly logical way with the social realism of Bardem, Berlanga, and Ferreri. Yet, tellingly, Saura rejects the neorealist label, preferring, instead, to see *Hooligans* as "a search for and the molding of a Spanish reality" (Rentero 1976, 12).[1] About the time he started to think seriously of a career as a commercial filmmaker, shortly after completing *Cuenca* in 1958 and while continuing to teach at the National Film School, Saura became interested in a series of newspaper articles about youth gangs in Madrid. He invited the author of these articles, Daniel Sueiro, to join him and his collaborator and former student, Mario Camus, in developing a film script around this material. Unable to find a backer for the project among established Spanish producers, Saura and Camus made contact with Pedro Portabello who, late in 1958, was forming an independent production company, FILM '59. Saura was able to enlist the Catalan producer's support to develop a modest, low-budget film based upon the Sueiro material.

Saura's inexperience in commercial scriptwriting was painfully apparent from the very start. Most of his knowledge of film production up to this point had been the result of either his own documentary project months before or his earlier work on the filming crew of Eduardo Ducay's never-completed documentary, *Letter from Sanabria*. Coming from a documentary tradition, he felt himself most comfortable in theoretic reflection on film, in the strategies of editing and composition that would, in fact, show up in the strikingly original narrative structure of *Hooligans*, and upon which he comments in an essay on the film (Saura, *1962*). In their conception of *Hooligans* both Saura and Camus consciously sought to break with the visual style of the banal studio-made films of the period. Camus says: "That picture calls your attention as a contrast with what was going on at the moment. Those films that were locked up in indoor settings, even when the film took place in a shantytown, were shot in a studio. And suddenly for us it was going out into the street" (Villegas 1976, 12).

A detectable spirit of defiance against the Francoist social ethos runs through *Hooligans*. There is, for instance, a brief scene where Juan (Oscar Cruz), aspiring to a career as a bullfighter, views the skyline of downtown Madrid from a hilltop in one of the dreary working-class suburbs of the city. He bemoans his fate to one of his comrades: "It's really hard to become someone here." Though the scene was later deleted by the censors

---

[1] Agustín Sánchez Vidal reviews the polemics of stylistic classification that surround *Hooligans*, variously described as a Spanish variant of Italian neorealism, a continuation of the harsh picaresque realism that inspired many of Buñuel's films, finally, a coincidence with the French New Wave. He concludes that the hybrid nature of the film derives less from any particular intellectual project than from the young director's documentary style of recording action in combination with the need to respond to the practical problems of film production (31–32).

from the copy of the film authorized for domestic distribution, it crystalizes much of the thematic structure and conceptual strategy that mark Saura's formative approach to social cinema. For that one fleeting moment the film's protagonist becomes spectator to the design of his life, as if realizing that the deceptive allure of the material world he sees is a bait to snare him and not a promise of success. He views the world with a detachment that is equivalent to lucidity and just the reverse of the position and consciousness he and his comrades assume once he returns to the action.

Juan's telling distance from within the narrative exposes at once the director's own impulse to stand back from the space of containment and view dispassionately the world that ensnares him. If it were not for the insistence upon the figure of spectators dramatized within a sizable number of the film's major sequences, this one brief scene might appear to be only a mark of Saura's indiscreet introduction of social criticism into his film. But within the larger framework of *Hooligans*, there can be little doubt that the vignette works as one link in a chain of meta-commentaries on the nature of social representations which operate as a form of mystification for the Spaniard.

A series of cultural, psychological and even political texts spring from the first implicit opposition between the stark, dreary Madrid Saura's camera documents and the landscape of contrivance and artifice that audiences had come to accept as the only possible setting of a Spanish film. There had been, of course, Spanish films earlier in the decade that included authentic locale shots. One could trace a direct line of precursors to Saura's film beginning as early as José María Nieves Conde's *Surcos* (1951: Furrows) and including sequences in *Muerte de un ciclista* (1955: Death of a Cyclist) and Marco Ferreri's *El pisito* (The Little Flat) in 1959, all of which involved authentic working-class urban locales. But something quite new and startling surfaces in the introduction of urban space in *Hooligans*: What had previously been thought to be simply an authentic, realistic background to cinematic action is transformed into a critical mise-en-scène that is used to shape the action of characters and also to comment on their struggle. The city, in a sense, becomes a protagonist of the film. Whatever shots of the downtown area we glimpse are by way of reinforcing the film's strategy of situating the viewer in the place and perspective of characters who are marginalized within their own society. That marginalization is then used thematically within the plot as the members of a Madrid street gang recognize their own peripheral existence and struggle to break out of their marginal status.

In the earliest version of the script the youths were depicted as simply petty criminals living off the spoils of their daily robberies, but the censors objected to this portrayal of aimless youth, insisting that there had to be some "altrusitic" motivation to justify such antisocial behavior. The protagonists of *Hooligans*, as the title suggests, are street youths living in one

3. *Hooligans (Los golfos, 1959)*

of the poorest working-class districts of Madrid, all played by nonprofessional actors. Though the script omits reference to their Andalusian origins, their speech and avid interest in bullfighting enables the Spanish audience of the day to situate these characters within the contemporary
context of the massive peasant influx into Madrid which, by the mid-fifties,
was increasing at an alarming rate as Spain's agricultural economy wors-
ened. Of the gang members, only Juan appears to have steady employment
as a stevedore in the Legazpi produce market. In one of the film's most
poignant scenes we see him with his back bent over carrying huge crates
on his shoulders to load a truck, the weight transforming him into a beast
of burden. Devoting his free time to practicing bullfighting, Juan hopes to
train as a bullfighter and eventually to assume a professional career in the
bullring. At the instigation of Ramón (Luis Marín), one of the two principal rivals for leadership of the gang, the youths agree to help Juan enter
a *novillada*, a special bullfight for aspiring novices. They need to come up
with the exorbitant entrance fee for Juan and plan to raise the money
through a series of robberies.

Eventually, one of the victims of the gang's assaults, a taxi driver, recognizes Paco (Ramón Rubio), a gang member, and chases him through
the city streets. Passers-by join in the pursuit until, finally, Paco takes refuge in a sewer. His dead body is found the next day on the outskirts of the
city. By now the police are closing in on the gang and trace them to the

bullring, arriving just as Juan is about to make his entrance into the arena. The film ends as the police and gang members view Juan's *corrida* amidst the shouts and jeers of a disapproving crowd. Juan's performance is a disaster and the film ends with a freeze-frame of the bull's head in its last agony, the emblematic image of the failed effort by Juan and his friends to realize their illusions of success.

A rigorous structure of narrative causality informs the development of action in *Hooligans*: the story of the characters' plight as they struggle to break out of poverty; the cultural mythology of the torero as heroic emblem which the gang members have each absorbed; finally, the scenario in which ingenuous youths are led to believe the myth of their own power only to be ensnared and contained by the repressive social machinery which that myth masks. These three levels are so intricately interwoven into the narrative and visual fabric of the film that one must take with reservation the claim by both Saura and Camus that the film was largely improvised.[2] What is clear, however, is that what started out for Saura as a documentary on slum life in Madrid evolved into a complex narrative structure through a series of critical interactions between the filmmaker and the censors.

The government's bureaucratic control of film production through what was called "prior censorship," submission of a script in order to obtain a license to shoot a film, emphasized the importance of a skeleton shooting script. Because the censors were not necessarily knowledgeable about film construction other than plots and dialogue, most of their objections related naturally to narrative construction. Though Saura's interests in *Hooligans* did not at first focus on questions of narrative, the arduous process of at least four major rewrites moved him to a deeper understanding of the ideological function of narrative as perceived in the censors' minds.

In particular, the censors' "suggestion" of giving the protagonists a socially redeeming motive for their crimes led Saura toward the first of a series of radical textual strategies that would alter his very notion of filmic structure and style. He took the minor element of a narrative revision—the cultural symbol of the torero—and transformed it into a symbolic narrative of its own. The final reworking of *Hooligans* in the form eventually authorized by the censors is the tale of the ideological "usage" of the torero's story. Saura treats that story as a symptomatic expression of the cultural blockage that besets the Spaniard in coming to grips with his own social and personal plight.

---

[2] Saura recalls how he and Camus would meet each morning for breakfast during the shooting and write the script for the scenes they were to film that day. (Author's interview with Saura, June 14, 1989).

The Individual and the Crowd

Hemingway's vision of heroic death in the afternoon aside, the corrida has long been viewed by Spanish intellectuals as the emblem of all that is regressive in Spanish culture, a combination of a debased romantic impulse toward individualism and traditonal Spanish machismo. Certainly, by the time Saura and Camus started to revise the script of *Hooligans*, it was a commonplace that bullfighting was at best a reactionary art that catered to the basest values and instincts of the Spanish lower classes and, at worst, for its emphasis on virility, sex, blood, and death, a uniquely Spanish expression of fascism (McCormick and Sevilla 1966, 199). Since the end of the last century, writers of the famed Generation of 1898, especially the philosopher Unamuno and the novelist Blasco Ibáñez, equated the bullfight with political and social stagnation. In Blasco's novel *Sangre y arena* (Blood and Sand) this argument is given elaborate narrative focus.

Saura's evocation of the system of exploitation of lower-class youth by the greedy impresarios emphatically draws on that strain in Spanish cultural thought that sees bullfighting as connecting all too logically with the reactionary and authoritarian tendencies of Francoism. The successful torero is viewed as the personification of the hero as plebian; adored by the crowd, he embodies in his daring and exaggerated nonchalance an almost mythic quality of individualism that is the symbolic incarnation of everything that is denied the audience in their everyday life: self-definition as individuals and recognition by others of that individuality. In short, the torero is seen to be the product of a socially symbolic activity where social contradictions, insurmountable in their own realm, find a purely formal resolution in the aesthetic realm (Jameson 1981, 79).

Saura says of the choice of the bullfighting motif as a backdrop for the film's action: "We looked for a kind of profession or occupation that supposed the possibility of instant success, keeping in mind that our protagonists were from the lowest social stratum and that, as in our earlier study for the script, they had come from Andalusia. So it seemed natural that in the context of the period, one of the most brilliant and most rapid channels for their hopes would be in bullfighting" (Brasó 1974, 65).

In a most basic way, the torero myth always implies its social audience, those who will "bear witness" and admire the prowess of the individual. Thus the landscape of social artifice sustaining that myth in the film comes into focus tellingly through the image of crowds. The recurrence of crowd scenes throughout, while seemingly an element of authentic local color, ultimately emerges as the symbol of everything the dream of individuality opposes. The torero aspires to the cheers of the crowds; and, within the bullfighting ritual, it is the crowd as much as the bull who seals the bullfighter's destiny. Through the portrayal of the crowd and its antithesis, the strongly individualistic torero, Saura conveys the sense of a cultural dilemma lurking beneath social facades. The youths' struggle for achievement is itself born of a tacit recognition by each gang member that he is merely an inconsequential element in an anonymous mass. Yet the crowd is used by these characters in an effort, ironically, to redefine themselves as individuals. It is as much the status of the crowd as of the false self-definition of individuality embraced by the protagonists to which *Hooligans* gravitates thematically.

We see this tension woven through different narrative and visual threads. Juan's effort to succeed as a bullfighter, defining success in terms of a recognition by the crowd, is perhaps the most conspicuous statement of that duality. In a less obvious way, Ramón and Julián (Manuel Zarzo), the rivals for leadership of the gang, reveal an awareness of the meaning of crowds in their desire to be leaders. The internal tension of the gang itself, built around the interaction of the three principal figures, is eventually shown to be a single struggle: characters trying to manipulate others in an effort to forge their own identity as individuals.

The recurrence of the crowd as a backdrop to much of the film's action brings this psychological and social tension into focus as the ubiquitous subtext of *Hooligans*. The Legazpi market scene, where Juan is shown working, the later scene in the flea market where Ramón goes to dispose of stolen goods, and the soccer stadium where we see the youths robbing parts from parked motorcycles all work to define the crowd as a force that gives a social definition to the youths as manipulators and shapes the course of their upward struggle.

A number of scenes portray a more explicit understanding of the meaning of the crowd by the gang members. Ramón, for instance, convinces the other members to help Juan only after he has viewed his friends in a crowded dance hall. Saura seems to be telling us here that the real inducement to action is less a matter of camaraderie with Juan than the oppressive knowledge Ramón achieves of the inconsequential status that they all share. Later scenes will reinforce this urge by the gang members to achieve individuality as a response to the faceless, docile mass in which they find themselves.

By the midpoint in the film, however, it becomes apparent that the easily manipulated crowd has somehow changed, and these changes prefigure the final sequence in which the gang is encircled in the bullring. The first point at which we see the youths beginning to sense their own ensnarement comes when Ramón and Juan are at a cocktail lounge preparing for what Julián has assured them will be an easy job of pickpocketing. The plan is for Juan to stand guard at the entrance of the crowded lounge and cover Ramón who is seated near Visi, (María Mayer), a girlfriend of one of the

gang members. As Visi passionately embraces her escort, Ramón is supposed to pick the man's wallet from his pants pocket. But, at the crucial
moment, Ramón panics; he looks around and sees a room filled with staring eyes. He leaves the lounge in failure, visibly shaken by the recogniton
of his cowardice.

This scene is constructed not only as an image of Ramón's social encirclement, but also as a characterization of the crowd as a protean eye that
controls individual action by the force of its admonishing gaze. In the rapid
series of cuts from Ramón seated near Visi to Juan and the hat-check girl
looking at the crowded room, Saura situates the spectator in the place of
one of those customers peering around the lounge. We are, in effect, made
to see ourselves as both members of the anonymous mass who can be manipulated and also as the agent of sight, trapping Ramón in his attempted
robbery.

From this point on, not only Ramón, but all the gang members find
themselves unsuspectingly encircled by mobs whose presence carries the
ambivalent mark of easy manipulation and of retaliatory ensnarement. We
can best see that duality and the basic reversal of the youths' hopes of success in the scene in which Paco is recognized by the cab driver whom he
had earlier assaulted and robbed. He stands in front of the bullring the day
before Juan's debut, distributing flyers that announce Juan's novillada.
When he approaches the cab to give the driver an announcement, the man
recognizes him and there begins a frantic pursuit through the city streets.
People join the driver until, at last, in an overhead panning shot, we see an
angry mob in hot pursuit of the desperate youth.

If at the beginning of *Hooligans* the crowd had posed the immediate
personal motivation for action by the protagonists, by this decisive juncture we see the crowd as the source of the youths' entrapment. The chase
scene, in particular, recalls Walter Benjamin's discussion of nineteenth-century depictions of urban crowds in London and Paris as reflecting a crucial
moment in the history of fascism (Benjamin 1969, 166–75). These agents
of order are themselves the pawns in a more elaborate ideological maneuver when they block from movement other individuals, like themselves,
who are struggling to break out of the trap of their collectivized and manipulated existence.

By the time we come to Juan's fateful debut, we have already sensed that
lurking in the idea of the crowd is both the possibility of a legitimate
achievement of individuality for the youths and also the risk of ultimate
entrapment, a social denial of each member's claim to individuality. That
risk finally crystalizes in disaster for Juan as the crowd rebukes his performance. Yet as Saura's plotting so carefully establishes, the underlying entrapment for the gang members has been constructed by the chain of earlier contacts with the crowd. The destiny of failure they confront at the end

has, from the start, never been a question of individual performance, but a fatalistic scenario that they have been unable to decipher adequately. The film ends by joining the privileged myth of the virile, heroic, individualistic Spaniard, as embodied in the bullfighter, with the image of the crowd, whose mindless conformism to the myth frustrates the individual's efforts to liberate himself from anonymity.

Looking *At*; Looking *For*

Saura describes the plot of *Hooligans* as "thematically, an instance of the fight for survival, the confrontation between a group of youths and the society that has abandoned them to their first impulses" (Saura 1960, 7). What we gradually discover as we examine the choice of visual techniques employed in *Hooligans* is a crucial link between the way the spectator is manipulated to view that fiction through cinematic conventions and the ways the characters look at the world around them. Indeed, the impossibility of empirical truth in the web of social artifice becomes one of the dominant social-stylistic bridges out of which the film establishes its discourse. In describing the nature of his collaboration with Saura on the film, Mario Camus explains: "Two distinct mentalities clashed there: Carlos's, which tried, let us say, to erase every vestige of logical order of scenes, which broke completely with the narrative thread. I'm accustomed to telling a story in a very orderly fashion so as to later on disorder it. But he made those brusque cuts and avoided any kind of sentimental posturing" (Villegas 1976, 12).

Indeed, a certain emphasis on disruptive, fragmenting devices in the film's narrational scheme seems pointedly designed to draw the spectator to a correspondence between the type of repressive, manipulated sight that defines the characters' way of seeing and the patterns of social sight that have positioned viewers to submit tacitly to the illusion of a congruent, stable world in their own interaction with their social environment. Our attention is insistently drawn to the way in which our "gaze" and the social position it implies blind us to the opaque patterns of social constraints to which the film's protagonists are subjected.

Saura defines the geography of social interaction in the film in terms of the "looks" of the various characters as these looks inscribe places of intelligibility, of narrative, representational coherence from which the spectator "reads" the fiction of the filmic text. These are, by and large, the "looks" of authority, each defined textually as the character's manipulation of another character's sight. The opening sequence establishes such a pattern. The film begins abruptly with a precredit shot of Ramón preparing to assault a blind lottery vendor sitting in her booth on a street corner. When she screams for help, the image cuts rapidly to a high-angle shot of a bullring where we see a youth (Juan) putting a young bull through its moves in a practice corrida. Just before the credits appear, we locate the origin of this shot as a place occupied on screen by a group of youngsters, no more than ten or eleven years old, who sit in the grandstand and admiringly follow Juan's every movement. Thus the spectator comes to occupy a place of sight that enables him to look down on the actions within the fictional space from a position of authority. Eventually, we will understand that this constructed position emblemizes the assumptions of authority that propel the young protagonists in their actions. But it is at best a figurative assumption of authority, for these ingenuous youths do not recognize the limits of their power.

The audience orients itself to the fiction initially through the classical conventions of on-screen "spectators-in-the-text." Nick Browne has described this type of visual-narrative enunciation so common to classical narrative cinema: "An impression of perceptual authority which the spectator assumes presents itself as being derived from places of characters within the fiction" (Browne 1981, 258). Tellingly, the first of these on-screen surrogates for the real spectator is an innocent child beguiled by the impression of prowess of Juan's bullfighting gestures and movements.

Our sense of perceptual authority is, of course, only metaphoric, yet Saura attempts to rechannel that metaphor into a specific textual project. The viewer is often made to stand back and observe, to question the meaning of actions, something that the characters are seldom willing or able to do, and, finally, to view the contradictions inherent in such socialized sight. The very concreteness of the material world in which these youths find themselves blocks from their view the manipulative force that is at the root of social positionality. Importantly, the terms of this blockage are introduced to us in the condition of blindness of the gang's first victim, the lottery vendor; for their own blindness to their true relation to society is the essential feature of all the gang members. What they cannot see is that, for whatever presumption of autonomy or power they may have over their immediate milieu, theirs is an atomized view, locked into an invisible system of snares that mask from them their true relation to the underlying system of authority and power in this society. It is ultimately an insight into our own social blindness to which the film inexorably leads us.

Disruptive editing and eccentric framing of a number of scenes work to thwart our normative reading of the film and to bring us to recognize that we have been placed in cinema as well as in culture by a chain of conventions that lead us to accept and internalize limited and skewed representations. A simple if somewhat forced example of the effort to dissociate the spectator from the illusion of naturalized fiction occurs in a scene described by Enrique Brasó (1974, 54–55) in which Juan comes to ask the bullfight

promoter, don Esteban, if he can have his name placed in the next fight
program. We see Juan approach the older man and ask: "Don Esteban,
Can I talk to you for a moment?" Don Esteban replies: "Yes, what do you
want?" The scene then cuts swiftly to a shot outside the bullring where
Juan is now speaking to his friends: "Don Esteban let me down. He told
me no." Such an editing device, common to the French New Wave style,
was, however, all but unknown in Spanish films at this point. When read
against the classical narrative practices of Spanish film of the day, it is particularly jarring in its impact on the spectator since the rapid projection
forward in time implied by the second scene is only coherent as the spectator retrospectively pieces the two fragments together in a congruent narrative whole. Saura's aim is clearly to engage his spectator actively in the
process of inquiry which begins with a visual decipherment of action.[3] A
most essential part of that involvement is exposing for the audience the
ways in which their prior conditioning to certain habits of social as well as
cinematic sight have led them into a number of critical impasses in their
reading of the film's narrative scheme.

   An elaborate sequence detailing the gang's robbery and disposal of a box
of tools reveals the progressive nature of the spectatorial hermeneutic. The
sequence begins as the gang gathers at a truck stop on the outskirts of
Madrid and members assume preassigned positions in preparation for the
theft of the toolbox from a parked truck. Chato is seated at a table inside
the restaurant; he peers out the window as the truck that the gang plans to
rob approaches from the distance. Other gang members are situated in
strategic positions both inside the restaurant as well as at the entrance. The
camera cuts rapidly from Chato looking through the window to Julián
standing guard at the doorway, then to a prostitute working with the gang
who attempts to divert the attention of one of the targeted truck drivers.

   In the next shot two members of the gang are seen in the parking area
in front of the restaurant; they are kneeling at the side of the truck, attempting to break open the toolbox. Because of the position of the truck,
the two youths are in constant danger of being seen by any of the unsuspecting customers. A series of eyeline shots from inside the restaurant to
the parking lot emphasizes the tension of the scene; each of the gang mem-

---

[3] In one of his rare essays on his theory of filmmaking, *"Por una mayor libertad de cámara"*
(For More Camera Freedom), Saura focuses on the relation between narrational innovation
and the audiences's absorption of such innovations: "Newspapers and newsreel techniques
have given to film new procedures of montage. Spectators have easily accepted the shifts of
image in movie newsreels as just another convention of the medium. The newsreel regularly
gathers fragments of the same event from different angles and points-of-view, without the
need for continuity in phrases or movements in order to establish [the scene's] continuity"
(31).

bers actively looks for potentially straying eyes of customers who might interrupt the robbery.

After a close-up of the two youths working furiously to dislodge the toolbox, the camera cuts abruptly to a medium shot of two unfamiliar faces, peasant women leaning against a wall and singing a folk song. This shot is particularly disconcerting since it is in no way localizable within the previously established narrative space. The tension of the robbery, made all the more dramatic by the play of glances through which the scene is articulated, lures the spectator into an anticipation of the outcome, only to have that resolution thwarted by the disruptive cut to the singers. Yet, as we will belatedly realize, this disruption has its place and purpose within the denouement of the robbery sequence.

From the close-up of the two singers we are introduced to a panoramic view of Madrid's Rastro flea market, unrelated, it would seem, either to the scene of the robbery or to the previous shot of the two women, although their song is still heard as the camera pans across the market area. Gradually, we discern the familiar figures of Chato and Julián moving through the crowd, one of them holding what appears to be the stolen toolbox under his arm. They walk up to a middle-aged stranger who is apparently waiting for them at the door of a building. The camera lingers on the facade of the building after the three men have gone inside. At last we locate the two peasant singers who have been standing against the wall.

Only retrospectively can the coherence of the sequence be grasped. The first scene, the robbery, has engaged the viewer in a simple but dramatic way in the tension of the action. We observe the action, but also share the gang's expectancy, as each glance shot carries with it the potential for a disruption of the robbery. With the elliptical jump-cut to the two street singers, the spectator's normative activity of *looking at* images and action in film has been transformed into an activity of *looking for* characters, continuity, or meaning. The viewer has, in effect, been repositioned by the enunciative scheme so as to replicate in his own viewing the perceptual activity of the gang members in the previous scene. When, at last, we are able to reduce the two scenes to a single, congruent, narrative scheme—a robbery and the disposal of the stolen goods—it is with the recognition that the perceptual placement of the fictional characters coincides with the position we have intuitively embraced as our own view of the later action.

In the flea market scene we once again confront the specter of the crowd, the anonymous mass of proletarian society, and we struggle to individuate characters within that mass. Our conditioned passivity to the visual field of conventional narrative film has momentarily been altered. In a literal sense we are involved in the tension that underlies the gang members' story, a tension between one's habits of passively *looking at*, and the possibilities of rechanneling those habits in such a way as to move one beyond contrived cultural representation to an activity of *looking for*, with all the cultural and political implications that such an activity necessarily implies in the Spain of the fifties.

Saura's underlying strategy in *Hooligans* is a deceptively simple one: pairing the cinematic fictional looks of his characters with his spectator's socially determined habits of looking. It is a strategy aimed at realigning the relation of the viewing subject to the world which, through his gaze, he embraces as normal and natural. This strategy becomes apparent even to the resistant spectator in the final sequence of the film in which Juan's debut at the novillada becomes the scene of his personal failure and, as well, the foil through which the gang members are ultimately trapped. One senses in the way Saura has invested the scene as the crucial moment in the fortunes of the protagonists and in the way he stages that moment of truth, that he is as much interested in demystifying the underlying patterns of ideological "blindness" as in depicting what is finally only an isolated instance of self-deception.

In the final corrida the contrived positionalities of the spectators in the stands at the bullring and of Juan, all living the illusion of individuality, are juxtaposed against a third perspective: the authoritarian look of the police investigators who have come to apprehend the gang members. Whether the police disrupt the corrida by arresting Juan before his debut or wait for the ill-fated conclusion of the fight, their authority is never in question. By waiting, they are, in fact, flaunting their sense of an invisible but all-pervasive social power, even beyond the encircled heroic ritual of the bullfight.

In progressive moves Saura's camera occupies first the position of Juan and the gang members who await, with unquestioning assurance, the inevitable success that they are certain the corrida will bring; then a series of shots of the disgruntled spectators in the stands who are now viewed explicitly as part of the elaborate social machinery blocking the gang's dream of success. That social machinery is ironically paired with the presence of the police as they wait at the arena barrier, looking at the corrida whose real outcome—the containment of the adversaries of social order—has already been predetermined. The denouement of the bullfight crystalizes in microcosm the fatalistic structures of ensnarement that lie hidden throughout this social landscape.

The arrangement of an audience of on-screen spectators dramatized in the final scene suggests once again that the depicted action is a simulacrum of the spectator's relation to the visual performance of cinema, with all the connotations of social blindness such a homology implies. It is the force of such illusory cultural narratives that blocks social sight and makes the audience victims and accomplices of their own social manipulation.

Hooligans ends with a freeze-frame shot of the bull's head as it lies prostrate in the sand. As an ironic twist, Saura shows us the glassy opened eye of the bull, seeing nothing and thereby replicating the deeper social blindness of those who have valorized this "moment of truth." In being forced to see the final image of the film as a photograph that exposes the true two-dimensionality of the screen space, the audience is thus returned to the awareness of their own position in the web of social representations. What we have taken for the represented social world is only a small fragment of a larger, contrived mosaic of actions.

In his treatment of the various spaces of action as fragmented, prismatic spaces of assumed authority and control, Saura reveals to us the conceptual heart of *Hooligans*: the exposure of the atomized world of the street gang and the implicit meaning of that atomization. Each member of the gang forges an illusion for himself of "making it" in a world that is there before his eyes, but from which he senses he has been excluded. What the characters never see, but what the spectator through the intervention of self-referential cinematic practices is brought to perceive and feel, is that the isolated individual is really trapped in place, not only by his social and economic circumstance, but also by the popular cultural ideology that induces him to live the illusion of his own autonomy.

When *Hooligans* was completed, a recently established government board selected the film as Spain's official entry to the 1960 Cannes Film Festival. Though the general audience reaction to the film was favorable, Saura was to learn that the official censorship review board had deleted ten minutes from the copy of the film authorized for domestic distribution and had given it its lowest possible subsidy rating, thus signaling to distributors the censors' assessment of the film as undesirable for public viewing. A Madrid booking for *Hooligans* was not possible until the summer of 1962, nearly three years after the film's completion and two years after the Spanish film journal *Temas del cine* had already devoted an entire issue to the film and its director as the bright new hope for Spanish cinema.

New Openings

In 1960, when Saura was at Cannes for the screening of *Hooligans*, he had the occasion to meet Luis Buñuel. Saura spoke to Buñuel of the latter's importance as a symbolic figure for a new generation of Spanish filmmakers, trying to persuade the legendary director to break his twenty-five-year exile and return to Spain to make a film. Buñuel's first and, up to this point, only film shot in his native country had been the 1932 *Tierra sin pan* (Land without Bread), banned successively by both the Republican and Francoist governments. Saura must have left a profound impression on Buñuel, for the famed surrealist later wrote to his family: "If Spanish youth is like those I have met here, Spain is saved" (Aranda 1969, 231). Saura described the

fateful meeting which would lead to the filming of Buñuel's most contro-
versial film, *Viridiana*, this way: "When we spoke to him about Spanish
censorship, Luis Buñuel decided not to make *Viridiana* in Spain, and only
our insistence succeeded in convincing him. Up to that time, the only one
of his works that had been shown in Spain was *Robinson Crusoe*, and even
that in a conveniently falsified version where the majority of the dialogue
was twisted. The ignorance of who he was was such that only a small number of young people and some film people knew of him" (Saura 1961, 28).

Buñuel was, of course, eventually persuaded to return to Spain to shoot
Viridiana as a coproduction for Portabello's FILM '59 and Bardem's production company, UNINCI. Owing in part to the original Cannes encounter and the subsequent *Viridiana* "affair," Saura's name would be linked to
Buñuel's over the next two decades in a variety of contexts, most often to
the political detriment and artistic disparagement of the younger director.

To the surprise of nearly everyone involved in the production, the script
of *Viridiana* was approved by the Spanish censors with only minor modifications, the most striking of which was a change in the very last scene of
the script, that only added more bite to what was already a film replete
with cynical and sarcastic aspersions to Spanish Catholic dogma and practice. To the disbelieving audiences at the 1961 Cannes festival, the completed version of *Viridiana* appeared to have the official endorsement of
the Spanish government. But when the film won the coveted Gold Palm,
the festival's highest award, only to be denounced by the official Vatican
newspaper, *L'Osservatore Romano*, as blasphemous, the Spanish government's response was to repudiate all connection with the film. Government
retaliation against those who it appeared were responsible for the production was swift and decisive. The film was banned in Spain, and even mention of it in the Spanish press was prohibited. Buñuel, it seemed, had once
again become the invisible man of Spanish cinema. José Muñoz-Fontán,
the under secretary of the Ministry of Information's film section, was dismissed from his post, and the Spanish coproducers of the film, UNINCI and
FILM '59, were disbanded.

Viewed as an accomplice to the *Viridiana* "affair," Saura was unofficially
blacklisted by producers who feared that any collaboration with him might
well lead to government retaliation against them (Alonso 1968, 3). His
career, which had started out with so much promise, appeared to have
quickly and unceremoniously ended. But then, in July of 1962, a radical
reshuffling of government ministers took place that included the removal
of the intransigent Arias Salgado as minister of information and the appointment of Manuel Fraga Iribarne in his place. Fraga soon named José
María García Escudero as the director of the ministry's film division. García Escudero had held that same post briefly in 1951 under Arias, but was
forced to resign because of the harsh criticism generated by his support of

Nieves Conde's *Furrows*. A liberal and a pragmatist within the doctrinaire ranks of the Francoist bureaucracy, García Escudero had also been one of the most prominent advocates of censorship reform at the 1955 Salamanca Conversations. Reassuming the position of government policymaker for the film industry, he was now able to put into practice many of the proposals that only a few years earlier had been viewed as dangerous and subversive by his predecessor. García Escudero's task was clear-cut: he had to revitalize the film industry. Such a radical shift in policy regarding film was altogether consistent with the spirit of change ordered by the technocrats who now held the decisive hand in running the government's key ministries. Thus began the seven-year period in Spanish cultural politics called *aperturismo*, the active policy of opening Spain up to the outside economic, industrial, and even cultural modernization, that carried with it an unheard-of liberalization of the means of public expression within the country.

Among the approaches García Escudero employed to energize film production over the coming years were two that were to give definitive force to Saura's career: the drafting in 1963 of a set of explicit norms that the censorship boards would utilize in the review and classification of Spanish films; and the establishment of a "special interest" subsidy, intended to promote high-quality cinema not so tightly bound up with the government's ideological penchants as the old "national interest" subsidies of the forties and fifties had been.

It was through this latter program that Saura came to propose the idea of a historical adventure film to the Spanish producer José Luis Dibildos. Dibildos was an unlikely partner for the independent-minded Saura. Though he had been an advocate of the liberalization and "Europeanization" of Spanish cinema for nearly a decade, the kind of films that his production company, Agata Films, favored seemed to have less to do with the legitimate aspirations of an authentic national cinema than with an enterprising plan to exploit commercial film properties by spicing them with a few suggestive, topical references to political and social themes. Dibildos had produced a series of mildly daring topical comedies that had raised social themes of the day in innocuous, lighthearted ways. Beginning with *Viaje de novios* (1956: Honeymoon Trip), he had produced eight such social comedies, all of which proved commercially successful in Spain but were ignored abroad precisely among the audiences for whom Dibildos had intended them. With the government's new subsidy scheme for "special interest," or art, films, as the phrase was commonly interpreted, Dibildos saw a way to continue his effort, while Saura looked at the arrangement as the only way of returning to filmmaking. Though obviously the result of a forced marriage of intellectual filmmaking and commercial contrivance, *Lament for a Bandit*, the sole product of their collaboration, is nonetheless a watershed in Saura's early development. For here, in a crucial way, he was forced to confront the tensions between his own ideas of what film might do and say, and the commercial and political constraints of the Spanish film industry.

Llanto por un bandido (1963: Lament for a Bandit)

A commercial disaster in its Madrid opening, *Lament for a Bandit* failed to impress even those Spanish critics who were so lavish in their praise of *Hooligans*. The problems with the film have often been attributed to certain incompatibilities between Saura and Dibildos, the unwieldy scale of a production that included hundreds of extras, and finally, the actions of the censors who deleted a substantial segment from the opening sequence of the film, thus rendering the narrative largely incomprehensible.

But beneath these obvious problems, *Lament* also suffered from Saura's overambitious conception of his project. Constructing an intellectualized biography of the legendary Andalusian bandit of the nineteenth century, José María Hinojosa, sung about in Spanish ballads as the heroic "good bandit," Saura invested the script he and Mario Camus developed with a cluster of abstract themes related to the concept of distorted and falsified Spanish cultural history. But beyond seeing Hinojosa as a victim of social ideology as the gang members of *Hooligans* had been, the script also sug-,gests that he is a figure wrongly appropriated by subsequent generations as part of the progressive mythification of Spanish individualism. The focus of Saura's conception of his character and story is clearly a reflection on the deceptive constructions of history that contemporary popular or mass culture has mobilized to orient modern Spaniards to a fraudulent notion of their own cultural history.

The film's action is situated in one of the most chaotic periods of Spanish history of the last century, the "ominous decade" of the 1820s, as historians call it, when, after the defeat of Napoleon's armies, the Andalusian population was torn between the tyrannical order of the armies of King Fernando VII and the insurgent liberal forces who attempted unsuccessfully to overthrow the monarchy. During this time, there arose a number of guerrilla fighters who, having helped to expel the French, now remained outside the law as *bandoleros*, brigands, courted by both liberals and monarchists who sought domination of the region. The general lines of this historical conflict seemed to lend themselves to a symbolic tale in which Saura might draw parallels to a wide range of contemporary political themes and situations. Speaking to an interviewer in the early sixties about his initial motivation in selecting a historical project, Saura says, "For a long time, Camus and I had been looking for a film that would appeal to a larger public. . . . We wanted to make a film within a popular vein, in which we could introduce real Spaniards, the Spanish people [*pueblo*], and our landscape, and at the same time to develop one of my own interests, which was to make a film in color in which I could work out some of the experiences I had already touched on in *Cuenca*. In this way, we chose the theme of "*el Tempranillo*," because he was a type of nineteenth-century myth who had been converted into a kind of superman, a popular hero who fought against absolute power . . . an individual who lent himself to this kind of film" (Egea and San Miguel 1962, 33).

Saura sketched the general outline of the script around details he was able to piece together from the life and legends associated with José María Hinojosa. Some of these were of purely popular inspiration, such as the Andalusian folk ballads still sung in many villages in southern Spain; other sources were part of the literary archeology of nineteenth-century romanticism: Théophile Gautier's and Natalio Riva's picturesque depictions of everyday life in Spain in the nineteenth century, and Prosper Mérimée's letters and articles on his travels in southern Spain. Similarly, the pictorial style that dominates the film is an effort to render cinematically qualities of the two most influential visual renditions of Andalusian life of the period: those of Goya and Gustave Doré.

As Saura says, *Lament for a Bandit* was ". . . a film about the nineteenth century . . . about a bandit, but it was the thematics that interested me, within the social problematic of the nineteenth century, but with repercussions in terms of the situation in which we currently lived" (Alonso 1968, 3). The details of Hinojosa's life and exploits are well known to Spaniards familiar with the ballads about the "good bandit," a sort of Spanish Robin Hood. In Saura's version, however, a decidedly antiheroic perspective is established from the very start. The story begins when, as a fugitive from the law, José María (Francisco Rabal) is taken in by a gang of highwaymen headed by the cruel chieftain, Lutos (Lino Ventura). José María witnesses a number of Lutos's acts of sadism and finally challenges the leader's authority. Killing the bandit chief in a brutal fight, José María assumes leadership of the gang. In time, he and his men gain control over a vast portion of Andalusia, opposing the king's authority by demanding tribute from stagecoaches that pass through their territory.

As an enemy of the king, José María gains the admiration of the long-suffering peasants who see him as their defender. He befriends a rebel soldier, the liberal Pedro Sánchez (Philippe Leroy), whom he makes his personal secretary. Through Sánchez's efforts, the bandits eventually ally themselves with the liberal army. Sánchez understands José María's petty vanity and flatters the chieftain into making a number of political alliances which further the liberal cause. But there is a decisive crisis in the bandit's life when the king's soldiers burn his farmhouse and murder his wife (Lea Massari) and newborn baby. From this point on, José María is a changed man, despondent and taciturn, given easily to extremes of cruelty.

Now markedly aged and spiritually broken, José María accepts the king's offer of a pardon if he will lay down his arms and disband his gang. His men, however, decide to continue their fight under Sánchez's leadership. In a final act of self-destruction, José María agrees to lead the king's troops to the liberals' mountain hideout. Having betrayed the people he once led, José María is now the victim of their revenge. He is murdered in ambush by one of his former comrades.

To interviewers of the day, Saura could only speak of a narrowly defined aesthetic objective in *Lament for a Bandit* that guided him in developing the film: to debunk the notion of "Spain as seen under the prism of foreign eyes, beautiful Spain in which everything was multicolored and a cause for marvel" (Cobos 1963, 414). He would describe his efforts "to make a film which would be more static than dynamic, one which you could *contemplate*, a film in which events occur with a kind of repose, a little like the films of Mizoguchi" (Brasó 1974, 86). His method was to intersect the simple and straightforward material of his narrative with a series of mediations, posing historical intertexts in both sound and image. Indeed, there is a constant emphasis of the artificial mise-en-scène of action throughout the film which serves to remind the audience that their notion of historical reality is continually mediated by contrived and often blatantly false artistic conventions. Beneath that simple aesthetic correction, however, lies a more potent political agenda that relates as much to the questions of the ideology of artistic form as to the more explicit theme of the Spaniard's age-old susceptibility to demagoguery.

A Political Film

In one of the more thoughtful discussions of the film at the time of its release, José Luis Egea suggested a contemporary analogue to the character of José María in Manuel Benítez, the "rags to riches" torero of the fifties and sixties, popularly known as "El Cordobés," and revered by Spaniards as a national hero (Egea 1964, 61). Saura's studied treatment of the historical genre was, in fact, widely interpreted as *film à clef*, with the most probable contemporary cognate figure of the bandit hero being Franco himself, although surely no one would venture such an interpretation in print. José María's achievement of the veneer of respectability through the aegis of his intellectual apologists, his transformation from the regional bandit to a symbolic figure of national liberation, and finally, his descent into self-imposed isolation, all seemed to have resonance in the anti-Francoist characterization of the Caudillo as a glorified bandit.

The censors were apparently uneasy with the film when it was submitted for final review to obtain a distribution license. A prologue sequence, not directly related to El Tempranillo's story but intended to suggest the cultural and political ambience of the period, was butchered beyond recognition. The sequence was originally written in the following manner: "Seven bandits are carted into a town's main square while all the inhabitants watch, fanning themselves. A man reads a list of their crimes. The executioner asks pardon for what he is about to do, making the sign of the cross, and then, one by one, he kills all seven bandits. From there the film cuts to José María in the mountains, meeting up with the gang he later controls" (Bartholomew 1983, 23).

Saura calls this prologue as originally written and shot "a great ritual" (Brasó 1974, 91). The participants in the execution ceremony—the town crier, the executioner, military officers, even the prisoners—appear to our view to be lifeless mannequins, or actors in a poor performance that is being staged for the benefit of an on-screen audience, the spectators who view the proceedings from the balconies overlooking the square. It is from this position, in terms of both physical perspective and social class, that the real audience is positioned to view the action of the prologue. Much of what ensues in the plot will only confirm the particularity of a certain reading of Spanish history that either serves the interest of a privileged social and political class or, as in the case of José María, works to manipulate the individual to the expediency of that privileged class's objectives. The prologue inevitably places the liberal prisoners at a visual remove within the scene; the choice of camera placement robs their deaths of the aura of heroic sacrifice, thus introducing at the film's outset the central tension between the individual's self-deluding sense of his own power and worth and the fabric of representations that robs him of his stature as an individual.

It was assumed that the motivation for the extreme mutilation of this scene had to do with the fact that Buñuel played the role of the executioner. The anti-Francoist playwright, Antonio Buero Vallejo, played the town crier, and seven prominent opposition writers, including the outspoken playwright Alfonso Sastre were to play the seven bandits. Of the original sequence, only a brief set of images of Buñuel and Buero Vallejo remain. Saura later suggested that the censors' discomfort with the sequence lay, as well, in the obvious connection between the method of execution, strangulation through the medieval Spanish method of garrote, and the recent execution of a communist leader, Julián Grimau, which had provoked an interational protest against the Franco dictatorship (Bartholomew 1983, 23).

Portrait of a Victim

While the visual and narrative structures of *Lament for a Bandit* promote such analogical readings of the characters and the plot, there is a more sophisticated narrative conception operating here as well. The film insistently brings to the audience's attention the aesthetic and popular cultural motifs that have constructed the modern impression of José María's life and times. In this manner, the simple strategy of historical analogy in the film gradually cedes to a focus on the ideological appropriation of history. Saura brings us to see just how we, as spectators, have participated in the maintenance of a mythic archetype that invests history with a false coherence. The film thus ceases to be about the fortunes of José María, who is now seen as merely an "effect" of a contrived system of representation, and becomes the demystification of a false historical consciousness that presumably engages and shapes the outlook of the contemporary Spaniard. As El Tempranillo's story is treated by "history," which to Saura means the ideologically complicit Francoist history, we discern that historical representation, such as the modes of popular cultural representation the film utilizes, only masks and displaces contradictions from the consciousness of the contemporary subject in culture.

4. *Lament for a Bandit* (*Llanto por un bandido*, 1963)

The use of painting as the mediating structure organizing and regulating spectator sight is central to our understanding of this project. In the fight scene between José María and Lutos early in the action, for example, Saura conspicuously uses the iconography of Goya's painting *Pelea a garrotazos* (Brawl with Cudgels) as the artistic design of action. By stylizing the elements of the fight to evoke in the Spanish audience a recognition of the Goya painting, Saura inserts into his audience's view a subtle recognition of the schism between action and the aesthetic frames that stabilize our view of action. The film recreates Goya's image in which two combatants are buried in the sand to their waists. But where the painting suggested swift, violent action, the film gives a contrary impression. The other members of the bandit gang retreat to a nearby hillside from where they plan to wait out the conclusion of the fight. The dramatic intensity of the life-or-death fight that Goya depicted with bold and violent pictorial strokes is absent from Saura's scene as it quickly becomes apparent that the outcome of the duel will not be decided by a single blow by either man, but by a protracted, antiheroic bludgeoning of one or the other fighter during a period of minutes or possibly hours. Between the suggestion of a heroic combat to the death, which one has become accustomed to expect from historical adventure films, and the slow, tedious battle enacted before our eyes, we begin to sense the basic discrepancy between socially shaped expectations of representation and the events that those conventions are meant to enunciate.

Historical and cultural conventions have placed the narrative depicted in Goya's original painting within a decidedly heroic-epic context that Saura's cinematic mise-en-scène intentionally undercuts. The on-screen audience, physically and emotionally detached from the action (they know from the outset that the battle will not be decided with a single blow), constructs a new frame for the event, revealing to the real audience a historical inscription that effectively mediates their viewing of the action. As in the prologue sequence, a persistent camera play dwarfs would-be heroic figures, deflating their gestures and, importantly, drawing the audience's attention toward the underlying conceptual play between events and the cultural and historical *mise-en-cadre* that has constructed and fixed meanings extraneous to the depicted events.

The duel is only one of a series of scenes that debunk the exotic and picturesque renditions of Spanish folk customs that were the staple of foreign pictorial as well as literary treatments of Spain. Out of such contrived visions, nurtured from within and without by a chain of cultural and artistic clichés, comes the mythology of a Spanishness of rugged individualism against which the film works thematically. The brilliance of Saura's conception derives from the way in which he conceives of the linkage between the theme of artistic and cultural imposture and the ideology of a false individualism that has shaped contemporary social and political values for the Spaniard. To the annoyance of both his critics and audiences, he chooses not simply to tell the "true story" of José María in the conventional style of historical genre films, but to sketch in a few bold strokes the outline of José María's life over nearly twenty years, and then to intersect moments in that exemplary life with perspectives that underscore the film's larger message of the imposture of Spanish cultural and political identity.

After establishing José María's identity as an outlaw whose instincts are basically decent, the plot of *Lament for a Bandit* advances by dramatizing a series of critical contacts between El Tempranillo, now a rebel chieftain, and the two dominant political forces vying for his support: the liberals and the royalists. Saura seems to suggest through such plotting that an individual, even a social outcast, is always implicated and controlled by the structures that order society, even as it appears that the individual lives beyond such structures. In one elaborate sequence, he links the visual deceits of painting with the political and personal facets of his character by introducing a painter as the mediator of social illusionism.

Having gotten through the royalist lines in disguise in order to visit his wife, María Jerónima, El Tempranillo is en route back to his camp when he is stopped by an armed man, Pedro Sánchez, a rebel soldier fleeing from the royalists. After getting Sánchez's pistol, José María sits astride his horse, smiling cunningly. The image slowly dissolves into a medium shot of the brigand now decked in traditional formal attire, but with the same ironic expression and nearly the same pose he held in the previous close-up. His posture suggests the quality of a portrait, and in successive shots after the initial dissolve, we discover that he is in his camp seated for a portrait painting. The progression of a half dozen shots shows us first the nearly completed portrait of José María, then the English artist (Pablo Runyan), as he views his human subject in contrast to the images on the canvas, then with increasing distance from José María, a larger scene in which other members of the gang look over the painter's shoulder and comment on the obvious differences between the painted image and the real man. Through this series of shots, José María recedes further into the background, dwarfed by the camera's increasing distance in each successive shot.

The camera then cuts away to some other spot in the camp to show some of José María's men carousing in a playful manner. When a call for "pay" is heard, the men run to the site where the portrait sitting is still in progress. Pedro Sánchez is now located in the scene. He has apparently become secretary to José María and, as the men gather around a table in the clearing where a paymaster and Sánchez are seated at screen right, Sánchez reads a letter to José María who is still visible in his erect and stilted posture of self-importance on screen left. The letter is a request from the king, asking the bandit to allow mail coaches to pass through his territory without paying tribute to the gang. José María responds smugly that the request will not be honored. The scene ends with a final close-up of El Tempranillo in his self-satisfied portrait posture.

This sequence poses in microcosm the progressive transformation of the once-natural peasant into a hollow portrait figure. It further identifies the dual source of that denaturalization as the interaction between the protagonist's own narcissism and the web of created social and political interests that have nurtured his vanity: the gang, the king, even the liberal intellectual Sánchez. But the portrait is not some static object in Saura's view. It not only falsifies the image it portrays, but also transforms its subject. José María has clearly been seduced by the artistic conventions of romantic portraiture that image him as an idealized, heroic individual. While still in that pose, he will "act out" a response to the king's request that coincides with the bravado of his assumed persona in the portrait. Importantly, he is performing here for multiple audiences: the assembled gang members for whom he needs to act as a defiant and fearless leader, but also for an unseen, admiring audience who will someday view him as an important, heroic figure. In this, José María is really a hapless pawn in the same game of social illusionism that had motivated and finally entrapped the gang members in *Hooligans*.

The portrait scene crystalizes the dramatic and conceptual design around which the whole tale of José María's life will take shape. It binds the spectator's interest to the character, but at the very instant when it frames the character, we are drawn back in order to view the heroic construction as a deformation of our own popular idealization of the legendary bandit. It is here where Saura wants to make explicit the relation of political forces to the aesthetic conventions that shape popular cultural imagination. But, importantly, that recognition of personal snares in culture is consistently denied the protagonist who willingly embraces all the artifices of appearances that seem to him to confirm his own illusion of power. El Tempranillo's belated recognition of his own trajectory of failure and dissolution is implied in the final phase of the film that describes the brigand's dissolution after the murder of his wife and their newborn baby by royalist troops.

The murder is the culmination of a series of efforts by the royalists to capture José María; in each of these attempts, the plan was always to lure him out of hiding by capturing his wife. Such efforts suggest that the royalists understood that if they could contain and control José María's most intimate, instinctive side, they could control the man, as well. Though their plan fails, María Jerónima's death marks the turning point in José María's psychic and political fortunes. He becomes more blood thirsty than ever before and pursues a course of revenge against the crown. Finally, his oldest friend rebukes him by evoking the resemblance between José María's actions and the cruelty years earlier of Lutos, the sadistic brigand he had killed in a duel. José María pauses, as if to acknowledge the failure of his own life.

Ensnared in a world from which he is emotionally estranged, El Tempranillo no longer holds any allegiance to his comrades. He eventually accepts the king's amnesty, putting down his arms, willingly aiding the royalist army in pursuit of the liberal band. In the final sequence we see him lead a military escort out of his village toward the mountain hideout of Sánchez's men. As they leave the village, a soldier pushes an old peasant woman to the side of the road in order to let the horse bearing the bloated and decrepit José María pass. "It's always the farmers," the old woman moans. "What have we done that they treat us as prisoners?" Standing broken at the edge of the road as the entourage led by the grotesque figure of José María passes by, the old woman expresses the predicament of contemporary Spaniards, positioned as they are between the structures of power and the false illusions of a heroic ideal which they are supposed to accept as their own.

José María then leads the troops to the mountain hideout of his former comrades. In the ensuing encounter he is killed, and the image of his lifeless body draped over his horse lingers on the screen in a freeze-frame as we hear the off-screen voice of a folk singer chanting a lament for the death of the "good bandit," El Tempranillo. The final invocation of this ballad that accompanies his pathetic death works as yet another bridge between the historical past and the audience's position in the present. The audience, Saura hopes, will see through this distanced contemplation the truth of its position in a contrived historiography of false values constructed to manipulate it into social and ideological passivity.

Despite its conceptual rigor, *Lament for a Bandit* proved to be far better as an idea than as a film. Yet the experience taught Saura an important lesson about the nature of Spanish commercial filmmaking that would have critical impact on his stylistic development over the next decade. Nearly twenty years later, in his flamenco dance trilogy, *Blood Wedding*, *Carmen*, and *Love, the Magician*, he would return to the questions of the ideological underpinnings of artistic form that are at the heart of *Lament for a Bandit*.

Possibilities within the System

Saura interpreted the failure of *Lament for a Bandit* to have been the result of his inability to control the artistic development of the film in both its production and final editing. This led him to recognize the imperative of achieving greater authorial control over his work, thus setting the stage for his willingness to collaborate with Elías Querejeta on a film shortly after the debacle of *Lament*. Querejeta was as unlikely a partner for Saura as Dibildos had been. A former soccer player and successful scriptwriter, he had made two documentary films earlier in the decade, *A través de San Sebastián* (1960: Inside San Sebastian) and *A través de fútbol* (1962: The Ins and Outs of Soccer), encountering many of the same censorship problems that had hampered Saura's work. He was, like Saura, "tired of letting other people have the decisions about film" (Fuentes 1981, 12). Indeed, they shared a number of common impressions of the dilemma of contemporary Spanish culture as well as of the dire situation of Spanish film production. Somewhat impetuously, Querejeta had decided to pursue on his own the formation of an independent production company he hoped might facilitate more expressive, creative film productions. Though inexperienced in the financial aspects of film production when he began speaking with Saura about a possible collaboration, Querejeta was, nonetheless, determined to find a way to capitalize on the "special interest" subsidy and was further buoyed by the recently published modifications in the censorship review procedure that now contained a set of explicitly stated norms of acceptability upon which film scripts and final prints would be evaluated.

Querejeta's strategy was to cultivate, in both the form and content of a Spanish film, an "international" style, one that might address two well-defined audiences, one Spanish and the other a limited cosmopolitan audience abroad. Dibildos had only spoken of such a style but seemed not to know how to develop it in his own productions. Querejeta clearly recognized that serious Spanish cinema, the kind Bardem and Berlanga had attempted in the fifties, had a severely limited domestic appeal, mostly for university students and the intellectual communities in major metropolitan areas. If that audience could be paired with a larger but equally well-defined foreign audience through a rigorously shaped thematic focus, then a small-budget Spanish film might well prove itself financially self-sustaining as well as artistically valid.

Querejeta's plan took into account from the very start the fact of Spain's marginality in the world. To succeed with a film in Spain meant that you had to succeed elsewhere first. The key factor was to reach that foreign market through entry of the Spanish film in foreign film festivals, a strategy that required the film to receive more active support than government bureaucrats had previously been willing or able to provide.

That activism, however, had to begin with the producer and director; thus, Querejeta improvised an aggressive approach with the government's film administration on *The Hunt*, his first collaboration with Saura, that would become the hallmark of his successful managerial style over the next two decades. This involved what Querejeta called the "technique of the *fait accompi*" (Hernández Les 1986, *Personalidad* 4), maintaining two scripts, one for the censors' approval and one for actual shooting; then pressuring the censors to accept, even with modifications, sequences and dialogues that they would have rejected in the earlier shooting script. Querejeta's activism included every aspect of the government's contact with film production, from approval of shooting scripts to the classification of his films for subsidies. His approach perfectly fit the temperament of the García Escudero administration, which appeared to want to support the kind of films Querejeta was proposing.

What had always seemed to Saura an adversarial relationship with bureaucrats in the censorship and subsidy offices Querejeta now redefined as an active adjustment to the limits and controls set by the government—while developing a more subtle approach to cultural critique within the elaboration of the film script. Under Querejeta's stewardship, Saura was asked to conform to a production budget that was to alter the scale if not the substance of his work: scripts with fewer actors and settings, a certain vigilance with the general cost of production, and finally, a conscientious understanding of the multiple audiences within the government and outside to whom the film would ultimately be directed.

In exchange for accepting these limitations, which he understood to be more practical than conceptual in nature, Saura was given his first real experience of complete production control over a film. He would later observe, ironically, that with a smaller budget than he had had at his disposal in *Lament for a Bandit*, *The Hunt* offered him more flexibility and more control over his work. (Brasó 1974, 125). As well as authorial freedom, Querejeta provided Saura with a small, highly professional technical crew who would remain with him through many of his later successes. Among these were Luis Cuadrado, as director of photography, whose work would be praised as contributing in an outstanding way to the "Saura touch," Teo Escamilla as cameraman, and Pablo del Amo as editor. It was also part of Querejeta's plan to improve the technical quality of his films, for he firmly believed that part of the noncompetitiveness of Spanish film abroad was due to its mediocre production quality.

No doubt as the result of discussions with Querejeta, Saura shifted his conception of *The Hunt* away from the socially validated myths that seduce and manipulate individuals toward the profiling of the mental machinery of the individual in whose mind the norms of a constraining social order have been formed and naturalized. With Angelino Fons, another student from the National Film School, Saura drafted a loose version of a script about four weekend hunters even before he began to talk seriously of a collaboration with Querejeta: "The theme of *The Hunt* occurred to me when I was filming some scenes of *Lament for a Bandit*, precisely in the same place where later I was to make the film. The scenery of the game preserve impressed me from the start: without a single tree, gypseous and dry, crossed only by a shallow stream and lined with rabbit den holes, as well as the caves and trenches from the War" (Bartholomew 1983, 27).

Now, with certain modifications included to adhere to the constraints of Querejeta's plan, the script was presented to the censorship board for the necessary shooting license. But the censors objected to a number of political allusions within the script that had to be expunged before permission could be granted. The working title, *Caza de conejos* (Rabbit Hunt), was thought to contain a sexual reference and had to be changed simply to *The Hunt*. The name of the cafe, Bar España, where the first scene of the film takes place, had to be changed since it appeared to suggest a national allegorical dimension to the film. The censors also insisted that all reference to the Civil War be deleted from the dialogue. In a story about three men who had once been comrades in the war and now found themselves on a rabbit hunt in a valley where a battle in that war has been fought, such an omission seemed at first to be the kind of mindless obstruction that could only damage the film's impact and meaning. Yet, as Saura reveals, the result of this prohibition was just the opposite: " 'Civil War' is not mentioned at any point in the film because it was absolutely prohibited by the censors. Only the phrase 'the war' is used, and it winds up taking on a strange meaning. By way of this indirection one gets the feeling that this is an oppressive environment, that there is a sense of violence, not only in the characters but in the setting itself, because everyone understands that there's been a war; there are trenches, a dead soldier's bones, and all the elements that give the presence of 'the war' an abstract meaning if you like, but without any concrete allusion" (Alonso 1968, 7–8).

What thus takes shape in *The Hunt* is the unique self-referential status of a narrative within the film that operates as a dilemma for both the fictional characters and the spectator. "Since you can't tell a story directly," Saura observes, "you have to circle around it" (Gubern 1973, 19). This strategy, which in a less self-conscious way was present in his previous films, works now to demarcate in striking ways the contrived scenario of an imposed cultural narrative: characters are situated within the social scenarios that have been constructed for them and in which they are conditioned to "perform." In effect, Saura has turned the premise of social realism around in this approach by making social reality self-consciously a problem of representation for the characters in the film.

Social Pathology

The plot of *The Hunt* bears several unmistakable resemblances to the tales of male groups and their moves toward violence as recounted in the earlier *Hooligans* and *Lament for a Bandit*. But, whereas in those films Saura concentrated on the plight of characters who lived on the margins of society, who were, in fact, outcasts, in *The Hunt* we are brought to the very center of contemporary social respectability: the milieu, the values and, finally, the consciousness of the Spanish bourgeoisie of the sixties.

Instead of a rebellion against the injustice of an uncaring social system, we witness the evolving marks of an unmistakable social pathology that is at the heart of social normality. José (Ismael Merlo) has thought up the scheme of inviting his old war buddy, Paco (Alfredo Mayo), to his hunting preserve for a leisurely day of rabbit hunting in order to put the bite on him for a much-needed loan to keep his failing business alive. The two are accompanied on the hunt by Luis (José María Prada), another former comrade who now works for José, and Enrique (Emilio Gutiérrez Caba), Paco's brother-in-law, much younger than the other three and somewhat excluded from the trio's conversations about "the good old days." Removed from these matters, Enrique finds himself the unwitting witness to the progressively more volatile feuding among the three older men. Almost from the start of the outing, old tensions and conflicts surface. Paco and José treat Luis as the fool, just as they used to do in the army; a long-festering rivalry between Paco and José shows itself in their seemingly innocent conversation.

If the plot about four weekend hunters and their descent into a human hunt appears straightforward, Saura's treatment is not. Wherever possible, he strategically aligns cinematic and intertextual reference to the Civil War with the actions, words, and images of his characters. National history is thus textualized in *The Hunt* within the terms of cinematic history. A prime example of this centers on the actor Alfredo Mayo. As a young man, Mayo built his career upon a series of forties films playing the role of the stalwart Nationalist hero fighting the Republican scourge. By far, the most influential of these was the role of José Churruca in Sáenz de Heredia's *Raza*. Not only did Mayo play the part of the nationalist patriot; his role was fashioned as a sanitized version of the Caudillo, replete with narrative parallels to Franco's own biography. Nowhere in *The Hunt* is there any overt reference to Mayo's former screen persona, yet implicitly, the character of Paco seems to represent a sequel to the earlier Alfredo Mayo, film-actor-as-national-hero. It is a shattering statement of the passage of time and the transformation of a bygone mythic hero into a venal and narcissistic old man.

The film was shot in a valley that once witnessed a Civil War battle similar to the one described in the dialogue. But the ploy of making the game preserve a former battle site, while grounded in fact, works as yet another intertextual reference—an homage in this instance to Juan Antonio Bardem's *Death of a Cyclist* (1955). This work is perhaps the strongest, certainly the most daring, expression of anti-Francoist sentiment in Spanish cinema of the 1950s. As in Bardem's film, the narrative space of *The Hunt* implies that the mise-en-scène of all contemporary action is necessarily the suppressed battlefield of the Civil War, not merely as a passive setting to action, but as the absent cause of all the personal and collective moves we witness. In this way the audience is reminded of the origins of the power structure that has placed the film's protagonists in conflict.

Enrique's curiosity about the past is triggered by the cryptic references made by his companions to the war. Instinctively, he finds himself questioning the other men and thereby underscoring for his audience the allusions to the unnameable war which is the insistent intertext of all narrative action. The development of Enrique as a fictional character within the plot was Saura's most inspired response to the list of proscribed topics within the script, for while the principal lines of action and dialogue scrupulously follow the censors' advice, Enrique's constant presence works to remind the viewer of the insufficiency of what is presented and discussed. He is the opaque figure of inquiry into the habits of a false social normality, questioning by his gaze, as well as by his words, the reified social mise-en-scène that for the characters and the censors passes for the acceptable order of contemporary experience.

The only character truly born into Francoism, Enrique merely lives out the dictates of that definition of cultural ideology. Yet because he is endowed with an intellectual curiosity about the actions of people around him, he gradually leads the audience to share his own awareness of the constrained and finally fraudulent impression of the world that he has for so long accepted as natural. At first he appears to be merely a mechanical figure, a device through which to manipulate the audience's curiosity about the past and intrigue about the contemporary conflict. Slowly, the chain of his questions makes the real spectator aware of the frame of interdictions that cuts off a seemingly self-sufficient normality from the historical contexts that have given rise to it.

Saura's strategy is to endow his character with a curious form of cultural amnesia that itself reflects Enrique's status as the symbolic representation of a generation of younger Spaniards who have only the vaguest notion of the roots of their contemporary circumstance. More than any of the other characters, Enrique insists upon his own individuality and, as well, his own noncomplicity with the past. Living the illusion of order that the oppressive postwar dictatorship imposed upon Spain, he affirms as authentic a narrowly contrived vision of the world by disavowing the past and reasserting a false individualism born of his status as a "new" Spaniard. He even boldly declares to Luis at one point, "I don't have to depend on *anybody!*" By using such a normative figure of sight and cultural belief as the formulator of narrational coherence through much of the film's action, Saura is able to place in the foreground as drama the multiple insufficiencies to which the system of cultural representation and more, the Spanish ethos of the sixties, has moved.

The war generation, Paco, José, and Luis, is played off against Enrique's contemporary generation, ironically characterized by the song played by Enrique on the radio: "Loca juventud" (Crazy Youth): Having fought and won the war, the older men have unavoidably fallen into the trap of believing the myth of their own victory. The younger generation, embodied by Enrique, is the inevitable consequence of its forebears. Shielded from an understanding of the true terms of his historical position, he only sees the aging relics of the past which hold no interest for him. Saura's ploy is simply to play the two attitudes off each other and thereby to raise in his audience's mind a keener awareness of the problematic issue of historical consciousness which in the sixties remains the conceptual battlefront of Francoism.

The persistent interaction with Paco, José, and Luis only awakens in Enrique the gradual recognition that his own point of view is a narrow and finally false one, that he is less a detached observer than a victim of the history he so strongly disavows. Through this gradual shift in Enrique's awareness of his relation to history the spectator's sight and position are slowly redefined. For, inevitably, the viewer's claim to coherent, distanced authority and noninvolvement with the action he sees is intimately intertwined with Enrique's narrative destiny. The spectator will gradually come to see and to understand in a self-referential way his act of sight, of "bearing witness" to the film as a form of personal and historical correction, of historical reflexivity in its most profound sense.

Of particular note in Saura's equation of the conventions of cinematic spectatorship with social spectatorship is the way in which the credit sequence of *The Hunt* works to produce within the filmic discourse a "trace" of memory for the spectator that will parallel at the film's end a significant retrospection for the fictional characters. There is evidence as early as *Hooligans* that he conceived the precredits and credits of his film as an essential grounding element through which the conceptual project at the root of the narrative could work to construct a particular spectator disposition to the ensuing narrative.

The credits are projected against a close-up shot of caged ferrets in agitated movement as they attempt to break out of their confinement. The rectangular cage conforms in shape to the rectangular movie screen, thus giving the spectator a first inkling of the entrapment that will later be expressed as a shared condition of audience and fictional characters. The credits are accompanied by the ominous, rythmic drumbeat that will be repeated as the jeep carrying the four hunters makes its initial descent into the valley. This musical overstatement of foreboding and menace accompanying the images and related to the motif of entrapment—it is repeated again when Enrique first spies the holes in the hillside that were used as foxholes during the war—serves as a melodramatic cue to the spectator. It creates an intentionally conventionalized trope of narration that brings to the foreground for the audience the ritual, performative nature of all the actions they are viewing.

When the final deadly hunt begins later in the film, it is introduced by the gamekeeper's arrival at the campsite with the caged ferrets the spectator has already viewed passively in the credit sequence. The film's denouement is thus posed less as a sudden descent into violence than as a déjà vu of what the audience already implicitly knew was there from the very beginning.[4] The film evolves through stages of action that seem to be guided by the crescendo of heat and animosity in the external environment, but that also delineate Enrique's gradual move toward a recognition of his own relation to the gradually surfacing struggle. There is a morning hunt scene in which the men flush out rabbits that are hiding in the bush; they take a break at midday to prepare a meal, at which time José sends Luis and Enrique to a nearby village for bread so that he can talk to Paco about the loan. This is followed by a siesta, a pause in the intensifying emotions of all the hunters, then a late-afternoon hunt in which ferrets are used to flush the rabbits out of the lairs in a nearby hill. Paco's refusal to lend him the needed money makes José markedly more irritable. When Paco shoots one of the ferrets instead of a rabbit, an intentionally symbolic action to further humiliate José, José goes mad and takes rifle aim at Paco, killing him. Luis, now delirious, drives his jeep up to José, screaming "Kill me too, get it over with!" Enrique stands frozen, aghast, as José and Luis kill each other. In a state of bewilderment and shock, Enrique runs up the side of the hill to flee the valley. The film ends with a freeze-frame of Enrique's profile in flight.

Interrogations

In the first sequence after the credits, the breakfast stop at a roadside cafe, we begin to identify Enrique as an interrogator of the past, but only on the level of personal intrigues. Ignorant of the causes of friction between José and Paco, he asks Luis about Arturo, a friend of the three older men whose

---

[4] The American distribution copy of *The Hunt* inexplicably replaces the credit sequence as described here with shots showing the jeep with the four hunters approaching the game preserve. The background music of the original credits is retained. Since the caged ferrets again appear in a brief scene in the gamekeeper's house when the hunters stop there before they set up camp, the American version is able to retain some sense of the déjà vu in the final sequence. However, the explicit address to the audience's cinematic memory is less pronounced and, one may assume, the impact of the déjà vu is correspondingly less intense.

name José had just mentioned. The question immediately leads Luis to refer to "the war," the time when Arturo and the other three men had been comrades and friends. We find Enrique's identification with photography a visual correlative of his intuitive curiosity about the people and things around him. His continual use of field glasses and cameras makes him more a witness-observer than a participant in the action during much of the early part of the film. Through this visual and verbal interrogation we are drawn to a series of elements that cumulatively define a dimension of historical meaning present but otherwise ignored within the fabric of this mise-en-scène: a German pistol, like those used in the war; the appearance of the caves carved out of the hillside which at first appear to be natural rock formations but are later identified as bunkers; the remains of a body in one of the bunkers which prompts Enrique to ask if the body was that of a soldier. All these otherwise innocent references find a common thread in the persistence of the memory of the war which, despite the characters' efforts, cannot be denied. In fact, the attempt to repress these memories only triggers Enrique's curiosity to know more.

In the early scenes Saura gives Enrique a certain unobtrusiveness as a character. A first modification of that specular transparency occurs during the morning hunt as the four men, each armed with a rifle, treck through an area of brush heavily populated with rabbits, but also laden with rabbit traps which the hunters must avoid as they stalk their prey. Enrique walks apart from the others and, in the first voice-over monologue of the film, speaks to himself: "I have the feeling I've been here before." His previously untroubled status as a mere framer of the larger drama of his companions has, all at once, become disturbed. Once the theme of the déjà vu is introduced, it is picked up and expanded by the other characters. When José tries to organize his fellow hunters in the next scene to cover certain parcels of land so that no rabbit will escape, Luis balks: "What is this, a military operation?" The remark only further specifies the subtext of the unmentionable war as the principal force beneath the action. As the men prepare to scour the bush for rabbits, Luis begins to whistle "The Battle Hymn of the Republic," a melody easily associated by the Spanish audience with another civil war.

During a mid-morning break, Enrique is placed in the foreground in three seemingly disconnected and trivial vignettes which are tied together by his presence as the cameraman-in-the-text. These scenes draw the spectator's attention to the characters' attitudes toward the visual contrivances that have shaped their personal and social identity. They also work during this explicit pause in action to construct what will be the first of many photographic albums within Saura's films—photography constituting the cipher of a series of personal and collective patterns of identity formation.

In the first of the vignettes Enrique has set up a delay mechanism on his camera, and we see him adjusting the tripod that holds the camera and then running in front of the lens to assume a pose with the other three hunters who proudly display the spoils of their morning hunt. In the second scene Enrique hands a Polaroid photograph to José which he has just taken of him in a candid pose. José, unaware that he was being photographed, becomes angered and destroys the snapshot. In the final scene, Enrique catches Paco admiring the models in a girlie magazine. Carmen, the gamekeeper's niece, peers over Paco's shoulder at the pictures with an unconscious gesture of her hand on her own body to suggest that she is comparing herself with the images she sees. Enrique quickly snaps a photo of the two absorbed readers of the magazine.

Though Enrique will appear to assume the mask of the photographic non-involvement in what he photographs in two of these scenes, his very act of photography reveals his and other characters' identification with the socially imposed myths of identity. This point is vividly made in the first of the three vignettes. As the timer on Enrique's camera clicks, Saura freezes the image of the four hunters in their triumphant pose to show us the image as it might be seen as a photograph. Enrique is ambivalently positioned both inside and outside the frame of representation. Later in the film we will recognize this ambivalence as the hallmark of a historically defined generation of contemporary spectators who erroneously believe themselves disconnected from the war in which their parents participated. For the moment, however, we see an isolated photograph framed by the

5. *The Hunt* (*La caza*, 1965)

camera lens which constructs an exaggerated heroic posture of the four hunters, not as they are, but as they wish to be seen. The discrepancy between the camera's portrayal of the world and the characters' self-image is further delineated in José's rejection of the candid snapshot Enrique has taken of him. José's destruction of the photo carries certain symbolic overtones; the action dramatizes the individual's self-censoring, selective mentality in the face of the evidence that contradicts his self-image. In the last scene of the series we are brought to view the multiple subjectivities that converge upon a seemingly neutral photographic image. Paco's admiring gaze at the magazine images is an externalization of his pretensions of youth as commented on in earlier scenes by the other men; it works to supply a retrospective explanation of José's reaction to the candid photo as a denial of his own apparent aging.

The picture of the women in the pinup magazine functions for Carmen as a role model as she unconsciously mimics their poses, attempting to shape her identity as female out of the images circulated within popular culture. The old man and the young girl, victimized by the same type of social mystification of youthful attractiveness, suggest more than merely the conditioning of individuals to the lure of photographic fantasy. This is the critical moment in Spanish culture when the power of traditional models of conduct and identity has given way to the cult of youth, only marking dramatically the discontinuity between the repudiated national past and the individual's understanding of his present.

The three "looks" posed in this last scene, those of Carmen, Paco, and Enrique, are marked as the three generations of Spaniards of the post–Civil War period. From a different vantage point, each is locked into the same illusionist consciousness, shaped by the external appearances of normality that surround them. Of the three "looks," perhaps Enrique's is the most revealing. He stands between the two generations, looking at Paco looking back and Carmen looking forward. It is ultimately the struggle for a lucid understanding of history and identity where, Saura seems to imply here, the key to Spain's hopes must ultimately lie.

The preparation of the midday meal after the photography "album" sequence breaks the previous continuity of space and action by developing a contrapuntal narrative involving elaborate cross-cuts between two simultaneous scenes: Luis and Enrique's errand to the village and José's conversation with Paco about his business problems. Saura is able to transpose within the narrow limits of the earlier action a range of associations that have resonance for the Spanish audience in a broader historical framework.

After Enrique and Luis have departed from the campsite, José brings Paco to a cave dug into the hillside where he has found the remains of a soldier who died during the battle fought in this valley. The scene is crosscut with the simultaneous action in which Enrique pumps Luis for information about Paco's obscure past about which he, his own brother-in-law, knows nothing. Luis balks: "What is this, a police interrogation?" The scene then cuts back to the cave where José is showing Paco the bones of the dead soldier. Revolted by the sight, Paco insists on going back to the campsite. Meanwhile, Luis and Enrique have arrived at the village bakery and follow the townspeople to the courtyard where the baker skins a lamb in preparation for roasting. The image of the skinned carcass and the blood on the man's hands disgusts the impressionable Enrique, thus paralleling Paco's revulsion when viewing the soldier's bones. Read from the spectator's perspective, the Civil War has been defined as a sacrificial ritual which the individual instinctively disavows and, therefore, is involuntarily led to reexperience.

While the denial of the past for Paco is consistent with his persona, Saura makes Enrique's reaction to the sight of the lamb's blood the pivot of what at first seems an inexplicable set of personal associations. In his second voice-over interior monologue he says: "How many humiliations have I suffered? None!" referring to his earlier remark to Luis that he is unlike the others, that he is not dependent on anyone. Then, abruptly, he turns to Luis and says: "Tell me something about Paco. Why did he marry my sister?"

This question seems at first unmotivated by any of the preceding dialogue or action. Yet, in fact, it marks a critical shift in Enrique's relation to his comrades and to the world within which he is situated. For this is the first moment in which the young man senses his own complicity with the past. It is a moment of introspection, of personal revision triggered by the sight of a ritual slaughter. Against his own rational stance, Enrique is forced now to reason in a context that goes beyond his own immediate interests, forcing him to identify with a community.

The form of this correction in personal perspective is as important as its content, for Enrique's question interrogates an off-screen time and space, symbolically alluded to in the cross-cut scene in the cave, but never openly confronted by any of the characters. It suggests to the viewer the containment of experience both for characters and audience in a rigidly controlled present tense. All questions of the past have been intercepted and blocked off from interrogation by a tacit covenant which Enrique is only now beginning to intuit as the order of a contrived perception. The logic of the cross-cutting of the two scenes has been to formulate for the spectator some of these questions, and then to dramatize the patterns of the blockage that denies their answer, serving in this manner to draw the viewer more deeply into the historical reflexivity.

The midday lunch break and siesta, following the return of Luis and Enrique to the campsite, mark the midpoint in the day and, as well, the dead center of the narrative. By this point in the film, the spectator has been made aware of the two dominant forces of narrative and perception that have converged to establish the underlying tension that forebodes the fatalistic denouement. One force is an ever-narrowing focus on the present moment, spatialized by the oppressive mise-en-scène of the valley, the over-determined space of entrapment. Against this structure of confinement built into the landscape and perspective of the characters, we intuit a counterforce, a set of references and images that impinge upon the limits of the present tense. By a process of accumulation of references to the war and to the past relations among the three older men, we come to understand that it is historical memory that challenges the habits of this contrived normality that the characters outwardly seek to sustain.

From as early as *Hooligans* we have discerned Saura's interest in the notion of framing as a perceptual activity of the socialized individual's self-positioning in culture. For his characters, to frame is to exclude and, through exclusion, to secure a coherent perspective on the world. This desire to frame and to control a view of things is an essential feature of Enrique's way of seeing. But unlike characters in the earlier films, his desire to frame action as stability is joined with his counter-desire to subvert and reject the social position held by his comrades. With his privileged status as observer-protagonist within the fiction, the spectator thus comes more readily to accept and follow Enrique's subversions of visual congruence because they are always naturalized within the text.

In the afternoon-nap sequence preceding the final rabbit hunt, the characterization of Enrique as "camera-man" is given new emphasis as we follow his viewing of the landscape and his fellow hunters as they rest. We see the images of Paco and Luis asleep on the ground as Enrique slowly pans over their bodies with a telephoto lens on his camera. The "bigger-than-life" magnification of these images expresses the vain, egotistical, and inflated self-image each man has of himself, but the close-up of their wrinkled skin reaffirms Enrique's private view of his fellow-hunters as aging, weak men. Suddenly, he spots something moving on the hillside and puts the camera down, quickly taking up his field glasses through which he is able to identify Luis climbing up the hill. The shot of Luis dwarfs his image and, ironically, externalizes from Enrique's perspective Luis's self-image as a weak, insecure man.

These choices of scale in the view of the other characters work, then, to denaturalize the spectator's view of the three antagonists before their final encounter with one another. What is significant about this visual representation of social identity is that it is maintained through the agency of an on-screen fictional character and yet exposes a pattern of artifice which is directed to the audience at a vantage beyond the closed world of the fiction. Enrique thus reaffirms for us the curious ambivalence of his status: He stands beyond and yet within the social space of action in which he is pictured. This dualism as character and also as surrogate spectator-in-the-text joins the referential and the self-referential structures of the film in the final sequence where the long-festering animosities of the three old friends surface and implicate Enrique irrevocably as a witness-victim of this historically symbolic violence.

In the last sequence, two forms of retrospection—historical and cinematic—are conspicuously joined to make the viewer recognize that there is an implicit contextual tension between what he has been shown in the film and what resides with equal opacity in his own blocked cultural history. The sequence begins with the arrival of Juan, the gamekeeper, bringing the caged ferrets to the campsite for the final hunt of the day. This reintroduction of the caged animals is designed to trigger in the viewer a retrospective memory of the earlier image not unlike Enrique's own déjà vu when he first stalked rabbits in the brush. The induced retrospection prefigures the more violent regression of the three older hunters who find themselves now openly reliving their past animosities through the ritual of the hunt.

According to the hunters' scheme, the ferrets are to be used simply to force the real objects of the hunt, the rabbits, from their lairs. But Paco conflates the ritual of socialized violence with a personal agenda when he intentionally shoots one of the ferrets instead of a rabbit. His action sets in motion a chain of violent counteractions, and the long-suppressed hatred surfaces among the three men as a human hunt.

Though Enrique has receded from stage center for the final crescendo of violence, his diegetic marginality is transformed into a cinematic theme in the film's final images. As the three bullet-riddled bodies lie on the valley floor, he runs up the path leading out of the valley. The sound of his panting breath is heard over the freeze-frame of his silhouette, trapped in his flight as he flees into the setting sun. Enrique's flight constitutes his recognition of his own fall from specular innocence, for, as we now understand, he has been positioned by events as well as by his own dangerous innocence to "bear witness" to the effects of the history that he had previously refused to identify as his own.

This condition of bearing witness, a complicity forged in the gaze, is, finally, the meta-cinematic bond that connects Enrique as a spectator-in-the-text with his off-screen counterpart. The photographer is now trapped within the frame of this final simulated photograph. The image remains on the screen, inviting our reflection of the implication of Enrique's and our own earlier detached, contemplative position in relation to history. If the audience understands the meaning of the lingering image as a mirror of their own psychic profile in relation to history, they will begin to grasp the problematic relation of their position to the constructed impressions of contemporary normality that they have viewed through the eyes of their on-screen surrogate.

III

A New Spain for Old Spaniards

Another Country

To MANY *The Hunt* suggested the emergence of an important new political director. When the film received the Silver Bear for best direction at the 1966 Berlin Film Festival, the jury, headed by Pier Paolo Pasolini, made explicit its esteem for Saura's political contribution by citing him for "the courage and indignation with which he presented a human situation characteristic of his time and society" (Gubern 1979, 16). This kind of appeal to foreign audiences was part of Querejeta's calculation in pushing Saura to develop what he called an international style. But the underside to that strategy, as Saura was soon to discover, was that his reputation abroad became tied to a narrow topicality of themes related either to the dictatorship or to Spain's social backwardness.

In his films after *The Hunt* he concentrated on characters from the Spanish bourgeoisie, people not very different from the protagonists of *The Hunt*. Like Paco, José, and Luis, they only wore the mask of modernity, while mentally and spiritually rooted in the past. But unlike in *The Hunt*, what Saura was attempting to do in these films was to capture a dimension of the problematic question of national cultural identity that went beyond the simple stereotypes of the victors and victims of Francoism.

The rapid transformation of the Spanish economy and society undertaken by the technocrats who gained control of key ministries in 1957 had clearly produced a crisis in Saura's view. In ten years the "Spanish economic miracle" had radically reshaped, at least externally, a country that for centuries had been sheltered from fundamental economic and social change. All at once the picturesque backwater of Europe was assuming the outward appearance of an emerging industrial nation. Yet beneath that image lay a profoundly regressive cultural heritage, one that could not be eradicated simply by the influx of foreign capital or the massive development of the tourist industry.

Such rapid modernization had created a series of contradictions in cultural identity and direction. In the generational gap that, in part, defines the dramatic action of *The Hunt*, we can read some of this problematic state of affairs. In the trilogy on which he then embarked, Saura tried to bring to the fore that schism between traditional and modern Spain.

"What I'm trying to do," he told a *New York Times* interviewer, "is in the vein of *The Hunt*. It is the study of the crisis in a seemingly developed society. The crisis of the modern Spaniard who, underneath the new veneer, is still medieval man, who still has working within him the old taboos and moral repressions" (Bratton 1967, D13).

The fact that Saura had chosen to concentrate on the crisis of the bourgeoisie was, more than any intrinsic merit of the films, the basis for a general critical complaint both inside and outside of Spain that these films were elaborate variations of a status-quo cinema. Saura and Querejeta appeared to be merely the puppets of the regime's cultural politics, involved in ". . . a cinema made by and for a small fraction of the middle and upper-middle class which has no connections with any other group of Spaniards" (Font 1976, 336). Indeed, Saura seemed intent on focusing on issues that posed no immediate political threat or embarrassment to the Franco regime, but seemed, from a certain skewed perspective, even to authenticate life under the dictatorship by showing affluent Spaniards who appeared to be not very different from their counterparts in the U.S. and elsewhere.

Thus, only three short years after receiving the hearty applause of the Berlin audiences and critics, Saura found himself once again at the festival, but now on the defensive against those interviewers who doubted the political relevance of the image of Spain he had portrayed in his three most recent films. His response, best summed up in an interview for a French film journal, reveals something of the dilemma he had confronted from the very start of his career: that of his Spanishness, which both Spaniards and foreigners had come to understand either as a function of a cultural exoticism or else a naive concept of social realism: "I believe this obsessional search for a kind of simple, primitive realism is out-of-date. This is the same kind of reproach they gave me in Spain, but it's a false problem. In Spain they said to me 'You're Spanish. So you should present a Spanish reality, but not the bourgeoisie because the Spanish bourgeoisie is dead, past. We have to think about the future. You have to study the lives of the working-class.' I find such utterances stupid. . . . I'm not interested in making a film about a particular subject. I'm stimulated by something else" (Cohn 1969, 30–31).

Beginning with *Peppermint Frappé*, Saura enlisted the help of Rafael Azcona, a scriptwriter closely identified with the New Spanish Cinema (Marco Fererri's *El pisitio*: 1958 and *El cochecito*: 1960; Berlanga's *El verdugo*: 1963). The script of *Peppermint Frappé* was actually written by Saura and Angelino Fons, with Azcona brought in at a later stage to assist in reducing the script to a manageable length. The success of that first collaboration would lead to four other jointly written projects over the next seven years.

Peppermint Frappé (1967)

Speaking of the country spa which is the principal site of action of *Peppermint Frappé*, Saura says: "That old house represents *my* house, *my* family, *my* Spain. Above all, it represents a form of education. There is a lot of nostalgia in my home; it is something I both love and detest at the same time. It provokes conflict" (Cohn 1969, 30). Though the characters in *Peppermint Frappé* appear to act out of their own psychological motivations, by their placement within the symbolic landscape of Cuenca—the traditional Castilian city with its modern and ancient quarters—the spectator is invited to read these actions as symptomatic of the greater cultural schism between visions of old and new Spain.

After viewing *The Hunt*, Buñuel, recalling a promise Saura had made to dedicate a film to him, is said to have remarked that this is the film he would have liked Saura to have dedicated to him (Brasó 1974, 163). In 1966, while accompanying Buñuel to the latter's native town of Calanda to view the famous drum-beating ceremony during Holy Week, Saura conceived of the idea that would later shape *Peppermint Frappé* into the promised homage to his spiritual master: "It was in Calanda with Buñuel that I got the idea for the film. You know the story of the drums of Calanda. The year I saw it a beautiful young woman, she was one of Buñuel's relatives, was beating the drum with all her might. I kept that extraordinary image as a persistent memory. This young woman belonged to another world; while all around her thousands of people were playing, she also beat the drum. It was all the more impressive since it is usually the men who do so" (Cohn 1969, 29). The Calanda sequence, Saura's overt statement of homage to Buñuel, appears only once in the film, but the larger plot of *Peppermint Frappé*, hinging on the crucial erotic image of the woman during a religious pageant, is actually a reworking of the opening sequence of Buñuel's Mexican masterpiece, *El* (1952: This Strange Passion), one of the few Buñuel films Saura had seen in Montpellier and one he insisted had radically altered his own ideas about filmmaking. Like Buñuel's deranged protagonist, Francisco, Julián (José Luis López Vázquez) is a member of the conservative Catholic middle class. Also like Francisco, his life is a chain of conflicts between his repressive religious training and his own deformed sexual fantasies. Buñuel deftly constructed what appeared to be an external form of narration in *El* only to lead his audience into the twisted point of view of Francisco as he pursues and attempts to possess the ideal woman of his dreams. The evolving narrative of *El* cleverly situates the spectator's perspective almost exclusively in Francisco's seemingly normal point of view only to reveal the instability of that view of society through a series of macabre actions. Through this strategy, Buñuel brings us to see that Francisco is not merely an isolated case of a deranged character. His warped perspective is the product of his religious and social formation, and society, in the person of his family priest, willingly authenticates his deranged behavior.

The plotting of *Peppermint Frappé* works in a similar fashion to establish Saura's theme of the tortured individual trapped in the contradictions of his social formation in Spanish Catholic bourgeois order. Julián is a middle-aged bachelor, living a cloistered life in the provincial city of Cuenca where he is well established in a successful medical practice. One day the ordered pattern of his life is shattered when his childhood friend Pablo (Alfredo Mayo) returns to show off his new bride, Elena (Geraldine Chaplin). Julián and Pablo embody the film's cultural schism: Julián is introspective and laconic; Pablo, gregarious and high-spirited. Julián equates his own personality with the tempo of provincial life, while Pablo boasts that he left Cuenca precisely to get away from such dreariness and to enjoy life. Pablo's new wife symbolizes her husband's repudiation of traditional values and his flair for modernity. She is attractive in a cosmopolitan way and, like him, mocks Julián's traditionalist values. Despite her rebukes, Julián finds himself immediately drawn to her.

Elena reminds Julián of a mysterious woman he had seen beating a drum during the famous Holy Week ritual in the village of Calanda. She insists that she has never seen him before, nor has she ever been to Calanda. During the days following their first encounter, Julián becomes more and more infatuated with Pablo's new bride and finds pretexts to spend time with her. Despite her indifference to his attentions, Julián's obsession with Elena does not diminish. As a result of his contact with Elena, he begins to take note of his laboratory assistant, Ana, a frail and homely girl who has secretly pined for Julián. A sexual liaison between the two is soon established. The role of Ana is played by Geraldine Chaplin as well, a device that enables Saura to literalize for his spectator the perceptual distortions that had led Julián to confuse the woman he saw at Calanda first with Elena and then with Ana.

While involved with Ana, Julián continues to pursue the elusive Elena, but she resists his advances with open derision. After a practical joke by Pablo and Elena, aimed at humiliating Julián, the shy physician begins to plan an elaborate revenge against the couple. He lures them to his country house, poisons them, then disposes of the bodies so as to make it appear that they died in an automobile accident. Returning to his country house, Julián finds Ana now dressed as the woman of Calanda. The film ends as the two embrace in a manner to suggest their complicity in the crime.

6. *Peppermint Frappé* (1967)

Looking at Looking

As in Buñuel's *El*, part of the energy of Julián's destructive imagination lies in his ability to construct images and plots that will be accepted and valorized by the larger social community. Throughout the film, for instance, he remains the model of provincial bourgeois rectitude. What is important for Saura is to show that his character's pathological nature is the product of his provincial bourgeois environment. In bringing Julián to a crisis in his own fantasy life, Saura is really describing something beyond a mere sexual fixation. We view the tensions within a prototypical Spaniard shaped by traditional values and prohibitions. Out of his own repressive education Julián comes to disavow the real in all things and to prefer a tame although artificial illusion to an authentic reality. Sexual fetishism thus becomes the metaphor for a chain of social repressions, a theme that again is consistent with Buñuel's development over the years. *Peppermint Frappé* anticipates a group of Spanish films in the seventies in which the theme of sexual repression becomes the means through which directors formulate biting critiques of a more expansive Spanish cultural ethos.[1] Conditioned by his social formation to repress any but the most traditional elements, Julián has found a way both to maintain the facade of order and to work through covert means to express his own deformed consciousness. But finally he encounters in Elena a figure who cannot be so easily absorbed into the distorted patterns of his psyche. The tension of his mind and, consequently, of the narrative articulated through his point of view manifest this conflict through those features that both the audience and the character hold in common: the lure of visually enticing images, and the submission of perception to social conventions of constructed intelligibility.

Voyeurism is thus given a special privilege in the film's structure as the essence of narrative as well as of social conflict. This erotic lure becomes the source of a continuous fascination for both the audience and the character as established through the agency of Julián's gaze. Initial spectator identification with Julián's perspective is introduced in the credit sequence in which we see a collage of fragments of images of women apparently cut from fashion magazines: hands, faces, full bodies, but only in the most contrived, unnatural postures. These figures are made all the more artificial by the effect they produce as an ensemble of clippings placed together against a black backdrop. We later identify these collage shots as pages from Julian's album of magazine clippings. The final credit image is a close-up of a model's eye with elongated eye-lashes and eye shadow. In this way,

---

[1] This is particularly true of films by José Luis Borau and Jaime Armiñán: *Mi querida señorita* (1970: *My Dear Señorita*); *Al servicio de la mujer española* (1977: *In The Service of Spanish Womanhood*); and *Nunca es tarde* (1978: *It's Never Too Late*).

we are brought into the film's narrative with the strange realization of perceptual distance from images; we are not looking at images so much as at images of images. The cipher of that spectatorial distance is the final shot of the model's eye which announces the film's theme of the social artifice of sight. As much as it is a story of erotic desire and sexual repression, *Peppermint Frappé* is also the story of the social regulation of the scopic apparatus.

Tellingly, the close-up of the eye is followed by a rapid cut to the fluoroscoped image of a man's body. Gradually we locate the setting as a physician's office where Julián is carefully examinining a patient's chest and lungs. These two distinct orders of images—the constructed sensuality of the magazine model and the cold detachment of the scientific image—are cleverly elided through the agency of a single enunciative figure: Julián.

After the fluoroscoping scene, Julián says good night to Ana and retires to his apartment adjacent to his office. We see him changing his clothes in two crucial shots as he stands before a mirror and adjusts his tie. These narcissistic characterizations connect logically with the previous brief scenes: Julián shapes and controls his self-image just as he has shaped and controlled the images of others. In the next scene he goes to the home of Pablo's mother where a reunion of the two old friends has been arranged. Pablo offers him a drink as the family awaits the entrance of Pablo's new bride, who is upstairs dressing. From where Julián is seated on a sofa he commands a full view of the staircase from which Elena will make her entrance. The spatial arrangement is strikingly theatrical in that from the sofa Julián is given prominence in the frame as to suggest that he is an on-screen spectator awaiting the appearance of an actress on stage. Pablo hands Julián a drink, the peppermint frappé of the film's title, which Julián sips at the exact moment that Elena begins her descent. Her entrance is cross-cut rapidly with shots of Julián's face, first surprised, then outwardly pleased, finally astonished as Elena's full body comes into view. This brief but important scene progresses from an initial glance/object shot showing Elena's legs followed by her torso as she descends, then the changing expressions on Julián's face. The series ends with a close-up of Elena's face as we hear the off-screen rhythmic beats of the drums of Calanda.

At the sound of the drums, the camera cuts to a black-and-white shot of a young woman, the same Geraldine Chaplin who has already appeared as Ana, beating the ritual drum amidst the crowd at the religious festival. The camera slowly tracks away from her to reveal the crowd of men who surround her at the ceremony. The incessant cadence of the drum abruptly stops, and the scene cuts back to the living room where Pablo begins to introduce his wife to his oldest friend. The duration of what appears to be a flashback in Julián's mind is only a few seconds, but it marks a decisive cleavage in the narration.

This is the first scene in which the spectator discerns a fissure in Julián's persona and, as well, in the agency of narrative enunciation. It is also the first instance of the flashback device to express the conflation of past and present in a Saura film. Within the specific details of *Peppermint Frappé*, it marks the exact point in the narration where story and image are expressed self-consciously as a problem for the character. That problem is the struggle of the individual to locate his immediate visual experience through the agency of a mediated representation, here a remembrance which, because it is set off in black-and-white, becomes yet another self-reference to the cinematic apparatus.

From the reminiscences occasioned by his reencounter with Pablo as well as from the visit that Pablo and Elena make to the old spa where the boys once played, we discern the shape of a more generic biography of Julián. Julián brings the couple on two tours: the first, a car tour of the city of Cuenca in which he escorts Elena through both the old and the new sections of the city; the second, the weekend excursion to his country house. Julián's naive motivation in these tours is to get closer to Elena. What surfaces, however, is a vivid portrait of his constrained psyche returning to the sources of his mental captivity in his childhood. Through the use of the picturesque Cuenca cityscape and the surrounding terrain, the exact locale used as a setting for Bardem's tale of sexual repression in *Main Streeet*, Saura makes the point that the tension between the modern and traditional values of the community is a psychic conflict into which each individual, each Spaniard, is unconsciously drawn.

An important dimension of that conflict lies in the social status of the female. In this respect, the three characters depicted by Geraldine Chaplin come to embody three stages of the psycho-sexual development of the Spaniard. Julián's preference for the respectable traditional order of things is initially disrupted by the appearance of Elena. Her dress and demeanor announce a preference for foreign tastes and mark her presence as incongruous, even threatening, in the subdued provincial town. It may well be for that reason that he immediately identifies her with an image he can control, the girl from Calanda. Julián's intuitive response to Elena is to attempt to possess her in both figurative and literal ways. The narrativization of that pursuit of control, and of Elena's thwarting of Julián's efforts, is enunciated through a scopic register that, importantly, aligns the character's personal crisis with the larger issue of sexual politics that underlies traditional Spanish society.

We get a sense of that cluster of specular and social themes in the sequence in which Elena, flirting with Julián, asks him to drive her to her appointment at a local beauty salon. Sitting alone in the beauty parlor waiting room, surrounded by women who are having their hair dried, Julián can easily view Elena as she waits to be attended to in one of the booths.

It appears as though he has momentarily achieved a voyeuristic control over Elena's image. When no one is watching, he rifles through her purse, left on a chair beside him, and finds a set of false eyelashes, which he quickly places in his pocket. Recomposing himself, he picks up a magazine to pass the time. The camera then begins a slow tracking around Julián, describing a visual circle in which he is now perceived to be the object viewed by the women who encircle him. The camera movement has effectively reversed Julián's assumed power by now making him the object of the female glance. It will be this reversal of Julián's traditionalist position, strongly identified with Elena's presence, that eventually throws him into a state of panic.

At the end of the tracking shot, Julián casts a furtive glance at Elena, now becoming a bit impatient as she waits; he sees her playing with her wedding band. This image triggers the memory of a scene from his childhood that crystalizes the contradictions of chastity and eroticism embedded in the Spanish psyche. Dressed as a bride and groom, a young boy and girl stand in a garden before a third child garbed as a priest. This clerical figure looms considerably taller than the other two and seems to be supported on the shoulders of a fourth youth concealed within the priestly cossack. The priest gives the groom a wedding band which he places on the girl's finger; the two children kiss. As the groom embraces and kisses the bride, the head of the concealed child pops out from beneath the robes in order to observe the kiss. The scene quickly cuts back to the beauty salon. Given his already established timidity in the face of an erotic presence, we easily identify Julián as the child peeping out of the priest's cossack. The combination of the beauty parlor and flashback scenes suggests a psychic profile of the character that will be developed further in later sequences. Having been formed by the repressive social and sexual order of Catholic provincial life, Julián has come of age replicating in his outlook that Catholic bourgeois ideology as well as his own contradictory relation to it. He is unprepared either to confront his sexual desires except in function of his repressed childhood, or to understand the changing social and sexual order of society. For that reason Elena's presence signals a critical disruption of the order Julian has achieved.

In the next major sequence, when Julián invites Pablo and Elena to his cottage for a weekend, we gain a more detailed sense of the weight of the past upon his present state. The very fact that he has chosen the site of his childhood sexual fantasies for a vacation cottage suggests the psychic subtext that continually informs his actions. When he takes Pablo and Elena on a tour of the grounds of the abandoned spa, he shows them a hole in the wall of the old bathhouse where he and Pablo used to spy on naked women bathing. Later on, as the three explore the main house, they go to the room that was the boys' bedroom during summer vacations. Julián shows Elena how his aunt would spy on the boys through a keyhole to make sure they were sleeping and not engaged in masturbatory sex. Through this second tour Saura underscores the patterns of repressive sexuality, of prohibitions and lures, which clearly have a resonance on the ways Julián perceives the world and himself as an adult. The spa is the prismatic world described by Julián as a place where one sees and, in turn, is seen. In his adult life he has absorbed those same patterns of scopophilia into his way of being, acquiescing in, even supporting, the self-censoring structures of a seemingly chaste existence—but continually eroticizing the world around him.

The Closed World

The erotics of sight is the hallmark of Julián's being in the modern world, but for him sight insistently carries the mark of its own prohibition. He is the epitome of a constrained spectatorship as social identity, actively maintaining his own captivity by segmenting, atomizing, and visually circumscribing all the elements of an instinctual order that attracts him. The spectator understands only retrospectively that his actions in everyday life have been metaphorically stated in the credit sequence shots of female figures.

No more striking example of his ambivalent psychic status is to be found than Julián's response later in the afternoon when Elena decides to practice modern-dance exercises on a small circular stage in the middle of the garden. He takes out his camera and slowly circles her as she dances to the music of a tape recorder. His response to her alluring body and movements, made all the more enticing by her dance leotard, is to mask himself with a photographic camera, to reinsert the mediation of artifice over the instinctual attraction he feels. He slowly moves around the stage photographing Elena from various angles, capturing but also intuitively containing Elena with his own countermovement. This scene, of course, inverts Julián's sense of violation as the object of the look of the women in the beauty salon. With camera in hand, he anthropomorphizes the specular apparatus in the text, containing and controlling images. When his tracking and photographing have completely described a circle, we have, in fact, reached the next crucial juncture of the film: the shift from the delineation of the social mentality to the activation of what Saura calls "the destructive imagination" of his character. Julián ceases to be merely the observer of illusion; he is now its author.

That shift becomes more apparent when Julián later presents Elena with the photographs he has taken of her. The action takes place again in a space that symbolizes the contradictions between tradition and modern Spanish values: the famous Hanging House of Cuenca (*Las Casas Colgadas*) only recently converted into the Museum of Modern Spanish Art. Overlooking the Castilian landscape from the side of a huge gorge, the traditional facade of the building masks the extreme modern style of its interior. When they first meet, Elena receives his photographs with cordial indifference. Later, as the three leave the museum at nightfall, she tells Julián to wait with Pablo at the side of the pedestrian bridge. She has a gift for him which she has left in her car. Elena crosses the bridge and drives her car up to the other entrance of the bridge so that the headlights glare into Julián's and Pablo's eyes. Then Elena emerges from the car wearing clothes similar to those of the mysterious woman of Calanda as described by Julián. In further imitation, Elena appears with a huge drum which she beats violently as she approaches Julian. Julián now feels all the more humiliated as he understands not only that Elena is mocking him, but also that Pablo's light derision earlier in the day had been part of the prank the two were plotting for him. The scene, dramatic in terms of Elena's cruel rejection of Julián, seems also to dramatize the film's thematic conflict between antithetical cultural styles, the gorge symbolizing the schism between new and traditional Spain.

Provoked by Elena's cruel burlesque of his desires, Julián conceives the idea for a "perfect murder." Saura observes with ironic relish that the censors deleted nothing from the script of *Peppermint Frappé*, and thus allowed the film to stand as the first conspicuous example in a Spanish film of the period of crime without punishment. Indeed, this perfect crime expresses the architecture of the closed world view that marks the contrived image of everything in Julián's life. Like the framed images of fashion models and the encircling of Elena as she dances at the spa, Julián's act of revenge against the couple reveals a destructive impulse folding in on itself. Picking up Elena's curiosity about his relationship with Ana, Julián invites Elena and Pablo to join him and Ana in his country house. Before Pablo and Elena arrive, Julián places what appears to be a poison in the decanter containing the drinks he plans to serve his guests. The drink is the peppermint frappé of the film's title, popularly believed to be an aphrodisiac. When Pablo and Elena arrive, Julián tells them that Ana will be a little late and offers them the beverage. After a few sips, the couple begins to ridicule Julián once again.

When they finally succumb to the poison, Julián carries their bodies to their car which he manages to drive off a cliff, giving the appearance that the couple had died in an automobile accident. Returning to the house, he is only mildly surprised to discover the fireplace ablaze even though a fire had not been lit when he left the cottage. He hears the approaching sound of the Calanda drums. The front door opens and Ana appears, now dressed in the identical fashion of the woman of Calanda. Julián embraces Ana as the camera circles the couple, giving closure to the film.

Ana's appearance in the final scene is ambiguously set so as to elicit a process of questioning by the audience. There is no dialogue in the final scene; therefore, the final appearance of the woman of Calanda inevitably raises for the spectator the question of which of Geraldine Chaplin's three roles this character is intended to be. At what should, in classical terms, be the decisive moment of cinematic narrative closure, we are led instead to acknowledge after the fact the complicity of our own sight in sustaining the illusionism of Julián's way of being in the world. Conventional cinematic closure is thus replaced for the spectator with a moment of hermeneutic distance. The final scene of the film inevitably prods us into a retrospective reflection on the social meaning of action in much the same way that the powerful finale of *The Hunt* did. The two films, in fact, work along similar conceptual lines, attempting a disalignment through visual narrative of the audience's identification with and confinement in a narrowly defined image of Francoist social normality.

Peppermint Frappé proved to be Saura's first film not to be altered by the censors in any form. Ministry of Culture archives indicate that some of the censors were vexed by the Buñuelian influence in the narrative, but this did not produce the kind of retaliatory attack that had occasioned the mutilation of *Lament for a Bandit*. Though all the censors noted the marked erotic nature of the plot (Hernández Les 1986, 169), they still classified the film as *apto para todos los públicos*, equivalent to the "G" rating in the U.S.

The technical quality of *Peppermint Frappé* represented an obvious improvement over the majority of Spanish films of the period, and this fact enabled Querejeta to argue with the government for a "special interest" subsidy as he would later do for more politically objectionable Saura films. Of those production values, special note should be made of the film's splendid use of color photography, the striking camera work by Luis Cuadrado, and the appearance of Geraldine Chaplin in the cast, which gave the film an additional international aura which Querejeta hoped would make it more marketable outside of Spain. Though Saura remained faithful to a critical conception he had begun to explore in *The Hunt*, to all outward appearances he and his producer had simply receded from the battle lines of opposition cinema in Spain and become that much more window dressing for the government's claim that the old Spain of political repression was gone.

Stress es tres, tres (1968: Stress Is Three, Three)

The Spanish audiences of *Peppermint Frappé* may well have been more seduced by the narrative premise of the film—illusion tranformed into life—than by any statement of the deforming patterns of repressive, conservative

culture. The strong box-office showing in Madrid may also have had something to do with the favorable critical reviews that gave prominence to the
film's erotic theme. Yet, even this commercial and artistic acclaim did not
satisfy Saura. "I had the sensation at the end of *Peppermint Frappé*," he says,
"that I had told a story. I mean, a story has been recounted with a very
concrete plot. . . . At the root of it I had the sense that in *Peppermint Frappé*
I was constrained by story and I wanted to unbind myself. So, I made *Stress
Is Three, Three* as a kind of liberation" (Brasó 1974, 206–7).

Stress Is Three, Three (the film's curious title is a verbal conceit which,
when pronounced in Spanish, means "It is three, it is three, three") was
the occasion for Saura's renewed experimentation in cinematic narrative.
In attempting to frustrate his audience's conventional expectations of cinematic plotting, however, he moved away from nearly all the formulas that
had given him success in his two previous works. Though *Stress* is generally
conceded to be the weakest of his films made during the Franco years, a
number of elements become prominent in the film which, in fact, provide
the impetus for his later work. Among these is the growing influence of
Geraldine Chaplin in the development of script ideas, and, owing to her,
the emergence of strong female characters in Saura's films of the seventies
(Brasó 1974, 198). In *Stress*, however, the female figure is still secondary.

Key to an understanding of *Stress* is an appreciation of Fernando, the
film's protagonist, played by Fernando Cebrián. For the first time Saura
presents a character who recognizes the traps of his way of seeing and
makes that troubled consciousness a self-referential component of the narrative. In providing Fernando with an understanding of the snares of illusionist social representation and yet making him unable, even unwilling,
to disengage himself from those images, certain of the ideological ambiguities of *Peppermint Frappé* are resolved to the director's satisfaction.
Gradually the spectator of *Stress* comes to intuit that Fernando is not some
eccentric, pathological figure, as was Julián, but a prototype of the "new,"
progressive Spaniard of the sixties and, as well, an amalgam of socially
grounded habits of perception and belief that coincide with dominant
bourgeois values. Saura describes Fernando, the central character of *Stress*
this way:

> He is . . . a successful industrialist, a man of great earning power, the owner of
> several factories—one of the conquerors in life. And yet he is completely inca-
> pable of solving his relationship with his wife. He veers away. Their relationship
> and the possibility that his friend might be her lover are problems that he does
> not know how to confront or even present to himself. Here is a tremendous
> insecurity. He is maimed in his emotional life, this very successful modern man.
> In a way, it is the problem of urban industrial society everywhere. First neglect,
> then disregard of, then incapacity for the emotional side of life. But in Spain this

industrial society and the world of objects which are its indispensable products and its fetishes, all this is new. And it adds a new dimension, the stress of external substitutes, to all the old, inner, one-dimensional moral strains and stresses. And so you have a man who becomes a compulsive voyeur, who wishes to assure himself . . . [of an adultery which in the end he himself provokes]. (Bratton 1967, D13)

Following the linear sequence of a day-long car trip made by Fernando, his wife, Teresa (Geraldine Chaplin), and his best friend, Antonio (Juan Luis Galiardo), who is a few years younger than Fernando, the film traces a symbolic regression by the three from civilization, as characterized by the urban sprawl of Madrid, to the primitive, as embodied by the coastal beaches of Almería. During the trip Fernando's anxieties surface: his suspicion that his wife and best friend are lovers; his feared loss of virility; and, finally, the anxiety of approaching death. What little sustained narrative there is in the film comes from the crescendo of emotional conflicts that punctuate the trip. Thus, as a plot, *Stress* appears to be similar to *Peppermint Frappé*, an indictment of the false impression of rapidly acquired Spanish modernity.

Depriving Fernando of the privilege of enunciation that was so decisive in the development of Julián, Saura, instead, endows his character with the organizing consciousness of a *metteur-en-scène*, perhaps the origin of the figure of the director-in-the-text that will eventually generate the Antonio Gades roles in *Blood Wedding* and *Carmen*. Fernando frames scenes as though, metaphorically, he controlled a camera, or perhaps *were* a camera, focusing on other characters, inventing the points of view and scenarios within which his wife and best friend find themselves hapless performers. At key moments, he unobtrusively sets up Teresa and Antonio in potentially compromising situations as though "framing" an image that will confirm their complicity in an adulterous relationship. Self-consciously standing back from such events, Fernando's actions suggest to the spectator a number of pivotal themes regarding the individual's relation to social representation.

Fernando's approach to his emotional problems, that is, his mimicking of the objectifying strategy of the cinematic apparatus, is itself revealing of the symptomatic condition of his modernity. His problems, Saura would have us believe, derive from the mask of modernity that Fernando assumes in an effort, ironically, to resolve the crises of his life. Yet he is endowed with one telling feature: He has discovered positionality as the signifier of meaning within the social world and he is not indifferent to such knowledge. As the trip progresses southward, he follows a symbolic trajectory through the prismatic views and framings that will reposition Teresa and

Antonio in scenes that give Fernando the visual confirmation of their adultery.

The thematic premise that provides narrative cohesion to the film is simple enough. In the credit sequence, as we see Fernando's car moving through the smog and congestion of a Madrid expressway, a voice-over narration explains the meaning of social stress: "Stress, this term means literally force, effort, tension, but it is used colloquially as a synonym for violent stimulus, a stressful factor is one which affects, which produces discernible consequences. Included in this concept is boredom, disagreeable work, difficulties of any kind in life; that is to say, anything that might bother someone is a stress factor to the spirit" (Brasó 1974, 194–95).

In the ensuing actions in which Fernando, Teresa, and Antonio find themselves in a series of stress-bound situations, Fernando becomes a demonically possessed figure, slowly stripping away the mask of social postures in others and revealing at the same time his own inner conflicts. As the three move to more and more primitive terrain heading south to the Mediterranean coast, Fernando seems to regress first into adolescent behavior, then into childish rivalry with Antonio, finally into a savage hallucination in which he fantasizes murdering his assumed rival.

While this portrait of Fernando's reversion seems to provide a semblance of narrative logic to the film, the real drama takes place in the way he comes to reveal a less obvious dimension of his identity. In one of the earliest episodes, for example, Teresa asks Fernando to stop the car along the highway so she can get some fresh air. Antonio asks to accompany her. When the two get out of the car, Fernando precipitously drives off, leaving the stunned couple at the side of the road. He drives to a nearby hilltop where, unseen by Teresa and Antonio, he can observe their actions, hoping to confirm his suspicion of their adultery. He sees nothing and reluctantly returns to pick them up. Fernando's actions are telling of a convoluted perspective toward his own consciousness. Rejecting the merely visible, he is nonetheless trapped in a belief that he can obtain empirical, visual proof of his suspicions. Even more pointedly, his seemingly spontaneous action of abandoning the couple on the roadside reveals his own understanding of the ways of manipulating a world so as to produce the desired appearance.

Like Saura's earlier "specular" characters, Enrique and Julián, he too likens his own perceptual apparatus to that of a photographic camera. In several pivotal scenes Saura provides dramatic evidence of the ways in which a photo-ontological and/or cinematic consciousness has been internalized into the dominant pattern of Fernando's perception. When, for instance, the three are forced to make a detour to a small town so that Fernando can make an official statement for the local *Guardia Civil* about a ghastly auto accident they witnessed on the road, Antonio and Teresa wait for Fernando in the village plaza. As he sits in the Civil Guard office, he peers through the window and sees the couple seated together on a bench under a tree. The window frame appears to simulate a camera viewfinder, perfectly centering the very image his earlier contrived efforts had failed to produce.

Viewing Fernando viewing the couple as he tells the Civil Guard officer his age, profession, and marital status, the spectator begins to appreciate some of the complexity of Saura's conception. The juxtaposition of Fernando's official identity with his sentimental identity suggests one of the schisms that informs all the film's action. Similarly, the intersection of multiple social and personal perspectives on the characters—those of Fernando, the official, and the spectator—clearly establishes the prismatic distortions of human sight that undercut the technocrat's insistence upon empirical, verifiable social and personal truth. Truth, as Fernando comes to see, is always thwarted by the relativism of multiple perspectives, as well as the emerging sense of the vulnerability of his own perspectival position.

At their brief rest stop at the farm owned by Fernando's aunt, Teresa retires to one of the upstairs bedrooms of the huge house. When Fernando decides to follow her upstairs, he hears Teresa's voice on the other side of a partially opened door, and then views her speaking gently to someone else whom he cannot see. Her words are a confession of love which, as she says, she has not been able to express earlier. Certain that he has at last caught Teresa in a compromising situation with Antonio, Fernando rushes into the room only to find her alone, speaking into a full-length mirror which the door had masked from his view. She explains that, because he has become so tense and anxious in the last several weeks, she felt a distance between them and was only trying to find the words to express her love to him. Fernando is unmoved by what he perceives to be a mere ruse.

One of the significant features of this scene is the manner in which the spectator is positioned to "construct" along with Fernando a narrative confirmation of Teresa's infidelity, based upon the chance synchronization of words and a narrowly framed image. The logic of the momentary deception is a striking example of the meta-cinematic inscription that continually informs Fernando's view of the action: the positioning of an innocent subject before the constructed illusion whose verisimilitude is forged by the fortuitous synchronization of sound with image. The textual motivation for such an elaborate scene seems to be to draw the real spectator to an awareness of the invisible cultural apparatus that has positioned Fernando to absorb personal scenarios in ways that correspond to the cinematic ontology. For one instant, as the spectator occupies Fernando's "place" in the scene and hears Teresa's words through the half-opened door, he, too, is made to believe the coherence of what will shortly be revealed as the protagonist's warped image of his wife.

7. *Stress is Three, Three* (*Stress es tres, tres*, 1968)

The images and "plot" Fernando stages in his mind are the time-worn clichés of the jealous husband and the unfaithful wife, a social scenario of traditionalist Spain that belies Fernando's otherwise convincing appearance as a modern, progressive-thinking Spaniard. In Fernando's insistence on the adulterous relationship between Teresa and Antonio, Saura updates the blackest of Spanish literary traditions—the seventeenth-century honor plays of Calderón de la Barca such as *El médico de su honra* (The Surgeon of His Honor) and *A secreto agravio, secreta venganza* (For a Private Offense, Private Revenge). The pivot of these plays is the husband's right to punish the presumed authors of any stain, imagined or real, to his honor. The spirit of just vengeance by the protagonists of Calderonian honor plays is a mark of the spiritual medievalism with which Saura characterizes Fernando.[2]

The arrival of the three characters at a secluded beach on the Almería coast provides Saura's most elaborate treatment of his meta-cinematic and medieval themes. Like the previous settings, the primitive beach begins to shape the action, first in the infantile jousting of Antonio and Fernando, then in a race across the sand as if two rivals were vying for Teresa's affec-

[2] Robbin Fiddian and Peter Evans observe that, throughout the film, Fernando's treatment of Teresa appears to be a crude parody of Spanish male chauvinism and thereby contributes to his depiction as the modern-day exemplar of Calderonian patriarchal fiction (77–78).

tion. Finally, it appears that the two have reached a quarrelsome point in their social relations where open conflict must inevitably erupt.

As in *The Hunt*, there is a precipitous pause in the action just as the menace of violence becomes clear. Fernando declines Teresa's invitation to go snorkeling with her and so, clad in a wet suit and snorkel, she sets out with Antonio, leaving her husband to ruminate over his own self-doubt. Fernando then dons his own wet suit, produces a menacing spear gun, and begins searching the nearby inlets and coves for Teresa and Antonio whom he expects to find in amorous embrace. Spying upon them from behind a huge rock in a scene that recalls the first scene of his voyeurism, he sees Antonio and Teresa kiss. Fernando now seems prepared to avenge his honor. What was in the early stages of the film a story about the breakup of a modern marriage all at once reveals itself to be an all-too-familiar Calderonian plot in which the cuckolded husband claims the right to avenge his honor by killing his rival.

Rather than interrupt the couple, Fernando returns to the blanket and sits on the beach imagining Teresa and Antonio's return. In this sequence the view of the couple emerging from the water is shot in overexposed black-and-white stock, giving the jarring impression of the violent nightmare that, in fact, is evolving in Fernando's mind. This is a sort of hallucinatory film-within-the-film in which Fernando as author-spectator images the denouement of the scenario he has previously concocted: As Antonio approaches in his wet suit, Fernando suddenly leaps to his feet and shoots a spear into his side. Teresa screams in disbelief as Antonio writhes in pain. His agonized body penetrated with spears replicates the image of Ribera's painting of the martyred Saint Sebastian, a copy of which appeared on the wall of the farmhouse. Fernando shoots more spears as the violent shots of the attack are matched with Teresa's shrieks. Abruptly, the hallucination ends as we return to Fernando sitting on the blanket on the desolate beach as the sun begins to descend.

After a moment of silence, Antonio and Teresa now come out of the water. The scene is identical to the first shots of Fernando's daydream, but, instead of picking up the spear gun as Antonio approaches, Fernando only sits sullenly and asks Antonio how the snorkeling went. The sun sets, and the three prepare to leave. As the car drives off into the night we hear Fernando say to Antonio, "We have to come back here another day, you and I." "Me, too," chimes in Teresa. And the film ends in a total screen blackout.

Fernando, who from the beginning of the film has lived the scenario of his own suspicions about Teresa and Antonio, seems to have located himself in a number of self-referential illusions that he has come to acknowledge as false. His manipulation of the social setting, for example, revealed his will to artifice. But at no point did he realize that he was also living the illusion of his own control and mastery of situations, the illusion of his own power. This final, striking sequence works not only to reveal the power of Fernando's imagination, but also to suggest through the hallucination scene that his condition is in some way analogous to that of the real spectator, and that cinema is only a metaphor for the chain of fraudulent illusions that have provided the modern Spaniard with the impression of perceptual and social stability and power.

Most of the reviews of *Stress* were resoundingly negative, critics having made little effort to understand the film as a form of experimentation in Saura's work. It is all the more ironic, therefore, to discover in the recently published censors' comments on the film a brief discussion that attempts not only to assess the film's merit, but also to situate it in terms of Saura's recent development. One censor writes: "This script is a second version of *The Hunt*. Only there the squabbling among the protagonists was economic, here, it's sentimental. If there they were conditioned by political ideology, here it's their own bourgeoisness. The fundamental difference, however, is that *The Hunt* is totally plausible as a plot while for me the plot of *Stress* is implausible" (Hernández Les 1986, *Singular*, 172).

La madriguera (1969: The Bunker)

La madriguera (1969: The Bunker), gives closure to the cycle that began four years earlier in *The Hunt* with the development of Enrique (Brasó 1974, 162). Yet, while thematically another view of "old Spaniards in a new Spain," the real significiance of *The Bunker* lies less in its relation to the films that precede it than in the nature of some of Saura's formal experimentation in this work. These include the privilege now accorded to the female subject as discursive and thematic center of the film, and the delimitation of all action to a single house. This latter feature, seemingly a new twist to the theme of mise-en-scène, at first gives the impression of being merely part of the cinematic vogue of modernity that became a fairly constant motif in Spanish films of the late sixties, particularly in the films of the so-called Barcelona School, such as Vicente Aranda's *Fata Morgana* (1965; Mirage) and Carlos Durán's *Liberxina 90* (1969).

But what distinguishes Saura's film is the self-consciousness of the modernist setting; this is not merely a surface embellishment to a conventional story, but in many ways the setting *is* the story. The conflicts within the plot arise from two characters having been "placed in the scene"—in the imposing modern fortresslike mansion in an opulent suburb of Madrid—in ways that are symptomatic of their problems as individuals as well as of the cultural crisis of Spain's sudden and contrived modernity. If the imposed mise-en-scène strikes one as a contrivance of plot, it also reverts back

to the larger social contrivance of the Spanish "Economic Miracle." At key
moments Saura has his actors, Pedro (Per Oscarsson) and Teresa (Geraldine Chaplin), gaze out from the huge wall-length window of their house
as if to remind the spectator that these characters have conflated their way
of seeing the world with the prismatic view that their position in this constructed illusion of modernity has afforded them.

What little there is to the plot of *The Bunker* is a dramatic situation:
Teresa lives what appears to be an ordered existence as the attractive wife
of an important industrialist, Pedro. Her stability is shattered when old
furniture from her parents' house arrives one day and she has the delivery-
man store it in the cellar. Stimulated by these relics from her past, Teresa
becomes entranced by the memories of her childhood. When she orders
her servants to bring up all the furniture from the cellar to redecorate the
house, displacing the contemporary decor, both she and Pedro find themselves reliving moments from their past. Through a series of seemingly
improvised playacting games, the two begin to dress up and act out events
from their married life. Finally, when they enact the breakup of their marriage and Pedro's abandonment of her, Teresa kills him.

The underlying strategy of *The Bunker* seems to be the gradual elaboration of the mental machinery of constraints and inhibitions that have constructed a trap within which the individual is immobilized. Some of the
process of containment is personal—the individualized traumas that have
been long suppressed; other aspects are societal—the repression of the individual within an authoritarian order, the sanitized notion of modern existence that isolates the individual from him or herself. Gradually one recognizes that the house is merely the facade of an illusory modernity
intended to cover personal conflicts and contradictions of its inhabitants—
in short, an allegorical milieu within which the psychic crisis of old Spaniards in a new Spain is once again reenacted.

Saura describes the project of *The Bunker* this way: "I find myself with a
world to develop [in the film], and a world which is, at the same time,
contemporary in Spain, because, besides, the 'Middle Class' or the Spanish
bourgeoisie, it seems to me, finds itself in a basic predicament; it's a class
still quite dominated by medieval structures that are in contradiction with
what has been called 'industrial development.' There's a kind of industrial
boom, and the technocrats are appearing, etc., but at the same time a whole
series of taboos and earlier structures are preserved. And that, in a short
number of years. And so, beginning from here, the engineer from *The Bunker* and his wife respond in a certain way to that contradiction" (Brasó
1974, 237–38). Within this allegorical mise-en-scène which emblemizes
Spain of the sixties, the characters move instinctively through a series of
simulations of scenes from their lives, through which process they gradually intuit the real structures that have ordered their existence. Those struc-

tures have been masked by the language of artifice which is the indelible mark of their social submission to order.

The bulk of the film, in fact, is dedicated to the series of games through which we witness Pedro and Teresa learning to speak their desires and hatreds to each other. This game motif dramatizes on one level the deformed and suppressed communication between two individuals who, in their repressive social milieu, have become alienated from their inner selves. But self-referentially as the agency of filmic narration for much of *The Bunker*, the game motif points outward to the no-less-deformed system of visual and narrative allusion Spanish cinema is forced to adopt in order to communicate with its audience. Román Gubern has called this latter phenomenon, developed as a response to Francoist film censorship, "a pathology of expression" (Gubern 1974, 296), in which allegory, symbolism, parable, double meanings, and metaphors replace the clear and direct presentation of a social reality. In *The Bunker* that pathology of expression is wed to the theme of the falsified language and images that construct the simulacrum of experience for each individual.

The precredits and final images of *The Bunker* address the spectator as the self-conscious "reader" of the social language of constructed images. In the precredits, for example, we have the first distanced shot of the fortress house. We view through the huge living-room window the first shot of the couple embracing and kissing. The terms of a certain cultural illusion of the ideal marriage are established: Matrimonial harmony is paired with the affluence of the attractive couple. The window "frames" the couple as a photographic camera might and thereby constructs the ideal image of the successful marriage in the modern world: youth, beauty, affluence, love, etc.

At the film's end, after Teresa has shot Pedro as the culmination of their games and has apparently killed herself also, a snapshot appears on the screen of an earlier Pedro and Teresa, smiling into the camera arm in arm. This last shot, maintained as a freeze-frame, serves as a coda, as it reveals prominently the power of the artificial frame of the photograph to capture a segmented and partial image that falsifies the lives we have, by this point, come to see in full.

The Female Subject

The Bunker represents an important thematic shift in Saura's development toward a greater appreciation of the female subjectivity. Though the presence of female characters has grown progressively more important with *Peppermint Frappé* and *Stress*, this is the first of his films to give thematic and discursive centrality to the female character. As Saura readily acknowledges, that growing importance of the female derives from the influence of Geraldine Chaplin in his work: "The entrance of Geraldine in my work— and also in my life—changed my way of looking at women. It changed it considerably because the women I knew up until then—some more intelligent than others—generally came from a Latin, or Spanish education, with the woman being a little more passive. . . . Today all of that has changed with the years, of course, but thirty years ago the bourgeois Spanish woman, which is what interested me in my work because it was what I knew the best, generally did not have a job and dedicated herself to getting married, to having children; she dedicated herself to the house" (Bartholomew 1983, 29).

The development of the script for *The Bunker* repeats that bourgeois scenario, but, importantly, undercuts that narrow Spanish definition of the woman by giving centrality to Teresa's growing consciousness of her entrapment in a constructed social identity. "*The Bunker* owes a lot to Geraldine," Saura says, "because many of the things that are in the film are things which she either lived directly or were recounted to her, school memories, conversations with her friends" (Brasó 1974, 236). Though there are striking points of thematic coincidence with his two earlier films, Saura's new focus on female consciousness is established from the very start with the series of isolated shots that follow the credit sequences. We see a furniture van on the highway, then a shot of its arrival at the house, finally a shot to a dark corridor in what appears to be a convent school where a nun is dragging a young girl before a priest. The girl screams, and the scene abruptly cuts to Teresa's awakening in bed in the middle of what is now understood to be the nightmare we have just witnessed. A later sleepwalking scene, what Saura calls Teresa's involuntary somnambulism, is occasioned by the impact on Teresa of the mementos of her childhood. That plunge into the past initiates a progression of instinctive moves by her to reconstruct moments from her childhood through simulated reenactment of scenes as triggered by the objects that the moving van has delivered to the house. Like Julián in *Peppermint Frappé*, Teresa acts out a number of traumas of specific repression in her religious and family past. The predominance of the authority figures of priests and nuns, and later of the father, suggest a traumatic submission by her to figures of authority.

The Bunker derives its dramatic impact from a sequential progression that clearly traces Teresa's destablization and immersion into psychodrama. The first somnambulism ends after Pedro has been cajoled into interpreting the role of Teresa's father. When, on the next night, Pedro follows her to the cellar where the furniture has been stored, it appears not only that the obsession with the past has taken over Teresa's very being, but also that the force of her will is beginning to take over her husband's imagination as well.

The next morning, when Pedro is at the factory, Teresa begins to rum-
mage through old mementos stored in the cellar. She finds a photograph
of herself as a child and attempts to simulate her childish smile as she sits
in front of her bedroom vanity. There is a first suggestion of theatricality
in this scene, as though she were an actress attempting to make herself up
for a character role she is about to play. This is, in fact, the first explicit
moment in the film when the spectator can discern the character's move to
theatricalization of her own previous life. In Saura's next film, *Garden of
Delights*, the parodic theatricalization of a man's life will begin with a scene
strongly reminiscent of this one.

With the image of Teresa sitting before a mirror and attempting to re-
create her own past image, Saura once again dramatizes the illusionist apparatus in the text by drawing the audience's attention to the figuration of
a *regressus in infinitum* in the scene: We view the filmic representation of
Teresa's simulation of the image of herself as a young girl in what is an
already theatricalized photograph. In that original image, she had propped
her long hair under her nose to appear as an incongruous moustache, thus
pointing ironically to the fact that the child in the photograph was also
trying to simulate another identity. With this final layer of the regressus,
Saura appears to suggest that, as in a Borges story, individual identity is
only part of an infinite chain of simulations of other texts, other adjustments to social identities. Equally revealing is the scene's mirroring of Teresa's impulse to mimic others, both as a child and now as an adult. Her
underlying crisis, we begin to intuit, derives from her awakening to the
social identity a phallocentric social system has constructed for her.
Though the script of *The Bunker* understates the Spanish social context of
action, at various moments the Spanish audience is invited to read their
own regressive cultural experience into Teresa's and Pedro's actions. This
is particularly true of incidents depicting the authoritarian environment of
Teresa's childhood.

The mirror scene reveals Teresa's confusion between the terms of the
reality of her experience and the artifices through which she views those
experiences. Saura purposely maintains a pattern of radical juxtaposition
between interior, subjective perspectives and external, orienting shots of
the action. As with the nightmare of the convent school, such internalized
perspectives are always finally disrupted by a detached vision which recu-
perates for the audience the knowledge that they are looking at Teresa's
looking, examining the ways she sees herself through artifice.

Teresa's reawakening to her past through flashbacks of her childhood
occurs in the early stages of *The Bunker*, shortly after the arrival of the
furniture, and serves as a prelude to the games through which she engages
Pedro. After a troubled night in Teresa's parents' bed, Pedro oversleeps
and decides, quite uncharacteristically, not to go to work that day. The

stage is now set for a series of playacting situations in which the two appear innocently to be entertaining each other. Each of these theatrical simulations of stages of the intimate life of a man and a woman moves the couple further away from external reality and into a labyrinth of nostalgia and of sentiments that they have hitherto hidden from the other, and even from themselves.

Simulations

There is a total of seven simulations or games producing what amounts to the portrait of a woman gradually coming to a recognition of the social roles and role-playing that have constructed her identity within a phallocentric cultural order. The first game is innocent enough, a parody of childbirth initiated by Teresa and prompted by mention of her girlfriend who seems always to be pregnant. It is followed with the game of lovers in which Pedro accidently reveals to Teresa his previously unspoken erotic desires and possible infidelity. In ensuing reenactments a note of animosity and aggression begins to surface. After playing lovers, Teresa rebukes Pedro for his passion in playing the role, the implication being that he has been unfaithful to her. The game of Santa Catalina comes to an abrupt end when it appears that Pedro is about to strike Teresa with a yardstick. When they move to the game of the St. Bernard Dog in which Pedro, now on his hands and knees, plays the part of a humiliated dog, Teresa does strike him with a broom. After a reconciliation between the two in what is never clearly distinguished as their game or reality, the pattern of play changes precipitously to more immediately autobiographical themes: games of marriage, of separation, finally, of death.

  In the movement from one game to another, the two characters have apparently moved from simulations of past memories to indirect confessions of their unspoken animosities toward each other. With the games of marriage, separation, and death, they have reached a point where the constraints of socially masked meanings give way to the deformed expressions of their own mutual desires and hates.

  Teresa interprets Pedro's game of separation as his confession that he desires to leave her. As he packs a valise in the bedroom, she goes into his study from where a gunshot is heard. Pedro rushes to find Teresa slumped over the desk with his pistol in her hand and what appears to be blood on her temples. He hurries to the telephone to call the police, but suddenly stops when he notices a bottle of ketchup on the floor. Teresa sits up and looks at him. Outraged by her fraud, he rushes back to the bedroom and continues to pack. She follows him, but he rebuffs her: "The games are all over, Teresa," he tells her. Taking his valise, Pedro goes to his car parked in front of the house. Teresa, understanding that he really does plan to leave her, runs to the entrance of the house and shoots Pedro in the back with the pistol. His lifeless body falls on the pavement.

As Teresa views the corpse from the doorway of the house, the camera rapidly pans away to a perfectly manicured lawn and the close-up of a snapshot of the smiling couple is seen as an off-screen sound of a gunshot is heard, evoking the possibility of Teresa's suicide. In the film's final juxtaposition of the reality of murder with the artifice of photography, Saura reinserts the essential schism between the stabilizing illusions that fix false identities and the destructive imagination that such suppressions induce in the psyche of individuals. That image, standing outside the narrative as it does, addresses the real spectator and invites a reflection, not on the particular destinies of the protagonists, but on the process of cultural formation and deformation inextricably woven into these symptomatic destinies. For this is not simply a photograph of the couple in a falsified, "public" pose, as we now understand. It harks back to the earlier scene in which Teresa sits at her mirror and attempts to imitate her childhood expressions. Photography is the symptomatic mark of the forms of socially implicated representations that do not merely reflect, but construct and impose identities on the individual.

Like much of the rest of the film, this pensive moment with which Saura chooses to end *The Bunker* derives from a vision of the psychic burden of a cultural identity that is only incidentally Spanish. The result, as we see, is a film that clearly seeks to transcend the ghetto of its Spanishness and direct itself to a more universal spectatorship. Yet, by attempting to demarginalize the Spanish experience with *The Bunker*, Saura inevitably disappointed the all-important festival audiences and juries outside of Spain he was dependent upon for recognition. Reflecting on the hostile reception the film received in Berlin, he observed: "What they wanted to see was that in Spain people died of hunger in the streets. In terms of a political position, it seems to me essential that they should be able to make political films in Spain one day, but with seriousness. Of course, *The Bunker* had nothing to do with that" (Brasó 1974, 258). Though the film did far better commercially in Spain than any of his previous works with Querejeta (Hernández Les 1986, *Singular,* 310), *The Bunker* did not even have a commercial release in France until 1979—by which time critics had begun to perceive its importance as a prefiguration of key elements of Saura's seventies' works, *Ana and The Wolves, Cousin Angelica, Cría!* and *Elisa, My Life.*

IV

Victims

Martyrs as Models

THROUGHOUT the 1960s Franco delegated progressively more decision-making powers to Admiral Luis Carrero Blanco, an ultra-religious conservative and unconditional supporter of the Caudillo. By the decade's end, Franco's strategy for developing an institutional continuity in his regime would be made clear when, in October of 1969, he made what would be his final major cabinet adjustment, replacing thirteen cabinet ministers, and naming Carrero Blanco vice president of the newly formed government. In all but name, however, Carrero Blanco was now head of the government (Fusi 1985,194).

These were times of crisis for the country, as open signs of violent dissent became an increasingly common fact of daily life. The chief concern for Carrero was the restoration of the government's authority. In 1970 the

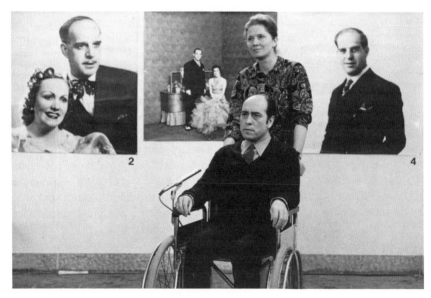

8. *Garden of Delights (Jardín de las delicias*, 1970)

trial in Burgos of Basque militants provoked an international reaction to the regime. But the government felt itself forced to do something in the face of increasing terrorism by various groups, the most prominent of which was Euskadi Ta Askatasuna (ETA), the clandestine Basque revolutionary organization. At the time, university strikes, press reporting of large rallies, and a general rise in public consciousness of the extent of dissent in the country as had never existed before created new pressures on a regime already shaken by the apparent dissolution of its formerly secure public acceptance. In part, the reason for this public awakening could be traced to the 1967 relaxation of press censorship, a liberalization sponsored by Fraga Iribarne.

Fraga's willingness to defend the right of the press to publish accounts of public demonstrations and even government corruption quickly made him a liability to the regime, and he was dismissed in October 1969, to be replaced by Alfredo Sánchez Bella, a man whose views of freedom of expression were much more in line with the new authoritarianism. Sánchez Bella remained in his post until June of 1973, during which time he supervised the return to the hard-line approach to censorship in the media that had operated with only minor resistance until 1963. There was not only a reinstitution of the vigorous surveillance of Spanish production, but also a stricter classification of foreign films shown in Spain and the altering of plots to adhere to the government's reactionary moral code. The mutilation of foreign films such as Altman's *McCabe and Mrs. Miller* and Bertolucci's *Before the Revolution* were common, as was the banning of other totally undesirable films: *Last Tango in Paris* and a group of Fellini films, including *La Dolce Vita*, which the government had steadfastly refused to approve for public screening for a decade in any form at all (Gubern 1981, 251–55).

Nearly a decade of *apertura* had made these repressive policies not only intolerable but even counterproductive, for they gave tangible evidence of the repression that was now being felt by larger segments of the population. Nor did the "big stick" policy change many attitudes among filmmakers. Suppression of particular films and the censorial mutilation of others was common knowledge and, rather than serving to deter filmmakers, seemed only to move some of them toward a more concerted political cinema. Saura would, in fact, become one of these politicized directors.

As Román Gubern documents in his exhaustive investigation of the erratic censorship policies of the period, *Un cine para el cadalso* (1976: Cinema for the Scaffolds), a number of Spanish filmmakers of this period were to find themselves martyred almost without provocation for films that only in a very narrow sense could be seen as detrimental to the status quo. Three of the most extreme and well known of these martyrdoms, which involved public announcements of film releases and subsequent suppressions, characterized the coercive climate of the times: Josep María Forn's *La respuesta* (1969: The Response), which dealt with student unrest and generational conflict in a Catalan family; Carlos Durán's futuristic science-fiction film, *Liberxina 90* (1970–71), which depicted a resistance movement against a government in a world of the future; and, finally, Basilio Martín Patino's documentary about post–Civil War Spain, *Canciones para después de una guerra* (1970: Songs for after a War). Representing three radically different types of filmmaking, as well as distinctive thematic and cultural visions, each film, nonetheless, within a period of two years (1969–1971) suffered arbitrary suppressions by the Information Ministry's subcommission on censorship.

Forn's film had no doubt raised questions for the censors because of its treatment of university strikes and the general tone of its dialogues involving a series of themes that challenged traditional authority and the values of middle-class Spanish society. Following normal procedures, the script was submitted for a shooting license. Forn learned that approval was contingent on his willingness to accept twenty-one cuts in scenes and dialogue. Once completed and, ironically, even before a decision was made by the subcommittee on censorship, the film was invited to be shown at the semi-official Molins del Rey festival devoted to new Spanish cinema. Though authorized for the festival, the film was simultaneously denied a distribution license for subsequent public screening.

Trying to force a reconsideration of this latter decision, Forn refused to permit the previously announced festival screening. Pressure from friends and government officials was exerted on Forn to relent, and he finally agreed to a deal with the festival director whereby *La respuesta* would be shown at Molins del Rey, but only if he could address the festival audience before the screening. His impassioned denunciation of censorship policies and the actions of the subcommission were to cost him dearly. After his fiery speech, Pedro Cobelas, then subdirector of the film commission, informed Forn that he would personally make sure that none of Forn's future films would ever get approved.

Over the next six years, Forn deleted scenes and retracked dialogue in an effort to placate the censors, but to no avail. *La respuesta* was to be rejected a total of twenty-four times by the censors.[1] The film was finally granted a domestic distribution license in 1976 but in a pale version of its original biting form. Not only had the film's time of contemporary protest passed, but the newly edited version appeared devoid of any of the force of the film shown years earlier at Molins del Rey.

Carlos Durán's *Liberxina 90* (1970–1971), a political fantasy that takes place in an imaginary country in a futuristic setting, went through an

---

[1] From personal interviews with the director, May 1987.

equally painful captivity. The script was delayed by censorial objections for nearly two years. Once completed, *Liberxina 90* was invited to the Venice Film Festival, but the Information Ministry denied the film an appropriate release, forcing the producer to alter a number of lines of dialogue that were deemed unsuitable. Finally, when it appeared that a public screening would be available at the San Sebastián Festival, the festival's director objected to the inclusion of newsreel footage of Soviet troops marching into Prague in 1968 and of the image of the Ku Klux Klan in the U.S. Dependent on the Ministry of Information for subsidies, the San Sebastián Festival had now become a new source of censorial intimidation for filmmakers.

By far, the most important of the martyrdoms of the period was that of Basilio Martín Patino's *Canciones para después de una guerra*. A nostalgic montage of songs and newsreel images covering the period from approximately 1936 through 1960, the film was really an astute invocation to the audience's memory of the hardships of the postwar period and the cultural infantilization of the Spanish people. Though scrupulously "correct" in not openly mocking the regime, the implied parody of Francoism often comes to the surface in *Canciones* through surprising juxtapositions of songs and images. For instance, the song "*Se va el caimán*" (The Alligator Is Going Away), placed at the end of the film, is easily read as a comic allusion to the inevitable death of Franco.

Originally approved for all audiences by the censors, but not without twenty-seven deletions of footage, the film was actually designated to receive the government's "special interest" subsidy. Upon its release, however, the right-wing newspaper *El Alcázar* violently attacked *Canciones*, provoking such a furor in official circles that Carrero Blanco ordered a private screening and then had the film withdrawn. Not only was *Canciones* banned, but when the American Academy of Motion Picture Arts and Sciences became interested in possibly nominating it for an Oscar in the Best Foreign Film category, they were informed by the ministry that no such film existed. Though not released in Spain until 1976, after Franco's death, the *Canciones* scandal, as well as the film's critical theme of recuperated memory, had already had its effect upon other filmmakers, most notably Saura and another Querejeta protégé, Victor Erice, whose *Espíritu de la colmena* (1973: Spirit of the Beehive) evoked memories of the dreary days of the immediate postwar period.

The mean-spirited policies of Sánchez Bella's ministry had, by this point, awakened a measure of political awareness in Saura that had not really been seen since *The Hunt*. Of course, his most recent work had dealt with the impact of a repressive climate on the outlook of individuals but, by comparison with the films of other directors, and, certainly, judged against his own earlier work, it appeared that he had retreated from the important political issues of the day. The increasing negative response abroad to his most recent films may also have prompted him to redirect his thematic focus after *The Bunker*. Whatever the motivation, however, the shift to a more politicized cinema was clearly evident in his next three films: *Jardín de las delicias* (1970: Garden of Delights); *Ana y los lobos* (1972: Ana and the Wolves); and *La prima Angélica* (1973: Cousin Angelica). Though distinct from one another in terms of character and situation, they form a political triptych, dealing with the twin themes of family and censorship. In part because of Querejeta's plan for an active engagement with the censors, in part because of the dazzling inventiveness of the three scripts, but most assuredly because of Saura's status as a noted director outside of Spain, these films avoided the martyrdom of others of the period while touching the very nerve center of Francoism.

Describing the ways in which the fact of censorship had shaped his style during this period, Saura observed: "Censorship obliges one to find a roundabout way of narrating things. This necessity of avoiding the facts without losing sight of them forces one to explore types of narration and plots which, little by little, shape the personality of the director and of his way of making films" (Gubern 1973, 19).

In each of the three films, Saura attempts to address a collective Spanish audience by putting into question the Francoist ideal of the unified, passive nation. In approaching each of the three films he implicitly utilizes the tradition of nationalist films dating back to Sáenz de Heredia's *Raza*, in which the ideal of the family is exploited as the emblematic expression of the nation. But that ideal family, already stereotyped by the right, is now stood on its head as Saura equates the family with the ideological apparatus of the state. In these three films the family insistently serves as the expression of emotional and political bondage, becoming the agency through which Saura dramatizes the involuntary submission of the individual to the constructed ideological discourse that is the nation as understood in Francoist terms.

"The Play's the Thing"

Speaking of his conception of *Garden of Delights*, Saura says that circumstances surrounding the death of Juan March, the notorious privateer and industrialist who helped bankroll the July 1936 military uprising against the Republic, were the inspiration for his conception of Antonio Cano.[2]

---

[2] For a thorough discussion of Juan March's rise to power and the extent of his financial empire, see John Brooks, "Annals of Finance," *The New Yorker*, Part I (21 May 1979): 42–102; Part II (28 May 1979): 42–91.

March's final words to the police who tried to extricate him from his car after a crash were these: "*Mi cabeza, mi cabeza. Hagan lo que quieran con mi cuerpo, pero no me toquen la cabeza*" (My head, my head. Do what you want to my body, but don't touch my head.) (Brasó 1974, 273). In developing a plot around a fictional industrialist who, like March, was influential in government circles, but who, in this case, survives the automobile accident although suffering amnesia and partial paralysis, Saura is clearly taunting the censors in ways that go beyond even what had been his most politically daring work up to this point, *The Hunt*.

The protagonist of *Garden of Delights* is unavoidably cast in a political light. Whether one traces his resemblance back to Juan March or reads into his amnesia and bodily incapacitation a coded reference to Franco's long-rumored mental and physical decline, the image is still a dangerous one never before posed by a Spanish filmmaker.[3] To balance the risks inherent in such a script, Saura, with the support of Rafael Azcona, produces an intricate, intentionally dense narrational scheme involving flashbacks and simulated memories, as well as a number of hermetic fantasy projections by the protagonist to suggest the kind of labyrinthine structure evoked in the film's title inspired by the Hieronymus Bosch triptych displayed in the Prado Museum.

The enunciative strategy of *Garden of Delights* goes back to the model of *The Hunt* in which an on-screen spectator, Enrique, was the source of a series of interrogations of a narrative mise-en-scène. That situation is considerably intensified, as the on-screen surrogate of the real spectator is now the Juan March character. The pivot of Saura's strategy lies in the fact that, from the very start, the protagonist, Antonio Cano, played brilliantly by José Luis López Vázquez, has been forced into a series of "therapeutic" dramatizations of key moments from his life, staged by his family in the hope of triggering the reawakening of his memory. Their interest in his condition, we quickly learn, is not familial love but the pressing need to locate Antonio's Swiss bank account so that the family can stave off a major takeover of their business interests. Individual tragedy thus carries with it a decisive measure of that peculiarly Spanish grotesque black comedy, the *esperpento*, epitomized early in this century by the works of José María Valle-Inclán.

The credits and first narrative sequence of *Garden* establish the film's enunciative design and comic grotesque tone while intentionally forcing the spectator into a pattern of visual interrogations of the spaces of representation. The credits open with a slow tracking of what appears to be the

[3] Juan Pablo Fusi describes how, by the mid-sixties, Franco's appearance had become markedly transformed from the earlier image of the virile soldier into that of a fragile and weak old man. This, in turn, gave widespread credence to the rumors of Franco's imminent death (184–85; 224–26).

interior of an abandoned warehouse. Eerie sounds like those of an electric saw cutting through wood are heard over the credits; the image then cuts to some other location, noted by the change of off-screen sounds. We see a dated family portrait situated on the edge of a dressing mirror as a woman in a red dress makes up her face apparently to coincide with the image of the woman in the picture. An elderly man oversees this operation, as the view of the larger scene widens gradually to reveal an ornate bedroom where the old man is issuing orders to both the woman and some servants. The setting is patently artificial, suggesting as much a theatrical set as a real bedroom. The scratchy phonograph music of the thirties' song "Recordar" (To Remember), sung by Imperio Argentina, is heard.[4] A servant leads a huge hog into the bedroom at the old man's instructions, and it appears the scene is now set according to the old man's dictates for some strange kind of ritual or ceremony. A wheelchair is then rolled into the

9.   *Garden of Delights (Jardín de las delicias*, 1970)

[4] While serving within the film to underscore the critical theme of the inducements to the character's nostalgia for past events, "Recordar" also addresses the audience meta-cinematically with a song from a popular thirties Spanish film, Florián Rey's *Su noche de boda* (1931: *Her Wedding Night*), inviting the spectator into the same retrospective flow dictated by the character. This is the first of a chain of textual commentaries to other films that abound in *Garden of Delights*.

room in which is seated the mute figure of a man who we later discover is the middle-aged industrialist Antonio Cano.

The curious preparations are part of a reenactment of a scene from Cano's early childhood. The elderly man (Francisco Pierrá) is his father; the woman in the red dress (Charo Soriano), an actress hired to play the part of Antonio's deceased mother. They speak to Antonio as if he were a child, for indeed, the staged scene recreates an incident that occurred when Antonio was five. He had made his mother cry and his father punished him, locking the frightened boy in a room with a huge pig, warning Antonio that the pig would eat his hands off. In the present-day simulation Antonio is wheeled into the room containing the pig, and the door is locked. Family members and servants listen at the door as Antonio stammers a few words amidst the pig's shrieks.

One of the assembled group, Antonio's daughter (Julia Peña), chides her grandfather for his cruel treatment of her father. "Don't you understand," he responds, "symbols are everything." His words, of course, transcend the context in which they are uttered, establishing the first of a series of links that will lead the spectator of *Garden* to recognize the actions of the elder Cano as synonymous with the process of ideological coercion of the Spaniard by state cultural apparatuses.

Saura cleverly delays divulging the full explanation of the family's plan. Instead, he gives us bits and pieces of the mystery that informs the therapeutic sessions: We learn that enacted scenes correspond to traumatic or otherwise significant moments in Antonio's life; that he has been incapacitated by some kind of accident; that he has lost his memory; and, more than anything else, that his father's and his wife's concern is for at least sufficient recuperation of his memory so that he will be able to recall the numbers of his Swiss bank accounts. By stringing out these details that, if presented directly at the outset, would orient us to a more linear reading of actions, Saura reveals one of the essential structural objectives of *Garden of Delights*: to make the audience identify with Antonio's position as victim, bringing them to share his sense of confusion and disorientation through much of the first part of the film.

The credits and first sequence focus on the paradigm of enigma/decipherment which operates throughout the entire filmic narrative to engage the spectator actively in the unmasking of the terms of his own relation to an all-pervasive cultural repression. The spectator is initially positioned to discover a confusing and disorienting space of action, the warehouse from which the mysterious noises emerge. Then the scene quickly shifts to a second, less ominous but equally bewildering, space where characters are involved in actions that appear enigmatic only because their framing context has been suppressed. This structured disorder entices the viewer to resolve the confusion as an act of "reading" contexts that operate around images and actions. Gradually, the spectator comes to sense that the fictional world portrayed within the film is divided into on-stage and off-stage spaces, the latter being suppressed spaces constituting the source of meanings for all the "staged" scenes.

The warehouse locale of the credit scene is, in this sense, one of the key off-stage spaces. Much later in the film, we will identify it as the storeroom containing props used in the theatrical representations of Antonio's life. Following a visual quotation from the final images of Orson Welles's *Citizen Kane* (Brasó 1974, 282), the warehouse is the place that contains the intimate mementos, the possible "Rosebud" that may answer for us the underlying question of the film: Who is Antonio Cano? The mobilization of the spectator in a hermeneutic activity is obviously an expedient strategy for presenting a series of otherwise "dangerous" images and scenes that, if presented in a more direct narrative style, would surely have been deleted by the censors. Saura and Querejeta seem to have been calculating that the hermetic style of *Garden of Delights* would lead the censors to conclude that the film would not appeal to a very large audience, and would therefore be lenient in their treatment of it.

The notion of the therapeutic theatrical performance is, for the Spanish spectator, an obvious borrowing from Calderón de la Barca's seventeenth-century tragedy, *La vida es sueño* (Life Is a Dream), one of several Calderonian plays Saura weaves into his plots over the next decade. *Life Is a Dream* tells the story of the captivity of Segismundo, the young prince of Poland, who is imprisoned in a tower at birth to prevent the fulfillment of a prophecy that he would one day murder his father and assume the crown. Repenting his cruelty to his son, Basilio, the king, has Segismundo drugged, then brought to the palace to be awakened and made to believe that he had only dreamt his captivity. When Segismundo, who has never been in civilized society, begins to act violently, he is again drugged and returned to his prison, now prompted to think that his experience of freedom was the real dream and his imprisonment is his reality.

The Calderonian analogy provides a politically volatile intertext that requires no explicit verbal cue for recognition by a Spanish audience. In *Life Is a Dream*, for instance, Basilio's efforts to trick destiny reveal him to be both a bad father and a bad ruler. By implication, Antonio's father, and the Francoist ideology that he embodies (Catholicism, patriotism, family), are all successively lampooned. The contrived representation of Antonio Cano's life according to the ideological expediency of the family is inevitably seen as congruent with the activities of the Francoist state, which holds the individual's mind as well as his body captive. By means of the Calderonian allusion, Saura also solves the important dramatic problem of making Antonio a sympathetic character for the audience by paralleling his dilemma with the tragic condition of Segismundo.

Memory Is History

The enunciative mechanism of *Garden of Delights* is, by far, the most complex Saura has developed to date. Two major orders of narration are quickly identified within the first few minutes of the film: Antonio's life as simulated for him against his will by his father and wife (Luchy Soto); and the series of memories and traumas that, on a deeply personal level, both he and we are made to review. The Saura-Azcona shooting script actually distinguishes five planes of action which cover periods in Antonio's life and present-day hallucinations,[5] both weaving his personal recollections with the reconstructed events his father has devised and framing these within the present-day context of his convalescence. Throughout the film, as Katherine Kovacs has meticulously documented, we move without transition from one realm of action to another, from reality to dream and back again (Kovacs 1981, 46–47). As described by Kovacs, the five planes are:

1. *The recreated past*: a series of scenes staged by Antonio's father, beginning with the pig incident and including Antonio's first communion in 1931, just as the Spanish monarchy was overthrown and the Republic was declared, and his mother's death, which apparently coincides with the victorious Francoist armies' entrance into Madrid on April 1, 1939.

2. *The present-day frame* of Antonio's convalescence under the care of his father and his wife, Luchy: During these sequences Antonio is pushed to remember his past through theatrical devices, as when his mistress, Nicole (Esperanza Roy), is brought into his bedroom to prod him as his family observes the scene from behind a concealed mirror, or as he is forced to submit to a memory lesson by reviewing a collection of photographs from his past.

3. *Evoked Past:* The contrived scenes are interrupted by Antonio's own independent memories of crucial moments in his life, the most important being his remembrance of a childhood illness when his aunt nursed him. The scene is presented with the pointed suggestion that Antonio's affection for his aunt, even as a small child, is tainted with erotic desire.[6]

4. *The "oneiric" world*: These are the eruptions of hallucinations which continually threaten Antonio as he sits in his wheelchair in the garden of his huge estate. In one of these oneiric scenes he imagines himself being violently pushed

---

[5] For a penetrating analysis of the five planes, see Katherine S. Kovacs, "Loss and Recuperation in *Garden of Delights*."

[6] As he evokes this memory, Antonio projects himself back in time, yet images himself as an adult playing the role of the child. The strategy of an adult impersonating himself as a child is a further dimension of the device of a single actor playing multiple roles in *Peppermint Frappé* and *The Bunker*. In important ways, it prefigures the critical use of this same device in López Vázquez's performance three years later in *Cousin Angelica*.

into the swimming pool. In another, the appearances of medieval knights and of
two combating armies are seen, each time driving him indoors.

   5. *A future plane*: As he gradually regains his physical abilities, Antonio demonstrates a more active concern for his own future, as when he attempts to drown
his wife during an outing in a rowboat, resisting the pattern of existence his
family has thrust upon him.

Of the various planes of action, the most easily identifiable for the spectator are those of the "recreated past." Moments of personal importance in
Antonio's life are continually matched with critical moments in the life of
the nation, particularly the upheavals of 1931 and 1936, and the fascist
triumph of 1939, thus creating a readability for the audience that many of
the seemingly more symbolic planes of action lack. In these scenes of the
re-created past, personal memory is grotesquely conflated with national
history. In part this is the result of Saura and Azcona's shaping of Antonio's rise and fall to parallel the rise and eventual decay of Francoism; in
part, it is a reflection of the conceptual design of *Garden of Delights* that
insistently identifies the Francoist family as the social apparatus that replicates on the personal plane the ideology of the state, constructing the prismatic frame of reference through which the individual's consciousness of
himself takes shape.

Film and Lucidity

The scenario in which the family is represented as the apparatus of ideological orientation within Francoism involves an elaborate spectatorial project
in which, at certain moments in the text, the real spectator is made to occupy Antonio's point of view, both figuratively and literally. We are made
to identify with Antonio, to see the world of the re-created past metaphorically "through his eyes," with the textual reinforcement of that identification underscored in those scenes in which Antonio becomes the dramatized agency of visual enunciation. This occurs, for instance, in those
seemingly enigmatic oneiric sequences authorized by Antonio's gaze. The
function of the spectator's sharing Antonio's way of seeing the world appears to be to simulate for the real audience their own cultural position as
subjects of the ideological message of Francoism.
   At various points in the text, however, this process of spectator identification with the sight and plight of the protagonist is disrupted by a mode
of address that functions in precisely the opposite way—that is, to undercut the force of given images and sequences, leading the audience to a
heightened sense of their own manipulation by the unseen agency of representation. This decentering of the audience from dramatic identification

with Antonio operates principally through cinematic self-reference, inter-textual quotes to other films and cinematic artifice in general. There is, for instance, an early invocation of the song "Recordar" and Antonio's imag-ing of himself in a lush seashell bed that serves to parody the visual style that prevailed in Spanish popular cinema of the pre–Civil War period (Ko-vacs 1981, 48). A later nightmare scene in which two opposing bands of children fight with swords and shields on a playing field to the accompa-niment of the music from Eisenstein's *Alexander Nevsky* continues the chain of cinematic allusions. Toward the end of *Garden of Delights*, Antonio at-tempts to capsize the rowboat in which he and Luchy are seated in appar-ent parody of the American film *A Place in the Sun*.

To this significant chain of film allusions must be added the obvious modeling of the narrative to copy in self-conscious fashion Orson Welles's *Citizen Kane*. Saura's objective appears to be to draw his audience's contin-ual attention, both in the form and content of *Garden of Delights*, to the condition of artifice and construction that orders the life and memories of a character, as well as the representation of that life for others. In totalizing that figure of artifice to include the very film the spectator is watching, Saura, in fact, raises the question of the audience's relation to the network of representations that shape their own perception of the social world of Spain in 1970.

In one key scene, in fact, the cinematic situation is depicted within the film in a manner that erases any doubt about the underlying significance of Saura's enterprise. A sequence begins abruptly with grainy black-and-white newsreel footage of the Nationalist soldiers marching along high-ways in defiant heroic swagger, suggesting the end of the Civil War in the early spring of 1939. A voice-over chants the words of Rubén Darío's fa-mous poem, "Marcha triunfal." All at once the screen rips open as in some Dadaist movie gag, and Antonio's father appears, dressed absurdly in an army uniform of the period, attempting once more to provoke his son's personal associations with a moment in the life of the nation, in this case a momentous national event that coincides with the death of Antonio's mother.

The scene that Antonio's father concocts is a grotesque parody of per-sonal history; but it is also a parody of a parody: the March of Time se-quence from *Citizen Kane*, which introduced the question of the individual behind the public image. In a manner similar to Welles's deployment of newsreel, the spectator of Saura's scene is initially led to believe that the newsreel is a direct address to him as audience, only to discover the real on-screen audience to which that newsreel is directed. In *Kane* the staging of the film-within-the-film operated thematically to announce to the on-screen audience the need to look beyond the false sufficiency of public im-ages to find the real man behind the mask. That invocation to look beyond the framable representations of cinema in *Garden of Delights* has a much richer trajectory than Antonio's father could have imagined. The inclusion of the newsreel in this critical context hammers home a number of anti-Francoist themes, of which the most devastating, by far, is the depiction of the ideologically complicit cinematic apparatus. The relationship between censorship and the war is central to that operation, as Saura puts into question the Francoist interpretation of all Spanish history in terms of the triumph of 1939, and the lives of all Spaniards in relation to the fortunes of that war.

Finally, what is at stake in this sequence and throughout *Garden of Delights* is the unmasking of the political relation of the spectator to history. Saura's ironic reversal—putting Antonio Cano, the heir of the fascist victory of 1939, in the place of the vanquished—seems aimed at motivating the character and, by extension, his audience, to sense a need for lucidity in recuperating a personal meaning in the collective history that has, until this moment, been massively recoded by state apparatuses to suit the political needs of the regime.

In a more elaborate scene near the end of the film, a meta-cinematic trope is joined to the theme of perceptual manipulation to produce another inventive sequence of black humor that once again pushes the spectator to a critical lucidity about his own relation to personal and cultural representations. Antonio's wife, Luchy, brings him to the gardens of the royal summer residence at Aranjuez in an effort to entice him to remember an earlier time when the two of them were happily married. The setting of the action, while itself indicative of the artificial cultural landscape, initially suggests, at least in terms of the sequence, a direct representation of action. The scene begins with a shot of the royal gardens at Aranjuez where Luchy leads Antonio from their parked car. The strains of Rodrigo's "Concierto de Aranjuez" are heard, as if Saura were giving a romantic ambience to the scene. But we quickly realize that we are not listening to mere background music but rather to a tape from the small cassette recorder that Luchy carries. Her plan is to soften Antonio and spark his memory with mood music.[7] Though the contrivance varies from the earlier newsreel sequence, the pattern of manipulation of the subject's memory through a technological invocation is identical, as is the simultaneous engagement/illumination of the spectator in that same process. Our first intuitive reading of the scene as a direct representation of action we are "seeing with our own eyes" is thus exposed as another trick of an off-screen apparatus which still seeks to manipulate the consciousness of its subject.

---

[7] At Geraldine Chaplin's suggestion, Saura used direct sound for the first time in *Garden of Delights*. The Aranjuez sequence indicates his obvious relish in experimenting with this new dimension of cinematic narrative effects.

In this sequence, however, it seems that the visual and auditory cues have finally succeeded in triggering Antonio's memory. He recalls the trees, the landscape, the water, a boat. Thinking that his desire to go rowing in one of the boats docked at the side of the lake is a recollection of their honeymoon, Luchy gladly accedes to Antonio's wish. When their boat moves away from the dock, Antonio begins to rock from side to side in an apparent effort to throw Luchy overboard; he even picks up the oar attempting to strike her, all the time muttering "*Una tragedia americana*" (An American Tragedy).

The cinematic intertext, though apparently devoid of political connotation, replicates on the level of family melodrama the patterns of ideological manipulation of individuals that we have previously identified with the state. The audience becomes increasingly aware of the weaving of referential and self-referential implications of the film's narrative. Through Antonio's story, we see the dramatization of the manipulation of the individual's sight and belief, his education in repression. But through cinematic self-reference, that story continually alludes to a broader complicity in the condition of the spectator who is made to believe in the momentary illusion of his own autonomous, detached sight, only to recognize its limits through the text's unmasking of artifices.

Garden and Lucidity

The Aranjuez sequence ends with a cut to what appears to be the lush gardens surrounding the Cano estate as the camera tracks to two cars on the verdant lawn which appear to have crashed head-on. One is a shiny Mercedes-Benz, and, as the camera tracks in, we discover Antonio crouched over the steering column, his head bloodied. Nicole, his mistress, who had appeared in one of the earlier theatrical scenes, is at his side; her thigh is wounded and bloodied. The two are totally immobile, giving the impression that they are dead. The camera then cuts to Antonio, once again in a wheelchair, observing what it now becomes clear is the oneiric re-creation of the car accident that had originally paralyzed him. It is at this moment that he speaks the March lines: "Don't touch my head! Don't touch my head!" As the camera shows Antonio's intense and pained facial expressions, we see other wheelchairs moving on the lawn behind him: his father, his wife, their two children, the actress who played the role of his mother, even his nurse. They circle Antonio as he sits transfixed by the image of the accident. Then the camera cuts to yet another image of Antonio—this time, standing erect on the terrace apparently looking at himself and the others in wheelchairs. He quickly retreats into the house, but then stops. The image cuts back to a distanced shot of the circle of characters in wheelchairs on the lawn. The film ends with this image frozen to produce a tableau effect approximating a contemporary version of one of Bosch's panels in his "Garden of Delights."

The reiteration of the garden as the space of represented trauma addresses the spectator rather than the characters. We become aware retrospectively that the garden has been, throughout, the locus of an insistent series of contrivances and manipulations. It was here where Antonio had been brought to be "retrained," to practice writing his signature, a reconstruction of his social identity. It was also in this very garden where he evoked his most terrible nightmares: being pushed into the swimming pool and viewing the battle enacted among small children. In another garden, at Aranjuez, we saw Luchy trying once again to manipulate Antonio's emotions and his own instinctive use of the garden environment in an attempt to murder her. Antonio, the involuntary spectator of most of the film, tellingly becomes the willful spectator of the family now viewed as crippled and catatonic. This final image effectively places the film's characters in a symbolically charged space. The reference traces back to the Francoist argument of Spain as a "peaceable forest" (Kovacs 1984, 2), untainted by the heathen, European world. Through the eyes of one of its victims, we come finally to see a vision of the whole at the film's end which reveals the price of that peace. The lingering freeze-frame of the paralytic circle, accompanied by Spanish medieval courtly music, invites the spectator to reflect upon the larger symbolic picture of the order of the world under this decaying notion of Spain.

Enter the Censors

The approval of the shooting script of *Garden of Delights* had been motivated to some measure by the censors' belief that the cryptic nature of the film effectively canceled out any political effect it might have. One censor wrote in his evaluation: "The advantage of such an intellectualized plot is that nobody can grasp the key to it, and the setups are so extremely limited in meaning that nobody can identify with anything" (Hernández Les 1986, *Singular,* 181). The argument was further made that a director of Saura's international status didn't need a government subsidy, but the decision regarding a "special interest" subsidy for Querejeta was put off until the film's completion. After screening that completed version, the board conceded only a minimum subsidy, even after specific cuts had been made to placate individual censors. These included the deletion of the Rubén Darío poem in the newsreel sequence, as well as a brief scene in which the maid exposes her breast in order to induce Antonio to drink a glass of milk.

While the fiery debates between Querejeta and the censors over the subsidy dragged on, the government blocked the release of *Garden of Delights* for the Berlin Film Festival, fearing the film's reception abroad at a festival known for its appreciation of political films might provoke another *Viridiana* scandal. Efforts to have the *Garden of Delights* screened at Venice and Cannes were also stalemated by Spanish officials. There was, of course, an irony in all these moves. For years the government had tried in vain to interest foreign festivals in Spanish films, with little success. Now, when the three most prestigious festivals came begging for a Spanish film, the government turned a deaf ear.

Only after long negotiation with the organizers of the noncompetitive New York Film Festival was *Garden of Delights* entered in the 1971 festival program, where it drew highly favorable reviews. This attention thwarted any government efforts to suppress the film in the pattern of either *Liberxina 90* or Patino's work. Reluctantly, approval was given to a domestic release of *Garden* but in a version that the censors deemed suitable. The ultimate irony, of course, was that the government's intimidating treatment of the film worked only to intensify the outside world's interest in Saura's work.

Ana y los lobos (1972: Ana and the Wolves)

Buoyed by the critical success of *Garden of Delights* abroad, Saura conceived of his next film project, *Ana and the Wolves*, as a direct provocation to the censors, incorporating into the script some of the hitherto "untouchable" themes of Spanish cinema. Speaking of his notion of the film, he said: "I had always seen the three great problems for the Spanish censors to be politics, religion and sex. And this bothered me until I came to the conclusion that the great 'powers' within Spain derived precisely from these taboos. Then it was a question of inventing a plot out of which came the gimmick of the film, the arrival of a foreigner to a house where those three powers are represented. Reigning above these [powers] there was a kind of mother figure. With that we had an obvious parable of a film, very easily schematized" (Lara and Galán 1973, 31).

From *The Hunt* onward, critics had remarked on Saura's penchant for symbolic narratives. In part, this development was the result of the peculiar scale and economics of Querejeta's productions. The strategy of a small cast and limited sets, as John Hopewell suggests, lends itself easily to symbolic readings: "Few locations and characters means that they have to become representative of larger historical realities if a film is to acquire a social relevance. And shooting in or around Madrid always located Saura's films in the symbolic heartland of the Francoist state: Castille" (Hopewell 1986, 72).

In *Garden of Delights*, as we have seen, that symbolizing tendency becomes self-referential ("Don't you understand? Symbols are everything!"). While at first appearing to be obscure and hermetic, some of these symbols are eventually demystified and shown to be merely the effect of the pathologically repressive society. Nowhere is the sham symbol more central to the conception of the film, however, than in the development of the Cano family. While symbolizing the forces of coercion, they also literalize the conservative bourgeois family as the agency of indoctrination of the individual toward Francoist values. Ironically, in a world where audiences and censors no longer believe in the self-sufficiency of direct representation, Saura's most potent weapons, and often his most startling gags, are this literalization of things.

This process of flaunting artifice through literalization continues in *Ana and the Wolves*, but on a grander scale. The family is represented by three generations. Mama, the matriarch (Rafaela Aparicio), has formed her sons, José (José María Prada), Juan (José Vivó), and Fernando (Fernando Fernán-Gómez), into three obsessive characters, each fetishizing one of the taboo topics Saura mentions. José represents the military, Juan is associated with lust, and Fernando embodies religious mysticism. We see the influence of these characters in shaping the minds of another generation—Juan's three daughters, Carlota, Victoria, and Natalia—toward the deformed perspectives of the world and toward themselves, which is, in Saura's thinking, the aberrant legacy of Francoism. Unlike *Garden of Delights*, *Ana and the Wolves* presents its material in what appears to be a direct, straightforward manner while continually feigning symbolic and allegorical intentions.

Ana arrives at the isolated country estate occupied by the ailing matriarch, her three sons, Juan's wife, Luchy (Charo Soriano), and their three daughters. Charged with the care of the three girls, Ana quickly becomes enmeshed in the fantasy life of each of the three men. José is the voice of order and authority in the family. With his fetish for uniforms—he tells Ana that "uniforms make the man"—he has set up a small museum of military dress in his study and recruits Ana to care for his collection. Juan, with his uncontrollable libido, tries to seduce her. So obsessed is he with Ana that at one point he sneaks into her bedroom to brush his teeth with her toothbrush. Fernando, by far the most subdued of the three brothers, has moved out of the main house to establish his residence in a nearby cave where he practices mystical incantations in an effort to levitate.

Between bouts of epilepsy and gout, Mama remains the protectress of the family unit. In the only scene where she and Ana engage in direct dialogue, the old dowager gives Ana a bit of the background of her three sons as she shows the governess their childhood clothing she has saved for years. "You must be understanding with them," Mama tells her, as Ana becomes interested in the absurdity of what up until this moment has only been a vexsome and eccentric family.

Ana now actively leads the three brothers on, playing to their fetishes and, at times, outwardly mocking them. When Juan starts sending her erotic letters, signing them as a secret admirer and delivering them with rare postage stamps from the family's collection pasted on the envelopes, Ana turns the matter over to José for disciplinary action. Only with Fernando does she develop a more intimate, although still platonic, relationship. As Saura says, that relationship is not based on physical attraction, but rather on Fernando's attempt to control Ana's imagination: "That's the idea of religion. That's why it is much longer and more laborious than his brothers' efforts" (Brasó 1974, 315–16).

When it becomes apparent that Ana has been leading her sons on, sowing doubts in their thinking and endangering the unity of the family, Mama orders that she be dismissed. The three brothers waylay her on the road as she leaves the estate. In actions that are dramatic expansions of their personal fetishes, the three assault and murder Ana. Forcing her to the ground, Fernando cuts off her hair; Juan rapes her; and José takes a pistol to her head and shoots her. The final freeze-frame is of Ana's agonized face in gruesome close-up.

A Repressive Education

In *Ana and The Wolves* the family, once again, is the agency of repressive education. As Saura sees it, the ultimate objective of such an education is to induce individuals to "learn their position," their "role" within a repressive social order. He focuses on this learning process in the very title of the film, evoking as it does a children's fairy tale. The fairy tale, a simplistic, straightforward narration, engages its audience in a fantasy. It is a genre that holds sway over the fertile imagination of the innocent mind. The three children who are wards of the foreign governess are metaphoric expressions of the innocence and vulnerability to fantasy that Saura wants the real audience to recognize as essential features of their own perceptual profile. On the most basic level of plot, the film presents itself as a cautionary tale to a gullible, innocent spectator: Beware of the devouring wolves around you.

Far more complex and biting is Saura's reshaping of the action within that black fairy tale into a parody of the religious allegory, the *auto sacramental*. The auto was a didactic religious dramatic form, developed in Spain as popular religious theater, which has survived centuries. Its object ". . . was to instruct the common people in the dogmas of the church and to show them their application to their own lives" (Brenan 1957, 297).

Saura's aim in simulating the didactic theatrical form is to posit a meta-critical referent within the film in which the spectator comes to recognize the underlying ideological basis of the relation between the forms of artistic expression and the social, cultural, and political climate within which those artistic forms operate and are authenticated by their audiences. In his demystification of the ideology of artistic form he takes his cue from one of the finest of Spanish religious allegories of the Counterreformation, Calderón's *Gran teatro del mundo* (Great Theater of the World). Gerald Brenan calls Calderón the "poet of certitude" (Brenan 1957, 298), and, indeed, *Great Theater of the World* is a perfect example of the Calderonian theology of predeterminism. The allegory centers on the presence of a character called the "Author," clearly intended to be God. In turn, a number of other characters who are the author's creations—World, Beauty, King—appear before him and are judged to be either sufficient in their performances or else lacking. When one of the characters rejects the lowly role assigned to him, the Author makes clear there is no place for free will in the theater of life; roles are fixed and one either performs well or not.

As the Calderonian Author necessarily speaks "down" in paternalistic tones to his creations, so his play inevitably does the same to its projected audience. Replicating the didactic style of the auto, *Ana and the Wolves* focuses on Saura's notion of the audience that has been invented and fixed by Francoism: Trapped in predetermined social structures (the family), assigned a specific number of social identities, the individual is constrained by what he or she can be or do and further victimized by the mythologies of the regime which continually reinforce the repressed, inhibited status of the individual vis-à-vis the power of the state. As Guy Braucourt observes, Saura and Azcona's particular achievement in their deft use of the Calderonian intertext lies ". . . in having found, for the purpose of illustrating this climate of inhibition and repression, a dramatic form in perfect harmony with the conditions of expression determined by the Spain of the day" (Braucourt 1974, 4).

The family in *Ana and the Wolves* parallels in striking ways the characters in *Great Theater*. With their mother as the Author(ess) of the grand design of life, each of the three brothers lives out his assigned obsessional role of power: sex, religion, and the military. Following a key detail of Calderonian theology in which the performance in this life becomes the basis for the final judgment in the hereafter, we find that the three brothers are not so much living as rehearsing their roles in the allegory of official culture. Frequent mention is made in the dialogue of the fact that a given action should not have occurred so soon, or a character will say, "So he's done that already, has he?" Devoid of spontaneity, each brother is a victim of his assigned role. The possibility of failed performance in life for Calderón thus becomes a comic inevitability for Saura's characters as allegory flirts with farce.

The ploy of the rehearsal of a preordained script has yet another subtle significance. From as early as *Hooligans*, Saura had depicted characters who were seduced by cultural myths of their own individuality: the bullfighter, the hero, and the hunter were the most symptomatic expressions of that myth. With *Garden of Delights* the notion of role-playing as the source of Francoist social identity was given a new prominence, although, owing to the parodic nature of the family members, we saw little significance in the choice of the therapeutic strategy of role-playing to trigger Antonio's memory. In *Ana and the Wolves*, however, Saura not only highlights the lack of spontaneity of individuals fixed into socially imposed roles, but also underscores the tyrannical operation of the family as the accomplice of the regime, inventing and sustaining the individual's dedication to emulating external role-models. This indictment goes far beyond Francoism and suggests, by implication, that the family is a historical matrix out of which the traditional repressive impulse of Spanish society emerges.

That broader historical focus does not suddenly erupt in *Ana and the Wolves* without conceptual motivation. As early as *Peppermint Frappé*, Saura suggested a broader cultural legacy—what he called Spain's medievalism—as the historical source of the individual's self-repressing mentality. In *The Bunker*'s opening flashback, we identify religion as a partial source of Teresa's repressive education. In *Garden of Delights* and again in *Ana and the Wolves* Saura's reliance on the Calderonian theatrical form provides us with the most revealing signs yet of his sense of the historically defined culture of repression. For this artistic structure embodies the ideology of constrained individuality, a hallmark of the Catholic orthodoxy of the Counterreformation that was to fix in place many of the repressive social, political, and religious situations that would eventually marginalize Spain in relation to the rest of Europe. In subtle ways over the next fifteen years he will return to different aspects of this theme of the legacy of Counterreformation ideology, finally culminating in *El Dorado* and *La noche oscura* (The Dark Night), Saura's only films to treat these questions explicitly as historical problems.

Anticipating a possibly violent rejection of the film by the censors, Saura employs a number of critical strategies to "lighten" the appearance of *Ana and the Wolves*. For instance, he insulates the brunt of his attack by distancing José from the army, making him only a collector of military uniforms; Fernando becomes a secular rather than a real priest whose goal in life is merely to achieve levitation. To further highlight the farcical over the conceptual critique, Saura selects a group of four consummate comedic actors to play the parts of Mama and her brood. Regardless of the mordant value of the role of the old matriarch, Rafaela Aparicio, the famed comic actress, still brings a sentimentality and tenderness to Mama which appears to deflect some of the obvious bite of her function in the film. Similarly, Fernán-Gómez, Prada, and Vivó as the three brothers must have appeared to the censors more as buffoons copying roles they had developed in lighter, popular films than as the material of a biting critique of Francoism.

The Personal and the Social

In response to one interviewer's questions about his attitude toward what has generally been perceived as his most cerebral, impersonal film up to this point, Saura reveals the personal connection between his characters and his own outlook: "I think the 'taboos' I present in *Ana And The Wolves* are the 'taboos' that afflict me directly, and which I have felt throughout my life since being a Spaniard resounds in me insistently. Keep in mind besides, that all of the films I make are in function of something very personal, and naturally, everything in *Ana And The Wolves* is part of me or of the 'taboos' that I have felt at particular moments" (Rentero 1976, 16).

His insistence on the personal dimension of social taboos hints at a complex human scenario that belies the film's apparently cold, intellectual design. As Mama's reminder to Ana to be understanding with her sons suggests, these are human beings who have been deformed by their assumption of the social masks they have been conditioned to accept as their only possible social and personal identity. The apparent model for Ana is Elena in *Peppermint Frappé*, the outsider as erotic bait whose presence within the closed world of traditional Spain poses a threat. But whereas the origins of the male's sexual obsessions are never clarified, Saura and Azcona make it clear that Ana's status as sexual object is a derivative effect of the deforming ideological apparatus of the family. Their antique values of family unity, military discipline, and religious zeal may appear quaint and amusing to Ana, but the social-sexual roles that she as the female subject must play in this ideological order eventually come to threaten her very life.

Up to a certain point Ana is successful at insulating herself emotionally from the grotesque antics of the three brothers. But when the children bring one of their dolls to her and tell her it was buried in the mud "by the wolves," her ironic distance turns to concern; for what she sees, and what the spectator necessarily intuits in his own reading of this world, is that there is a vital connection between the allegorical patterns of the film and the reality of real people. We begin to sense that the affective plight of these

10. *Ana and the Wolves* (*Ana y los lobos*, 1972)

"children of Francoism"[8] has emerged from the series of deceptively foolish and oddball antics of three seemingly harmless characters. Hidden in the broad theatricality of characters playing the role of actors lies the history of human generations who have been progressively deformed by the cultural patterns that will gradually transform them into the monsters who initially seem so harmless but who, in the final analysis, are predators. That is the point of the visual design of the film's beginning and end. The credits are shot against a background photograph of a family portrait which includes Mama, Ana, the three brothers, Luchy, and Juan's daughters. The lingering final shot, the close-up freeze-frame of Ana's agonized face at the moment of death, seems to suggest that there is a direct causality between the collective posturing of the family and the ultimate victimization of the indiviudal.

[8] Marsha Kinder argues that the figuration of this generation of "children of Franco" finds its source in the generational status of filmmakers like Saura and José Luis Borau, who were themselves the literal children of the dictatorship. The view of the emotional bondage that Francoist culture created in the young and vulnerable child is a fairly constant motif of many Spanish films of the seventies. For a stimulating discussion of the cinematic elaboration of the figure of the "children of Franco," see Marsha Kinder, "The Children of Franco."

Reenter the Censors

The version of *Ana and the Wolves* that was finally released in January of 1973 had gone through more censorial revisions than any of Saura's previous films. The details of that give-and-take of the censors' range of responses to the film at various stages of its development reveal on a very intimate level the complex of political and aesthetic positions that shaped much of Saura's film style during the final decade of the dictatorship. The Commission of Prior Censorship rejected a first script, pointing to its violation of published norms prohibiting the depiction of fetishism and unsavory social environments. It was in that early version where, as a precaution against negative censorial reaction, Saura proposed to have José as a samurai rather than a collector of military uniforms (Gubern 1981, 266). The censors rejected the entire script, however, on the grounds that it attacked the institution of the family. Four months later, when a modified version of *Ana* was presented, authorization was reluctantly granted for shooting, but with the strong admonition to the producer to make sure that Saura not stray from the approved script and that he avoid political, religious, and military symbols (Hernández Les 1986, *Singular,* 188). By this point, of course, the censors were well aware of the Saura-Querejeta ploy of the double script.

    The censors' understanding of their opponents is revealed in the written report to the full commission by one member who details for his colleagues his interpretation of the script's allegorical code: "The old mother is the regime supported by her sons: José, the military; Juan, money; and Fernando, the Church. These three wolves are the ones who undo Ana who is the monarchy. The three little girls, Carlota, Victoria, and Natalia, represent the *pueblo*, the people. . . . This is a negative script on every level which seeks to confuse the Spanish audience at a very delicate moment for Spain" (Hernández Les 1986, *Singular,* 188). Despite the commission's misgivings, *Ana and the Wolves* was granted a shooting license.

    When the definitive censorship judgment was made on *Ana* in December of 1972, the film was approved for release with no alterations, but it was restricted to audiences "above the age of eighteen," a final effort to limit the film's influence with the public. The logic of the censors' actions, which seemed to contradict their own inclinations as well as the policies of the Sánchez Bella administration, is best explained in the statement of the commission's vice president, Manuel Zabala, who wrote:

> A Saura-Querejeta film has to be, almost necessarily, a film of political and social critique focused from a peculiar point of view. Since circumstances do not permit them to make a direct critique, they do it through symbols. And that's what this film is: a pure symbol of Spain and her current "defects" as they see them. It is

clear that the film was made by altering the authorized script in some way. But the consequences of whatever decision is adopted will be the same as if they followed the script faithfully. If it [the film] is prohibited or mutilated, there will be a scandal inside of Spain and outside as well. If it is authorized there will be various problems that derive from that authorization. Now I believe that, in reviewing the various risks, prohibition is the heavier risk, for it plays right into the hands of the groups the author represents. The exhibition of the film in Spain will not change the convictions of anyone who isn't already convinced. And in the end, the film will pass without leaving a political trace. . . . That is what happened with *The Hunt* and *Garden of Delights*. Although abroad, some sectors will voice Saura's critique, it won't have the same resonance as a prohibition. We will have disarmed the opposition through authorization. Besides, there are more scathing and corrosive critiques and self-critiques than Saura's. In short, Saura's and Querejeta's vision of Spain, although we don't like it, lacks proselytizing, demoralizing force. If it is prohibited, it will lead to a scandal and to protests against the government. For that reason I would authorize it without cuts. (Hernández Les 1986, *Singular*, 188–89)

Zabala's thinking was to prevail with the commission, for the film was authorized for exhibition in Spain, and a "special interest" subsidy was even approved. These actions, while suggesting the privileged status Saura enjoyed even as he confronted the most aggressive and reactionary of censorship boards, also attest to the intelligence and perseverance of Querejeta. His unrelenting defense of the film with the censors helped save *Ana and the Wolves* from an all-too-familiar fate in the final years of the dictatorship.

Confrontations

For his next film, *La prima Angélica* (1973: Cousin Angelica), Saura took his narrative inspiration from an inconsequential bit of dialogue that occurs in the private conversation between Mama and Ana in *Ana and the Wolves*. The old woman speaks of a certain cousin Angelica who, as a small child, coquettishly played with Fernando. Building on that allusion, Saura and Azcona developed a script about the childhood memories of a man now in his mid-forties and his flirtatious cousin, Angelica, on whom he had a crush when he was ten years old. These memories become the lure for the protagonist's reencounter with a long-suppressed past and the spectator's recapturing of a banished phase of national history.

In choosing the theme of interdicted history—the Civil War years as remembered by a child of Republican parents—Saura pursues more than just the external demons of censorship that had suppressed all but the triumphalist readings of the war. He confronts the psychological and ethical traumas that the official distortions of the history of the war years in public discourse had conveniently ignored but that had scarred and even paralyzed a generation of Spaniards. Paul Ilie has spoken of this state of cultural affairs in which, even decades after the end of the Civil War, clearly half of Francoist Spain considered itself the victors of the war and the other half its captives. He calls this condition of captivity of the vanquished an "inner exile," ". . . a mental condition more than a material one, [removing] people from other people and their way of life. . . . To live apart is to adhere to values that do not partake of the prevailing values; he who perceives this moral difference and who responds to it emotionally lives in exile" (Ilie 1980, 2). *Cousin Angelica* is a dramatization of just such a condition.

Jaime Camino's 1968 film, *España, otra vez* (Spain Again), had daringly broken with the long-standing practice of dealing exclusively with the images and focus of the victors of the war. His film describes the return to Barcelona of a member of the International Brigade thirty years after his departure. Yet, owing to the protagonist's identity as a foreigner, as well as the film's focus on a melodramatic love story, *Spain Again* proved to be a more sanitized treatment of the theme of historical recuperation than many in the growing anti-Franco opposition would have liked. What Saura was looking for in his film was more in the way of an exorcism: the catharsis from a personal sense of alienation he had slowly been documenting in his films since *The Hunt*.

Cousin Angelica is precisely that expression of confrontation, recovery of personal and collective history, and catharsis. The film's sense of liberation comes from Saura's directness in depicting a number of scenes in which the Nationalist cause is either ridiculed or presented as inspired more by petty animosity than by patriotic or religious fervor. But more volatile than the treatment of the victors was the first compassionate view of the vanquished. Told as a labyrinthine montage of recreated memories that surface in the waking consciousness of the protagonist, the thematic and emotional heart of *Cousin Angelica* lies in the burden of remembrances that persist in the consciousness of the vanquished and that they still cannot bring themselves to confront.

Thanks to the violent press reactions from the Spanish Right, *Cousin Angelica* was to enter the public consciousness in ways no other Spanish film had. It was to cause a national furor as well, which surpassed in scope and intensity any of the previous scandals surrounding Spanish films during the Franco years. Given its political subject matter, it was not surprising that the first two versions of the script were rejected outright by the censors. A third version was finally approved and, after some delays, the finished film was accepted for distribution without deletion (Galán 1974,

43). But the real problems for the film were to come later. The Madrid opening was the occasion for violent audience reactions at a number of sessions. Newspaper reports of booing and shouting during the screenings and of menacing protests in front of the theater only seemed to fan the flames of public controversy. It was at about this time that Maurice Bessy came to Madrid to make his annual screening of a number of films as possible entries to the Cannes Film Festival. As improbable as it was, Bessy selected *Cousin Angelica* to represent Spain at the festival after having chosen *Ana and the Wolves* the year before.

The choice of a film that certain elements of the right-wing press considered injurious to the Nationalist cause to represent Spain at a foreign festival seemed an intentional provocation to the very honor of Francoist Spain. The authors of the first incendiary articles about the festival selection were film critics (Galán 1974, 44–51), but their protestations against the film seemed based more on political than artistic questions. Frequently cited as an example of the film's flaws was a single brief scene portraying a character wearing a Falangist uniform with his right arm in a cast from a war wound, thus forcing him to maintain a perpetual fascist salute. The effect of this first round of newspaper attacks on *Cousin Angelica* was to draw to the film the attention of more establishment editorial writers, who thus kept the controversy in the public eye.

In the middle of the Cannes festival, news came that the Madrid run of *Angelica* had been further marred when masked youths broke into the projection booth and stole two reels of the film. This kind of notoriety obviously created sympathy for Saura among the audience and jury at Cannes. Yet the festival judges chose not to award *Angelica* any of the regular prizes. Instead a special award was given to Saura. For right-wing elements in Spain, however, the result was the same as if the film had been awarded the Gold Palm. The conservative press attacked the award as part of a foreign conspiracy against Spain's honor by praising the detractor of the heroic struggle for National liberation.

By the middle of June 1974, Querejeta had been approached by the Spanish distributors of *Cousin Angelica* and asked, in the face of the violence and intimidation surrounding the public screenings of the film, if he would authorize a "cut" version in which the much-disputed fascist-salute scene might be deleted. It was assumed that the "suggestion" had come from unnamed officials in the government. Querejeta refused emphatically: "Legally, I'm the only one who can 'cut' the film and I refuse to delete even a single frame. Nobody but me can do it, and I'll start legal proceedings against anyone who tries to. I will not compromise in the face of the kind of intimidation aimed at suppressing what has been legally authorized" (Galán 1974, 144).

With the failure of external pressures on the producer, *Cousin Angelica* was eventually returned to more or less normal distribution in Spain, although newspaper attacks and protests at screenings continued. The Barcelona theater where the film was having a successful run was firebombed in July of 1974, and thereafter, domestic distribution of *Cousin Angelica* was suspended. Though never officially banned, the film clearly posed obvious risks to theater owners who had good reason to fear a repetition of the incidents that had hampered the Madrid and Barcelona showings. The combination of a small but active pressure group and the unwillingness of theater owners to book Saura's film only intensified the interest of foreign audiences.

Eventually the furor dissipated and it became possible to screen the film in more-or-less reasonable circumstances. Despite the climate of hostility that surrounded it, or perhaps because of the notoriety, *Cousin Angelica* was to prove to be Querejeta and Saura's first formidable box-office success, grossing eighty million pesetas by the end of 1975 as compared, for instance, to the second most profitable Saura-Querejeta film, *Ana and the Wolves*, which, in the first three years following its release, grossed a mere twenty-one million pesetas (Hernández Les 1986, *Singular,* 311).

The forces of negative publicity surrounding the film and, most specifically, the failure to persuade Querejeta to authorize cuts were to produce their own victims in the government. Assuming personal responsibility for the film that had been released during his tenure in office, Pío Cabanillas, the head of the Information Ministry, resigned his post at the end of October, 1974.

Another Family Plot

Hidden beneath all the controversy is a simple, indisputable fact: For the first time in thirty-five years, the Spanish audience, without benefit of sanitized editing by censors, was able to confront the uncomfortable and, for many, painful images of their own recent historical past. They were able to reflect upon their own relation to that past in ways that necessarily had repercussions in terms of their manner of looking at the political and cultural institutions of the present. In a way, this was what Saura had set out to do.

The narrative scheme of *Angelica* recalls that of *Garden of Delights*: the immobilization of the individual by the intricate machinery associated with the affective bonds of family; the victimization of that individual as much by the experiences he suppresses as by the imposed representations continually thrust before his eyes by members of his family. The casting of José Luis López Vázquez, who so stunningly conveyed the sense of the victim in *Garden of Delights*, in the role of Luis Cano, the protagonist of *Angelica*, only begins to suggest some of the affinities between the two films. But there are also some essential differences that the plot of *Cousin Angelica* clearly demonstrates, the most crucial of these being the distorted perspectives of the past that self-censorship inflicts on the survivor-victim of the war years.

Long after his mother's death, Luis fulfills her wish to be buried in the family crypt in Segovia. The middle-aged bachelor has her bones exhumed from a pantheon in Barcelona and heads by car to the Castilian city. In the middle of a lonely road, he stops and gets out of the car, recalling the same landscape at a moment in his childhood when he was being brought to spend part of his summer vacation with his maternal grandmother in Segovia during the fateful summer of 1936. He sees his parents before him, trying to soothe him after a bout of car sickness. Just days before they were to pick him up, the military uprising cut Segovia off from Republican Spain and Luis found himself trapped in the menacing environment of his mother's Nationalist relatives for the duration of the war.

After this first remembrance of his car sickness, Luis continues his journey. Arriving in Segovia, he makes contact with his Aunt Pilar (Josefina Díaz) and his cousin Angelica (Lina Canalejas), his sweetheart during his Segovian captivity. Angelica is now married to Anselmo (Fernando Delgado), a successful businessman, and has a daughter of her own, also named Angelica (María Clara Fernández), who is just about the age her mother was when she and Luis were sweethearts. These contacts rekindle old memories for Luis.

In all these remembrances, the past is not merely evoked, but reenacted, with Luis literally entering a kind of time warp. Characters Luis has met in the present appear to him playing the role of relatives he remembers thirty-six years earlier: the child Angelica of 1973, for instance, plays the role of her own mother, Luis's cousin Angelica, as he thinks he remembers her from 1936; Anselmo is imaged as Angelica's fascist father. In all these confused projections backward Saura implies ironic meanings. The most barbed, of course, following a line of thought first dramatized in *The Hunt*, is that the successful businessman of 1973 is one who learned how to exploit others during the war (Lara 1976, 158). Yet tellingly, Luis, the balding executive of 1973, plays the child Luis in all these evocations of his own past, thus blurring for the spectator the cinematic and narrative delimitations of past and present. The narrational strategy at the source of this technique—showing us the world through Luis's mind's eye—concretizes in a poignant way how the traumatic events of the war years have immobilized the individual.

Here we encounter for the first time Saura's depiction of the paradox of the act of memory. Luis finds himself able to conjure up the images from his childhood that have stymied his emotional growth for thirty-six years.

Still, these evocations are tainted and flawed by the insistent mental conflation of his contemporary experiences, thus rendering his past paradoxically
both persistent and irretrievable. This tension in the act of memory is, in
fact, the conceptual source for the structure of *Cousin Angelica*, as Saura
explains: "One day I looked in the mirror and said, 'My goodness, what
did I look like as a child?' I can't remember myself as a child in the mirror.
I have photographs, but when I look at them, I feel as if it's someone I
don't know" (Kinder 1983, 63).

This theme is pointedly dramatized in the scene in which Angelica shows
Luis a picture album with photographs from his childhood in Segovia to
prove to him that the resemblance he has imagined Anselmo holds to her
father is merely a trick of his memory. Before making his final departure
from Segovia, Luis relives one last terrible memory, the day when his
cousin Angelica told him that their grandmother thought the army officers
would kill his father. Luis even recalls having imagined his father before a
firing squad. This is obviously a faulty remembrance since his father appears alive in the first scene of the film.

On his return trip to Barcelona, Luis again pauses at the same spot on
the highway where he had his first reencounter with his childhood. He sees
the image of his parents and their car parked on the side of the road. He
turns his car around and goes back to Segovia. The second half of the film
details Luis's return to Segovia and his active confrontation with the relics
of the past that have continued to plague him in his adult life.

Distance

Despite the powerful emotional impact that the film clearly had on many
Spanish audiences (Buñuel broke down in tears when he viewed *Cousin
Angelica*), audience engagement is rationally calculated and developed
around a specific conceptual design of spectatorial figuration. The critical
point of framing of all remembrance is the roadside somewhere in Castile
where Luis first stops his car and gets out to view the countryside. It is here
where he is all at once engulfed by memories. The initial entrance into
illusion, cinematically rendered as a medium close-up of Luis pensively
looking off into the golden fields, is interrupted by the seemingly miraculous appearance of his mother in frame behind him. She is dressed in the
style of the 1930s. She calls Luis, and he turns around to the source of the
voice. We discover a 1930s car and a man dressed similarly in period clothing near the woman. The couple, Luis's parents, surround him, just as in a
sense the remembrances of the past now do.

No warning of the shift from experienced to remembered actions is
given so that, metaphorically, the viewer is made to share some of the char-

acter's own bewilderment at the sudden shift of temporal frames. To further emphasize this blending of time levels, Saura borrows and expands a device first used in *Garden of Delights* where, instead of having a child actor play the part of Luis in the retrospective moment, López Vázquez simulates that condition by a set of body and head gestures which suggests that Luis, for reasons not yet fully enunciated, is a frightened and bewildered child trapped in the body of an adult.

The cinematic simulation of the lure of the past is further emphasized through Saura's use of off-screen sound. As we have already noted, the off-screen voice of his mother calling his name as he stands facing the field of wheat introduces his first re-creation of the past. Similarly, the first recreated memory of his childhood days in Segovia is announced as Luis, Anselmo, and the priest talk on the patio of the church and Luis is drawn to a window by the sounds of musicians playing a familiar melody from an Easter pageant. By far, the most significant of these auditory cues is the Imperio Argentina melody of "Rocío"(Dew Drops), played as discursive background music at three distinct moments in the film: first, when Luis recalls his mother's farewell to him in his grandmother's house in 1936; then as an adult, when he and his cousin embrace and kiss on a rooftop as they apparently had done as small children; finally, in the last images of the film, as little Angelica's mother combs her hair while the two look into a mirror. In all three scenes, the sound track reinforces for the spectator the almost erotic lure of the past that entices Luis. The evocation of the voice of Imperio Argentina similarly creates cultural associations for a certain generation of Spanish spectators.

The lure of the past is finally broken when Luis is able to achieve a perceptual distance from his memories. That distance occurs only after he has begun his return trip to Barcelona and finds that he is able to reimage the experience of his parents taking him to Segovia in 1936. Unlike the earlier scene, images no longer engulf Luis. Rather, he seems able to dissociate himself from his childhood and view the past from a distanced position. Sitting in his car on a desolate Castilian roadside, he observes himself and his parents as though a spectator to his own life. This newly acquired distance symbolically states Luis's new relation to the images that have tyrannized him since childhood. He turns his car around and goes back to Segovia to exorcise these menacing images that had maintained him as a fearful child in the body of an adult.

Film and Memory

Luis's viewing of his past from a distance suggests a radical shift in his own personal attitude toward his memories. During the initial visit to Segovia he had found himself lured into the past as though a prisoner of those experiences that for so long had either enticed or threatened him. Though logically able to recognize the errors of his mental perception, as when he questions Anselmo about the latter's actions during the summer of 1936, Luis, nonetheless, seems unable during this phase of the film to achieve any kind of personal lucidity about his own relation to those often-distorted memories. He even makes a self-conscious connection between his memories and Proust's *madeleine*, as if to suggest that these memories were the inevitable result of the passage of time.

But now, with a physical distance that seems to embody an inner distance from his childhood, Luis sees the past, but he also recognizes *how* he was positioned to see it. This emphasis on the subject's positionality in terms of the intimate mind screen of personal representations is Saura's way of pairing a question of cinema—the relation of the viewing subject to images on screen—with cultural and ethical questions of that same individual's relation to his past and future. Tellingly, in one of Luis's first active explorations in the second part of the film, we return to the figuration of the literal film-within-the-film. Luis has gone to the school where he studied as a child in Segovia and takes a seat in the darkened auditorium where he relives the horrifying experience of a film called *Los ojos de Londres* (The Eyes of London), which priests had shown the young boys as a graphic demonstration of hell and damnation.

The film Luis reexperiences simply consists of a slow tracking across what appears to be a garbage dump with a gradual close-up of one of a group of sinister-looking male figures. The slow zoom eventually ends with the mysterious figure, actually Saura himself in a brief cameo, staring directly into the camera. Now voluntarily invoked, *The Eyes of London* proves naturally to be less menacing than it was when Luis viewed it as a small boy. But the real significance of the evocation goes beyond the mere fact of the impressionable child's fears which he has carried with him to adulthood. The cinematic apparatus within the narrative thrusts in the foreground two types of interrelated ideological coercion. The first is, concretely, the specific instance of how the young and impressionable viewer was tyrannized by the propagandistic deployment of motion pictures. The second theme, however, is a strikingly more original one which equates the positioning effect of the cinematic apparatus with the larger cultural apparatus that has subjected Luis to a reimaging of lived experiences as well as imagining of experiences yet to be lived. Because that other apparatus is so diffuse—it operates through his family, his friends, the Church—the distinction between representation and perception is blurred, making Luis fall into the perceptual trap of believing that he has actually seen things "as if with his own eyes." The re-creation of the scene in which he sees his father shot down before a firing squad, though patently false, shows us the profound impact that such a mind screen had assumed for the protagonist.

For Saura, the source of the individual's mystification lies in the deformed ways of seeing that have been absorbed by the subject formed under Francoism. The process of that deformation is concretized in the analogy between the indoctrinating apparatus of Francoism and the institution of cinema in which sight and representation are conflated, and where representation is confused with the viewing subject's own perceptions. By returning Luis to explore the cinematic experience, as he does in the *Eyes of London* sequence, Saura focuses on the perceptual shift that was subtly introduced in the second roadside encounter. Luis and, by extension, his off-screen counterpart now literally confront the cinematic instrumentality— its projection of images in the dark and its positioning of its viewing subjects to identify with those images. Personal lucidity for character and spectator alike comes to mean a recognition of the contrivances and manipulation of memory by an unseen, off-screen apparatus that masks the real terms of their relationship to their own experiences.[9]

The logic of Luis's trajectory following the second return to Segovia is an unmasking of those earlier confusions of meaning and perspective in which he continually saw himself as victim, prisoner, exile. The terms of his demystification relate back to the implied deconstruction of the paradigmatic perceptual apparatus that the victimized Luis has for so long carried with him in his head. The transcendence of that demystifying process beyond Luis to a larger Spanish audience is posed in the film's most violent and thematically most political sequence: his reliving of the bombing of his school in Segovia by Republican aircraft. The sequence is actually textualized in three different forms: the first, a slow-motion rendition of the bombing, serves as a credit sequence for *Cousin Angelica*. When the scene is again portrayed at normal speed late in the film, it parallels for the spectator Luis's sensation of déjà vu. Between these two literalizations of the bombing, we find a brief scene in which a priest in the school presents a sermon to the impressionable young boys in which he details the death of a small child by Republican aircraft in the Nationalist zone. The sermon, we understand, inscribes specific meanings on Luis's memory of the bombing of his school, which occurs shortly after the sermon.

The scene of the sermon is shot mostly in shadows to emphasize the fear and menace that grip the young audience as the priest describes the meaning of eternal damnation. As he speaks, the camera slowly tracks across the petrified faces of the boys seated at school desks; it lingers on the anoma-

[9] Saura's use of the cinematic analogy to dramatize the ideological coercion of his protagonist uncannily coincides with the theoretic description of the ideological effects of the cinematic apparatus as described by Jean-Louis Baudry and others. See particularly Baudry's *Le Dispositif*.

lous image of Luis, the boy in the body of a grown man, expressionless as he listens to the priest's words. Describing in gruesome detail the bombing of a school far behind the Nationalist lines and the death of an eleven-year-old boy, the priest uses the incident to emphasize the threat of eternal damnation for anyone who dies without having confessed his sins. At the end of his talk, the priest dismisses the boys and they march out of the classroom in regimental fashion.

The scene next cuts to the refectory where Luis is seated at one of the small tables. All at once the roar of approaching aircraft is heard. A bomb explodes, shattering the glass and throwing the boys across the room. Amidst the debris and bloodied bodies, Luis sits motionless, transfixed. The scene ends with a close-up of him and then a rapid cut to the same image but now located in his bedroom in his aunt's house in 1973. The entire preceding sequence, as we realize retrospectively, has been a flashback prompted by Luis's paging through one of his old school notebooks.

For the child Luis who experienced the bombing and obviously repressed his memory of it, the two-part sequence suggests the important conflation of personal memory with the weight of social ignominy. His father was part of the "red fury" of whom the priest spoke, who slaughtered his innocent friends and classmates. Yet, from his vantage point as an adult perusing the pages of an old notebook, Luis sees the sermon as a kind of framing device for the scene of the bombing. He seems tacitly to acknowledge the implied social contexts that have produced the meaning that he had, up to this point, accepted as his own sense of guilt and shame. Such an illumination is rooted in the kind of perspectival repositioning that Luis initiated in the second roadside scene. It was at that point only a subtle specular move, barely noticeable in the scene. Yet his willingness to stand back from his experience and analyze the sources, collective as well as personal, that had immobilized him, have made him progressively more aware of the false consciousness of his own experiences that have until now trapped him in the recurrent nightmare of the past.

Back to the Present

After his evocation of the school bombing, Luis has an emotional encounter with his cousin Angelica in which she speaks to him of her failed marriage. She intimates a reawakening of the affection she had once had for Luis. But he has already made the determination to leave Segovia once and for all, and his cousin's amorous overtures appear only to reinforce his self-distancing from the past. In that final sequence, the bicycle ride with Angelica's daughter triggers his memory of his thwarted escape with his cousin through Nationalist lines in an effort to rejoin his parents and their forced return to his uncle's house to be punished. In that final scene, his uncle brings him into a room and tells him to get on his knees. Luis lowers his head and his uncle begins to whip him with a belt. At first Luis holds his head up defiantly, but finally he covers himself with his arms as protection from the brutal beating. Slowly, the camera circles around Luis's body, then pans across the room away from the site of the violence, crossing into the next room where Angelica's mother is combing Angelica's hair as the young girl sits before a full-length mirror. The camera now occupies the place of the mirror so that in the final image of the film the two actresses look straight at the audience. The sound of the beating is drowned out by the off-screen recording of Imperio Argentina's ballad "Rocío."

The entire sequence is strategically placed at the film's end to thwart any sense the spectator might have of simple closure to Luis's remembrance of Segovia and the war. In not returning to the present-tense frame of action, the audience is left to ponder the significance of the Civil War as a yet-unfinished page of history that each Spaniard needs to confront on a personal level. Indeed, by ending the film with the dramatization of symbolic violence as remembered by Luis, Saura skillfully evokes his audience's recollection of the real violence of the Civil War. But a rekindling of long-suppressed memories is only part of what Saura seeks here. The final image of the film, that of the mother and daughter looking directly into the camera, effectively transposes Luis's troubled relation to a personal and collective past to the place of his spectator.

The glances of the two actresses as they look into the mirror seem to violate the cinematic illusion by addressing the audience just as they violate the historical assumption of a past clearly distinguishable from the present. For one instant the spectator shares Luis's original vision of the world, a vision in which present and past are conflated, where the individual and collective destiny of the Spanish nation is shrouded in the unspeakable war. Like Luis, who has projected into his recollections of the past certain notions of himself and his world derived from the present, the contemporary audience is also led to ponder their own personal and collective present—the very uncertain and troubling present of 1973—as an outgrowth of that unresolved, problematic historical period. This final image crystalizes Saura's underlying spectatorial project throughout *Cousin Angelica*: to trigger in the contemporary Spaniard's consciousness of history a recognition of that closed destiny that has shaped Spain since the war's end, and to trigger, as well, a desire for a lucidity about the burden of that history as it continues to shape the present.

V

Distanced Observers

Transitions

FRANCO's dream of a prolongation of Francoism beyond his own life by handpicking a successor ended dramatically with the assassination of Carrero Blanco in 1973 by members of the Basque terrorist group, ETA. The possibility of a replacement for Carrero by a political or military leader seemed quite impossible since the cult of personality of the dictator, carefully orchestrated for nearly forty years, had eliminated the possibility of the emergence of any new, charismatic leader. So, in Franco's declining years, as the rumors of his infirmities and senility continued to circulate, Spaniards braced themselves for the inevitable end. Not surprisingly, the news of his death on November 20, 1975, was less a national shock than the realization of a mythified historical juncture. Saura describes how champagne corks popped all over the country in secret celebration of the event.[1] But despite the preparations and anticipations, the real significance of Franco's death would be long in coming. Obviously, on the immediate level the question in all quarters was: What lay ahead for the country after the demise of the Caudillo? There would be no simple answer.

The immediate solution for a transition came with the naming of Carlos Arias Navarro as interim leader, a post he held from December of 1973 until June of 1976, when Adolfo Suárez, previously an obscure, local political leader from Avila, was chosen the first prime minister of a new constitutional monarchy. Under the agreement for an orderly, nonviolent transition known as the "Moncloa pact," Spain seemed headed in a precarious direction toward some form of institutional reorganization along democratic, if not necessarily liberal, lines. The immediate significance of these transitional moves was to give Spaniards self-conscious pause, to make them ponder their past and consider the options for the future. For political and military leaders, as well as for Spaniards of all social and political spheres, it was a time of awakened historical consciousness, a time to reflect upon the conditions of their present circumstance, and on the past that had led them to this moment.

In one way or another, the central focus of the four films that follow

---

[1] In an interview with John Darnton on the PBS special "Spain: Ten Years Later," aired nationally in March 1986.

Cousin Angelica is precisely this collective and personal questioning about what the future might hold for Spaniards beyond Francoism. It is also a question that has in some way been the driving force of Saura's films since *Garden of Delights*. Though eschewing a conventional political cinema, his insistent efforts to describe in his films the emerging consciousness of historical processes in individuals comes inevitably to be viewed in political terms as part of a "metaphoric tendency" in the cinema of the transition period (Monterde 1978, 12). In *Cría cuervos* (1975: Cría!), shot before Franco's death, for instance, there is a scene early in the film depicting the wake held for a military officer, which inevitably leads Spanish audiences to read the film's subsequent action as an exploration of a Spain beyond the shadows of the Caudillo.

That metaphoric reading coincides with the more ambitious historical project of Saura's work that comes more clearly into focus in his later films of the seventies: *Elisa, vida mía* (1977: Elisa, My Life); *Los ojos vendados* (1978: Blindfolded Eyes); and *Mamá cumple cien años* (1979: Mama Turns One Hundred). With the emphasis more on innovative narrational structures than political allegory, the films of the late seventies appear linked in their focus, however, on female protagonists who are each brought to confront the necessity of a revision of their sense of historical and personal time—the situation that so strikingly characterized Luis in the second half of *Cousin Angelica*.

A number of difficulties had apparently been festering for several years between Saura and Rafael Azcona. These had to do with the latter's well-known negative script treatment of women in Saura's films. The problems had come to a head with *Cousin Angelica*, after the completion of which the two men parted company. *Cría!*, therefore, was to be the first film for which Saura received complete script credit. This ultimate mark of authorial control is noteworthy as we observe some of the striking visual and narrative features that mark *Cría!* and the films that follow it in rapid succession. This is clearly a period of intense experimentation for Saura, particularly in terms of the use of cinematic point of view to help formulate a more aggressive questioning of historical consciousness as well as female subjectivity.

In a highly original and insightful reading of films by various directors of the seventies, Marsha Kinder makes a correlation between a generational self-definition of Spanish directors, particularly Saura and José Luis Borau, who described himself as a child of Franco, and the type of cinematic praxis involved in their seventies films. Picking up on the notion of these men as "children of Franco," Kinder sees the kinds of characters with whom they populate their films as the extension of the psychic profiles of their authors, ". . . emotionally and politically stunted children who were no longer young; who, because of the imposed role as 'silent witness' to the tragic war that had divided country, family, and self, had never been innocent; and who, because of the oppressive domination of the previous generation, were obsessed with the past and might never be ready to take responsibility for changing the future" (Kinder 1983, 57–58). For Kinder, *Cría!* is just such a symptomatic expression of the weight of political and social captivity that transforms certain of Saura's protagonists into "children of Franco."

A World without Franco

Following what is by now Saura's well-established strategy of constructing an on-screen spectator-in-the-text, *Cría!* is organized discursively around the presence of a child who, though only nine years old, embodies the emotional traumas and temporal consciousness that, as Kinder says, clearly link her with the adult generation who are the figurative children of Franco. From the very start, the spectator is positioned within the fictional space to identify with the enunciative coherence provided by Ana (Ana Torrent), whose very ingenuousness is equated at once with the passivity and innocence of the spectator as well as with the social ingenuousness of the Spanish audience of Francoism.

As the film opens, a stoic and muted Ana approaches her father's bedroom where she has heard a gasping sound and a woman's plaintive sobs. Descending the stairs, she spies an attractive middle-aged woman (Mirta Miller), hastily dressing and rushing from the bedroom to the front door of the darkened house. The woman and Ana exchange glances but do not speak. Once the woman has left, Ana enters her father's bedroom and finds the man dead, apparently from a heart attack. As if not really understanding the gravity of the situation, she unflappably takes away a half-full glass of milk which she carries to the kitchen and cleans. In the kitchen she sees her mother (Geraldine Chaplin), who chides her for being up so late and sends her off to bed.

Only much later is the full meaning of this brief but important scene illuminated for the spectator. As the film opens, Ana's mother is already dead; the image we see is only a fanciful illusion of the young girl's mind. Blaming her mother's illness and death on her father, Ana has dissolved a mysterious powder she believes to be a potent poison in his milk glass as a willful act of murder. Her belief in the powers of the poison are thus confirmed when her father dies. But the satisfaction of having rid herself of her father's presence is short-lived, for her mother's sister, her Aunt Paulina (Mónica Randell), soon arrives to set the house in order, turning out to be every bit the cold authoritarian Ana's father had been.

At the wake, Ana's father (Héctor Alterio) is identified for us as a mili-

11. *Cría!* (*Cría cuervos*, 1976)

tary officer, and the mysterious woman Ana saw fleeing his bedroom the night of his death, Amelia, as the wife of her father's close friend, another military officer, Nicolás (Germán Cobos). In the days that follow the wake, Ana remains tortured by the memories of her mother's illness. She rebels against her aunt's authoritarian style, and in bouts of loneliness, she variously imagines her mother's continued presence, or even her own suicide. Though diverted by the presence of her two sisters, Irene (Conchita Pérez) and Mayte (Mayte Sánchez), Ana's only truly close companions are the family maid, Rosa (Florinda Chico), and her pet hamster, Roni, whom she discovers dead in his cage one morning.

The motif of death clearly obsesses Ana: her mother's painful death from cancer; her father's presumed murder; her hamster's death; and her own imagined suicide. Ana even offers her grandmother (Josefina Díaz), ill and confined to a wheelchair, the opportunity of dying and ridding herself from loneliness by providing her a spoonful of her poison. The old woman turns down her granddaughter's offer. Events in this somber household come to a dramatic impasse when Ana, still believing that she has murdered her father, attempts to poison her aunt with the same powder. She repeats the preparation of milk with the mysterious substance, but the next

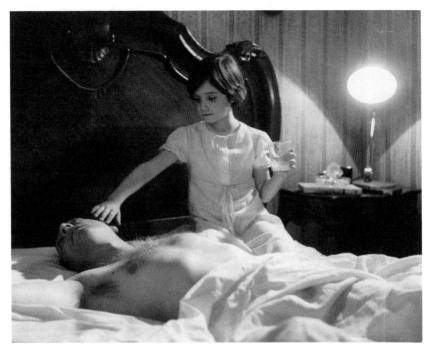

12. *Cría!* (*Cría cuervos*, 1976)

morning awakens for the first day of school to find that Paulina is still alive. Like *Cousin Angelica*, *Cría!* closes with a suggestive, reflective ending as we see Ana and her two sisters leaving the lugubrious family compound and marching into the vibrant and noisy city that has all but been shut out from their world up to this point. The action suggests that Ana, at last, has moved beyond the obsessional confinement both of family and of the memories of the past that had so tortured her consciousness, that, finally, she has purged those destructive impulses and is prepared to "grow" beyond them.

A History of Female Subjectivity

While this description of the plot line of *Cría!* appears linear and straightforward, the narrative is actually punctuated by a series of temporal jumps to key moments in the heroine's brief life. These scenes include moments from her parents' troubled marriage and her mother's illness and death, and flash-forwards to 1995, when the child Ana is presented as a woman of twenty-nine years of age, reflecting upon the "past" twenty years of her life. Geraldine Chaplin plays the roles of both Ana's mother in the flash-backs and Ana, the adult, in the flash-forwards, provoking at first a certain understandable disorientation for the viewer; for not only are the lines of identity blurred here, but the temporal shifts across past, present, and future are effectively dissolved. In this way, the film formulates the conflation of historical and personal time as a textual problem for the spectator to confront and decipher, that decipherment keyed to the historical issues that the Spaniard faces outside the film.

At various stages of the time shifts between past and present, and present and future, the child Ana shares the frame with one or the other of the Chaplin characters, walking into a scene, for instance in which her mother is writhing in pain, or rummaging through a storehouse in the family compound and standing next to the Chaplin figure as a projection of herself twenty years into the future. Whether evoking the present from the vantage point of 1995, or flashing back to 1975, Ana is continually cast in the role of historical witness, viewing, remembering, and eventually standing back from events to reflect upon them anew. In a series of on-screen spectator-witnesses spanning fifteen years, Ana stands as perhaps Saura's richest and, up to this point, his most complex character. Motivated by the oppressive environment of her family situation, her actions and perspectives can be read simultaneously on two distinct yet related levels: at once, as a moving tale of a sensitive child's loss of innocence; but also as a brilliant allegory of Spaniards trying to "reason" their own emotional liberation from captivity in the prison-house of Francoist ideology. In either reading, however, the figure of the disempowered female confronting her impotence within Francoist society is still central.

The narrative complexity of *Cría!*, appearing in some ways quite similar to Chaplin's triple roles in *Peppermint Frappé*, actually owes its origin to Saura's reflection on the closing image of *Cousin Angelica* in which Angelica's mother is seen combing her daughter's hair before a mirror. In *Cría!* an almost identical version of that scene appears but is imbued with even greater narrative and dramatic complexity. On the morning of her father's wake, Rosa, the maid, combs Ana's hair before the bathroom mirror. Ana's mother appears and takes over the combing. It is not until the next scene that we learn that her mother is dead and that Ana's conversations with her mother are really only an obsessive fantasy. It is left to the spectator to conjecture about the reasons for the same actress playing the role of mother in the period prior to 1975 and the grown daughter in 1995.

In having Geraldine Chaplin appear as both Ana's mother and as Ana at age twenty-nine, Saura reasserts the temporal entrapment of the contemporary Spaniard we noted in the final scene of *Cousin Angelica*. If the film is understood as a projection from the present both to the past and future, then, clearly, Ana images her future self out of her recollections of the past—namely, her mother. If the film is read from the framing situation of a young woman in 1995—that is, from a perspective that "historicizes" the present moment by presenting it as past history—then Ana has merely grafted her own image onto the memory of her mother, in much the same way that Luis in *Cousin Angelica* transposed characters from his adult life onto the memories of his childhood (Kinder 1983, 65). In either case, the theme is essentially a variation on Saura's notion of the confining imagination of the individual whose access to the past or future is determined by the identity that has been shaped for him or her in the present.

The film's title, taken from a popular saying, *"Cría cuervos y te sacarán los ojos"* (Raise ravens and they'll scratch your eyes out),[2] suggests a black variation on that theme of education; for nearly everything Ana has experienced and observed in her brief life is channeled into the morbid images that populate her fantasies of power, escape, or the future. Gleaned in part from her mother's illness, Ana's concept of death is adorned with the details related to her father's identity as a military man, a former participant in the Blue Division which fought with Hitler's troops against the Russians in the Second World War. There is a scene, for instance, in which Ana, carrying her father's pistol over which she and Irene have been arguing, enters the living room and surprises Paulina who fears that Ana is about to kill her.

One of the insistent themes of the earlier political trilogy had been that one learns from one's elders. We note a further biting reiteration of that theme in the scene in which the three sisters play dress up, an imitation of a bitter argument between their parents. Ana assumes the role of her mother, and Irene is Anselmo. It is out of such models of the past that inevitably the child will learn the forms of behavior for the future.

These signs of Ana's morbid education are only part of the picture, however. Out of the alienation and isolation that characterize her life, we see emerge an incisive reflection on the nature of constrained female identity in Francoist society. In constructing the family in *Cría!*, Saura conspicuously gives centrality to the role and destiny of woman. Not only are the three generations of Ana's family portrayed through female characters exclusively—Ana, her mother, and her grandmother—but the principal signs of other social positions are embodied in female characters, such as her Aunt Paulina or the maid, Rosa.

The socialization of the female in Francoist society is made the focus of a number of scenes. In one sequence, in particular, Ana's historicizing gen-

---

[2] Virginia Higginbotham reminds us that the inspiration for the film's title comes from these words spoken by Angelica's father before he beats Luis at the end of *Cousin Angelica* (92). This cinematic self-reference on the margins of Saura's filmography parallels the origin of *Cousin Angelica*, whose title and motif of childhood eroticism derive from the dialogue between the dowager and Ana in *Ana and the Wolves*.

erational perspective is joined to the question of female subjectivity. We see Irene pasting photos of popular singers and models into a scrapbook, absorbing in this way the place in the adult world defined for her by social representation. When her grandmother calls, the heroine runs downstairs and moves her grandmother's wheelchair to where she may view a bulletin board on which have been tacked the postcards and photographs that remind her of her youth. In viewing her sister's and her grandmother's actions, Ana observes a dramatic opposition: In one scene she witnesses the individual's absorption of the socially defined placements constructed for her; in the other, a passive, immobilized position out of which there will remain nothing but hollow memories. In both of the uses of images described here, the family constructs the mise-en-scène of the female's imaging of her destiny.

Together, Irene and her grandmother dramatize the dilemma forming in Ana's mind. She is confronted with the images of her past, which grieve her, and the equally distressing images of a vague future in which she feels herself abandoned. Tellingly, when Irene comes downstairs to enlist Ana in the game of dress up, Ana chooses to play the part of her own mother, but as a strong-willed woman who defiantly confronts her husband with the truth of his infidelity in a manner quite unlike Ana's real mother. We are made retrospectively aware of that choice of an identity when, in a later scene, she evokes the memory of her parents' quarrel and we see how her mother's response to her father was considerably more passive than her own.[3] Ana's evolving consciousness as an innocent subject has obviously provoked her into an inquiry into the ways in which she can break out of the snares she identifies with both her family and her present condition as orphan. Out of that inquiry the young child begins to discover her own strength and defiance to break away from the emotional and even physical entrapment signified by the family, and to assume the kind of lucidity embodied in her self-image as a woman in 1995.

---

[3] The children's enactment of the quarrel scene is actually one of the most complex sequences of the film. Not only does it restage their parents' marital discord and reveal Ana's own defiant attitude, it also connects with a broader critique of traditional Spanish social attitudes that define the woman as mere object. Just before Irene enters the parlor to call her sister to play, Ana puts a tape recording of "Ay, Mari Cruz" on the cassette recorder to entertain her grandmother. The song, a 1930s evocation of the seductive Andalusian woman, is somehow related in the grandmother's mind to her own past. But it also connects for the audience with the traditional view of woman as object since, in a previously evoked memory of her father's infidelity, Ana witnessed her father's flirtations with Rosa as the latter sang this very melody. The contrast between the historically rooted role of the female as the object of male sexual and social domination and Ana's self-definition as a strong, defiant female is emphasized as we hear the strains of the grandmother's recording as background music to the children's preparations for their enactment of their parents' quarrel.

Beyond a Repressive Education

Our placement with Ana as the pivotal agency of narration is secured early on through a series of point-of-view shots in which we are brought to identify with her glance as the principal internal narrational authority of the film. Yet the text operates as a continual juxtaposition among various positions of internal coherence which are often in temporal and therefore narrative contradiction with one another. Combined with the recurring image of Geraldine Chaplin as both mother and daughter in different time frames, these shifts effectively transform the development of plot in *Cría!* into a hermeneutic rite of passage for the audience who find themselves in a process of continually "learning" and "unlearning" perceptual positions in the narrative. This is, by far, Saura's most innovative cinematic narrative since *Hooligans*, for it clearly calls upon its audience to abandon some of its conventional habits of cinematic viewing and to assume a series of "eccentric" positions which coincide, tellingly, with the young heroine's decentered perspective.

The film defines its spectatorial role in part as a form of decipherment, as was the case in the political trilogy, but also as a process of demystification which will parallel the heroine's psychic reeducation. That demystification consists of recognizing the positionings that have secured limited, atomized points of coherence within which to understand a narrowly defined world. We are engaged, in effect, in a reenactment of the cultural submission to the places of constructed coherence through which one has learned to accept external social definitions of him or herself, the very process that has been narrativized as Ana's problem.

Saura gives special emphasis to the significance of Ana's condition of innocence, particularly what we must recognize as her perceptual naiveté. Her ingenuous glance, the nondistinction between what she sees and the ways in which she has been positioned to see, is the ultimate source of her captivity within her family and within the world controlled by adults. Her narration specifies the dilemma of perception for the spectator first as a problem of temporal incoherence. Thus, during a number of sequences, the viewer is made to share her plight cinematically, eventually to achieve a narrative lucidity that is congruent with the heroine's eventual achievement of a historical consciousness of her own past.

At decisive moments, we are provided with placements that offer us a coherence over the limits of Ana's point of view: a distanced shot of the house as viewed from atop a building across the street; a clarifying view of events as now understood by the Ana of 1995. While stabilizing our view on the narrative, these points also define places of illumination to which Ana, in her own psychic crisis, must eventually move. She needs to be displaced from her family, which she recognizes as the source of her imprisonment; to assume a position of control over adults; finally, in some way to end her entrapment in the defenseless body of a child. These are solutions that Ana is able to simulate by means of her many waking fantasies. But what she cannot see, what the spectator is gradually positioned to grasp, is that Ana also needs a conceptual vantage point from which to recognize the contradictions that plague her perception and lock her into a series of static positions either in the present or the past.

To grasp the centrality of this specularization over mere narrative, we need only consider the critical sequence leading up to the first introduction of the future frame of the adult Ana. After the wake, we see the child Ana in the garden of her house, protected from the rest of the city by high walls that surround the property. She looks up across the street to the rooftop of a nearby building and sees the image of herself perched at the edge of the building, preparing to jump off. The camera cross-cuts to the point of view of the imaginary double as she looks down at the dwarfed image of herself in the garden below, entrapped within the family fortress. Suddenly, the imaginary Ana jumps from the roof, and the camera gives us a dizzying pan of the Madrid skyline, with sounds of car horns suggesting that the fallen body has halted the busy city traffic; the camera finally cuts away to a close-up of Ana in the garden with her eyes tightly closed.

This scene provides the spectator for the first time with a margin of sight within the film which is beyond the point of view of the narrator, and through which we may observe both her perceptual and social placement in relation to the external world. At this critical point in the story, and only after Ana has projected her own death as a solution to her emotional problems, do we follow her to the storeroom at the bottom of the empty swimming pool where she goes to check the poison she had hidden after her father's death. Standing in the storeroom, as if in a tableau, Ana faces the camera which slowly pans to a corner of the cellar where we see Geraldine Chaplin again, now speaking directly to us, introducing the future frame of 1995.

The adult Ana explains the notion of the mysterious powder that the child Ana had so dearly coveted in earlier scenes: It was nothing more than bicarbonate of soda that her mother once told her was a powerful poison. She further explains her motivation in wanting to kill her father: "The only thing I remembered perfectly is that then my father seemed responsible for the sadness that weighed on my mother in the last years of her life. I was convinced that he, and he alone, had provoked her illness."

The adult Ana appears only after the spectator has witnessed the child's efforts at a spatial self-distancing. What we now have is a similar form of self-distancing, only here it is in temporal terms. Arising out of the blank stare of the child Ana, the adult seems to have achieved a perceptual and

13. *Cría!* (*Cría cuervos*, 1976)

emotional control over the otherwise unresolvable problems confronted by the child. She reaffirms the possibility of a world beyond the confining limits of the family, embodying a point of view that masters the totality of events beyond the ingenuousness and vulnerability represented by childhood. The adult Ana is a surrogate, as much for the spectator as for the child Ana, for she embodies the possibility of standing back from life as a distanced observer to view the patterns of positioning, of sight and belief, that have ensnared one in the traps of a contemporary world.

The Possibility of Growth

The final major sequence of *Cría!* provides evidence that Ana has been able at last to shed the myths of desired power and control that had been the mark of her earlier destructive fantasies. Awakening on the first day of school, she discovers that her aunt has not died from the powder she had placed in her glass of milk the night before. Paulina's appearance in the children's bedroom effectively puts into question for Ana the illusion of her earlier patricide and all the other illusions of power and control that emanate from that initial myth. This is a moment of contemplative shock which is only intimated in the scene. Yet, linked as it is to the final scene of the film, as the three children are seen leaving the house and entering the noisy city on their way to school, the moment suggests that, at last, Ana is moving toward the ideal of lucidity that her future self in 1995 has already achieved.

Within that metaphoric code informing so much of *Cría!* we may read the scene of departure from the house as Ana's abandonment of the closed structures that had previously confined her. Moving beyond the protective walls of the house, she passes by huge billboard signs which, as they imply a new, modern Spain, also carry the challenge for Ana of a new order of images, appealing to her as a consumer of other products, other myths to shape her identity. Though she is going off to school, presumably another confining institution that will seek to impose a social identity on her, Ana, like Luis in *Cousin Angelica*, nonetheless appears to have shed the paralyzing emotional ties that entrapped her within the metaphoric house of the old Spain. In contrast to the somber and immobilized images of the orphaned child earlier in the film, her energetic movement, now underscored by the rhythm of a popular song "¿Por qué te vas?" (Why Are You Going Away?), suggests a more determined, self-confident Ana, one whose message to her audience is the achievement of growth and the self-distancing from the burdens of the past.

The ending of *Cría!* is suggestively ambiguous, leaving some viewers uncertain as to how to read Saura's view of Spain's future. To these ambiguities, the director seems only to add his own ambivalence: "I believe we live immersed in a society that has been built upon an accumulation of errors. Some of these errors, I have no doubt, can be corrected. From that fact comes my reasoned optimism in the future, starting from the base of where we are now. But other errors, fundamental ones, are in the roots of our evolution. . . . We are the products of a repressive education that has left us disarmed and defenseless in the face of many things" (Harguindey 1975, 119).

Cría! was the last of Saura's films to be submitted to the censorship commissions, which were disbanded in 1977. The commission's principal concerns with the film had to do with the presence of military officers in the plot and the fact that one of them, Ana's father, was an apparent adulterer. However, as the censors' reports concluded: "The figure of the military officers is only secondary and there is no effort to generalize from that situation. . . . Its focus of criticism is the bourgeois family, not the military class. The only problem is that an interpetation can be given that the protagonists are officers and not exactly models of morality" (Hernández Les 1986, *Singular*, 194–95).

Despite these elements of purported social and political critique in the film, the real substance of *Cría!* lies on a more intimate plane, in its confrontation with the burden of history on the Spaniard and the ways in which, harnessing the experience of fifteen years of filmmaking, Saura poses a new strategy through which the individual may rechannel that historical burden into a constructive self-illumination. Though the particular narrative embodiment of this cultural theme is transformed in each successive film, the dominant strategy of historical distancing from the weight of regressive education by narrativized female subjects remains a constant in Saura's films until the end of the decade.

   Cría! became Saura and Querejeta's most commercially successful film up to this point, going on to become the sixth-largest-grossing Spanish film of 1976. The picture made a similarly strong showing in foreign markets, including the U.S. where Saura's reputation as Spain's foremost opposition filmmaker continued to grow. The security that the commercial success of *Cría!* provided gave him the creative freedom to engage in his next film project, possibly his most highly experimental, surely his most intimate film so far: *Elisa, My Life*.

Shedding False Images

Cría! dramatized the individual's response to the immediate facts of a world whose center appeared lost with the death of Franco. In his next film, *Elisa, vida mía* (1977: Elisa, My Life), Saura acknowledged that with Franco's death he had become liberated from certain ". . . moral obligations, from certain responsibilities which might be called social. Starting with Franco's death, I felt myself freed of those obligations and I decided to bring myself to other aspects of my life which seem essential to me" (Brasó 1977, 5). As a result, he dispensed with the usual depiction of tradition-laden bourgeois society and began to explore a dimension that, as he said, had all too often been neglected by Spanish artists: "In Spanish cinema there has always been a strange fear of showing our sensibilities. One of the causes of that is that a false image has been given to us. Outside of Spain one supposes that being Spanish means being brutal, elemental, violent, when it would be just as easy to show the sensibility of our writers and our painters" (Brasó 1977, 4). That Saura had chosen to concentrate on nonpolitical themes does not mean that he had abandoned themes of Spanishness entirely. If anything, *Elisa, My Life* reveals an intensified exploration of a rich and diverse range of personal and cultural experiences. Having thrown off the chains of the narrowly defined, politically inspired experience of Spanishness, for the first time, he began to delve into the heterogeneity of the Spaniard's ways of being in the world. Agustín Sánchez Vidal calls the film "a countrapuntal and polyphonic mixture of po-

etry, novel, theater, opera-ballet, photography and moving images" (Sánchez Vidal 1988, 126). Indeed, the complex weave of multiple artistic
forms reveals Saura's effort to reconnect with aesthetic traditions that had
for so long been perceived as marginal to the Spaniard's cultural legacy.

The visual and narrative design of *Elisa, My Life* focuses on a number of
these traditions as a dialectical structure out of which emerges the central
plot. There is, for instance, the set of conflicting notions of human experience as represented within Spanish literature: one, an affirmation of individualism as crystalized in the verse from a sixteenth-century poem by
Garcilaso de la Vega; opposed to this, the now-familiar theme of
predestination embodied in the seventeenth-century Calderonian auto sacramental; finally, the seventeenth-century stoic subjectivism of Baltasar
Gracián's allegorical novel, *El criticón*, which, to some measure, shapes the
setting of the film. Against this backdrop, Saura explores an idea of Spain's
spiritual landscape unlike any we have seen in Spanish films until this point.
Obviously borrowing from the Generation of 1898 poets, Unamuno and
Antonio Machado, he highlights a Castilian landscape devoid of obvious
monumentality, yet seductive in its tranquillity. The pivotal force of this
striking mise-en-scène will be its incitement of individuals to reencounter
their own imaginative powers. Thus, we see the film progress as a series of
interactions of characters with one another and with this setting as they
gradually populate the landscape with their own memories, dreams, and
inventions.

Saura's inspiration for *Elisa* came from a number of "lyrical" sources: a
childhood photograph of Geraldine Chaplin given to him by her mother,
"a photo from which emanated a mysterious charm and that induced him
to imagine the encounter between a mother and daughter after a long separation" (Miret Jorbá 1977, 20); his chance rediscovery of the poem by
Garcilaso de la Vega from which the film's title comes; finally, his own
sense of the difficulty and differences between literary and cinematic material (Brasó 1977, 5).[4] The result of his efforts to blend these images and
ideas together is a film that, in its subtlety and ambiguity, makes even more
unconventional demands upon its viewing audience than had Saura's two
preceding films. "This is the story of a reencounter," Saura says, "but it is
also many other things, such as, for example, the process of vampirization,
of a father and a daughter who share experiences and knowledge with each
other. It could also be the story of one marriage that ends and another that

---

[4] To these inspirations Saura admits a more autobiographical one: "The idea of making this
film came in a very concrete way. My father became ill and was in the intensive-care unit. I
began thinking about making a film about such a man" (Sánchez Vidal 106). That preoccu-
pation with the theme of death is the focus of the nightmare that haunts the film's protagonist, Luis. The inspiration for the nightmare, Saura says, came from a recurrent nightmare
Luis Buñuel described to him (Sánchez Vidal 124).

begins; it could be a film about loneliness, the failure of death. . . . It might even be read as a reflection about the differences between literature and film" (Saura 1977, 5).

The film engages us in what at first appears to be a simple story, but then reveals a complex narrational structure that, in effect, demands that its audience actively choose a position of "reading" that story, which is to say, that we elect a way of looking at the world defined within and in relation to the on-screen fiction. Elisa (Geraldine Chaplin) and Isabel (Isabel Mestres) come to their father's cottage in the Segovian hills to join him for a birthday celebration. We see Luis (Fernando Rey) as a man in his seventies, weakened by a heart condition, but, nonetheless, obstinate in his determination to live as a hermit away from the conveniences of urban life. Twenty years earlier, after the failure of his marriage, Luis had come to live in this desolate area to reencounter his own sensibilities. The family reunion includes Isabel's lawyer husband, Julián (Joaquín Hinojosa), and their two small children. Elisa has only recently separated from her husband, Antonio (Norman Brisky), and so, almost as an effort to fill the new void in her life, she has agreed to visit her father whom she has not seen in years.

During this visit, we come to understand Luis's philosophy of life which is in sharp opposition to the pragmatic reality of his daughter, Isabel, and her husband, Julián. When Julián questions him about his misanthropic actions, abandoning family and society, and taking refuge from reality in an isolated cottage, Luis retorts: "Reality? . . . the reality of a society formed by individuals who accept social norms in order to survive? And who dictates those norms?" Later, Luis tells Elisa that he wants to forget everything he has learned in the social world. At the end of the afternoon filled with reminiscences of childhood, Isabel and Julián prepare to depart. Luis surprises Elisa by inviting her to spend a few days more at the cottage so that they can get reacquainted. Hesitantly, she accepts.

In the days that follow, father and daughter recount some of the experiences that have shaped their lives in the interval since they last saw each other. They hold in common a number of similar experiences besides their failed marriages. For one thing, each is obsessed with the thought of death: Luis, because he is in failing health and knows he will soon die; Elisa, as the result of a feeling of emptiness in her life. Spending time with her father, she feels her spirit strengthened by his sense of inner repose. Through conversations with him, she becomes determined not to return to Antonio, even though he makes a trip to the cottage in an effort to patch up their differences.

We see Elisa and Luis reflecting on their past in what appears to be a series of interior monologues. They also tell each other stories that, in contrast to the tranquillity of their immediate surroundings, are filled with violence and death. Luis tells of a brutal murder committed near the cottage; Elisa recounts the mysterious disappearance of her girlfriend Sofía. These stories seem to parallel each other in that each involves an unexplained murder of a woman and both have conjectural, "open" endings about what may really have happened to these women. In the last part of the film, Luis's health worsens. Elisa goes in his place to the nearby girls' school where her father's class is performing a play that he had previously rehearsed with them. In the final scene we see Elisa sitting at Luis's desk reading the lines he had composed in his private memoir during the preceding months.

This memoir plays a significant if not altogether clear function in the lives of the two characters. Through repeated reference to Luis's personal diary, we gradually come to understand that Saura has really constructed a circular plot that, as it progresses in what seems to the spectator to be chronological form, eventually doubles back on itself at the conclusion of the film. The film starts with Julián's car seen approaching Luis's cottage as Luis's voice is heard off-camera: "It had been years since I last saw my father. . . . His illness coincided with the crisis of my marriage, I mean with one of the crises of my marriage." The film ends at a point sometime after Luis's death as we see Elisa sitting in his study reading these same lines aloud. We now recognize the lines as possibly part of the memoir Luis had been composing throughout the course of the film's action. As Elisa reads, the image again cuts to the first scene of the film, that of Julián's car approaching Luis's cottage.

Meditations on Individuality

There is a moment toward the middle of the film when Elisa has adjusted to the rhythm of life at her father's cottage. Luis, who has gone off to teach his daily class at the girls' school, returns to find his daughter engaged in cutting and pasting magazine images onto paper and then, through a process of wetting the back of another sheet of paper, transferring part of the original magazine image to a second sheet. Significantly, all the images she has transferred in her collage art are of women. The scene self-consciously "holds in place," the way a cinematic mise-en-cadre does for the spectator to see, the terms of the crisis that Elisa confronts: the social representation of women and the more general canon of deforming social representations that individuals have been conditioned to absorb as the models of their own identity. Elisa's immediate crisis, as she acknowledges, is only symptomatic of the larger crisis of having recognized that her sense of individual identity as a woman has been nothing but a series of positions she has occupied in a world ordered by patriarchal structures of sight, meaning, and creativity.

The poster art in which she engages, an act of transposition of the same basic image in order to facilitate a new "view" on the already represented female figure, suggests Elisa's tacit awareness of the falsified position she has so long occupied within the patriarchy. That awareness may well be the diegetic source of the film's striking enunciative feature: the framing of all narrative action within the memoir first identified with Luis and then, gradually, with Elisa. This theme is reinscribed in a number of scenes that draw the spectator's attention visually to Elisa's struggle to discover her own identity beneath the masks that have been imposed upon her. At one point, for instance, we are brought to witness Elisa's discovery of a framed photograph of herself and her sister on her father's desk near strewn pages of Luis's memoir. As she reads her father's words, the camera picks up the reflection of the adult Elisa imposed over the glass frame of the childhood photograph (Sánchez Vidal 1989, 112). The recurrence of such scenes leads the audience to read *Elisa, My Life* as a woman's process of remembering positions she has occupied or actually occupying them in order to reject them. Her gradual move from being the object of representations to being the producer of such a representation would thus correspond to the shift from the opening images of the film, in which her father first narrates her experiences, until finally Elisa achieves her own "voice" in the final scene.

In effect, the ambiguous and unsettling enunciative strategy that begins with Luis's voice describing what is later revealed as Elisa's life brings to the foreground the question of the female's discursive position. As in *Cría!*, this moves the spectator to consider the underlying logic of action as the heroine's struggle to transcend the confines of her own ideological formation within the discursively constructed positionalities of a female within a conservative patriarchal order. Significantly, Elisa's gradual empowerment parallels her figurative assumption of "authorship" of the story of her own life, that is to say, her move toward identifying with the memoir that Luis has been seen composing. That move to liberation is represented as a move toward gendered authority, the female assuming the position of power occupied by the male. Yet, given the extreme complexity of the film's discursive and narrative moves, it would be foolish to imagine that there is any clear and indisputable meaning to that final image. Rather, like Elisa's transposing of the magazine images into different frames, all of which maintain the familiar image but "denaturalize" its context, the final scene creates a pensive moment from which to lead the spectator to reflect upon the constructed social and personal positions occupied by individuals. These intensified spectatorial "readings" create a densely textured film. Though seemingly a break from the conception of Saura's earlier work, the discursive antecedent of *Elisa* clearly lies in the future frame of *Cría!* and serves only to reinforce the thematic and visual figuration of the film around the rejection of imposed norms of social realism and the reimagining of the position and ethos of individuality.

Decentering the Subject

Luis's memoir strikingly embodies this rejection of the habits of normative behavior that shape both experience and the perception of that experience. The opening sequence, in particular, is used as an important pivot through which the process of spectator repositioning is gradually effected. The synchronization of the sound track with the cinematic image initially secures an impression of narrative continuity and coherence. Luis's voice is assumed to be the agency of enunciation that situates the visual action as some as yet unspecified flashback narration. Though on subsequent reflection there is reason for the spectator to be confused by the combination of Fernando Rey's voice and the words he speaks ("It had been years since I last saw my father . . ."), one readily absorbs any possible incoherence by subordinating that question to the recognizable conventions of classical cinematic storytelling devices. Indeed, Luis appears to serve a double function in the film, subverting the norms of traditional patriarchal order within the diegesis while embodying a discursive resistance to traditional norms of narration.

Of the material practices of securing the cinematic illusion deployed to disengage the spectator from a realistic reading, none is more crucial than Saura's emphasizing the synchronizations of image with sound track. Throughout *Elisa* the disjunctions between verbal and visual codes induce the audience to assume a series of realistic readings and then to "unlearn" these as they gradually grasp the shifting centers of meaning. In this same learning-unlearning process, we come to recognize that Luis's memoir is only partially a remembrance. The scenes in which we see him sitting at his desk, writing, introduce only a few of the film's flashbacks to earlier moments in his life. At other times his voice-over narration appears to be anticipatory, describing actions that will be rendered visually in the next scene. As well, certain of the lines he appears to be reading from his memoir have actually been voiced earlier in the action by Elisa, as when he takes up her lament about her failed marriage ("You can live so many years with a person and then finally realize that you don't know him") and incorporates it almost exactly into his own memoir.

To these image/sound disjunctions must be added the subtle use of musical motifs from Erik Satie which are variously identified with Luis's or Elisa's narration and thereby blur the lines of simple narrative identification. In all, however, the essential pattern appears to be the subversion of a realistic narrative impression by the internal framing of events from Luis's point of view.

This process is particularly pronounced in the case of the two interpolated stories told by Luis and Elisa to each other. Each narrative initially poses an instance of enigma and sexual fantasy. In the first, Luis and Elisa stroll at dusk in the field near his cottage. As they pass a particular spot, he remembers an event, the murder of a woman, which is said to have occurred there. The woman, a widow, was brutally attacked and stabbed, and her unknown assailant left her body in the gully that Luis and Elisa are now passing. Luis tells his daughter that each year, on the anniversary of the murder, a man comes and leaves a flower on the site where the widow's body was found. When Elisa asks if he reported the stranger to the police as the possible murderer, Luis merely shrugs his shoulders and says he can't be certain of the man's relation to the murdered woman.

In the scene that immediately follows this conversation, we see Elisa sitting up in bed at night, apparently beginning to fantasize about the widow's murder. The scene swiftly cuts to a reenactment of the attack with Elisa now playing the role of the widow, stricken and lying prostrate in the gully. Another rapid cut shows Luis standing in his study at dusk, gazing out at the fields that surround the cottage. The progression of the sequence, from Luis's telling of the murder, to the image of Elisa in bed, to the reenactment of the crime, to the final image of the pensive Luis at his window, describes on a micro-level the narrational features that control the entire filmic discourse. The spectator is led through what appears at first to be a linear temporal progression to construct a coherent narrative line. Yet, through key images, namely the shot of Elisa in her bedroom and Luis in his study, the impression of a realistic, linear action is subverted and finally displaced as the spectator comes to suspect that the visual reenactment of the murder has been imagined by Luis who has transposed Elisa into the role of the widow in ways that parallel the visual transpositions of Elisa's poster art.

In the second self-conscious storytelling scene, Elisa relates to her father an enigmatic episode in her troubled marriage. Father and daughter are seated at the table in the cottage as Elisa describes how she received an anonymous phone call telling her that her husband, Antonio, was having an affair with her best friend, Sofía. Elisa tells how she went to Sofía's apartment to confront her friend but was told by the porter that Sofía had left the country. At this point in the telling, the verbal narration is joined by a visual representation of Elisa's description, beginning with Elisa's arrival at the apartment building. Then all at once, Elisa stops her story and says, "I never saw Sofía again." But the visual track continues the narration, showing Elisa's entering Sofía's apartment, searching her bedroom, and finally discovering the putrified remains of a corpse on the bed. The final image of this sequence is a close-up of Luis's face as he looks across the table to Elisa, implying that the source of that visual telling is once again Luis's imagination.

There is a thematic reciprocity in the two narratives, both of which emphasize the sentimental themes that Elisa's life shares with her father's: betrayal, the obsession with death, and repressed sensuality. Importantly, that reciprocity is defined in specular terms as those of narrator and subject. In the first story, for instance, the shot of Elisa in bed after her father's narration suggests her intense identification with the murdered woman. It is this shot that "authorizes" the projection of Elisa into the role of the widow in the subsequent visual rendition of the murder, as though Elisa were now telling her father's story. Similarly, when she tells her own story, the visual narration is picked up and concluded by Luis. This blurring of the lines of the agencies of enunciation finds its source in the eccentric point of view of Luis's memoirs, which are similarly shaped by this notion of decentering the real enunciator and projecting the other into his or her place. More than just a baroque twist to the film, this dualism finds its conceptual origin in the philosophy of regeneration which Saura's creation of Luis embodies.

Creative Positions in Culture

The habits of learning and the need to unlearn, which are central to Luis's thinking, are situated by Saura in a specific context of Spanish artistic and cultural tradition. He juxtaposes two notions of the individual that arise out of Hispanic cultural tradition and situates Luis's creative imagination as a resolution of the opposition inherent in these. The film's title, for instance, derives from a verse by the sixteenth-century lyrical poet Garcilaso de la Vega.[5] Luis even recites Garcilaso's poetry to his daughter and thereby identifies his own spirit with the recognizable Spanish poetic tradition that esteems the lyrical, creative impulse of the autonomous individual. But that individualism, as Saura well knows, is denied by the conservative ideology of the Counterreformation, which sees the individual's

---

[5] The verse from Garcilaso's "First Eclogue" consists of the sweet laments of two shepherds, Salicio and Nemeroso. Nemeroso's verse contains the lamentations for his dead lover, Elisa, which includes these lines: *¿Quién me dijera, Elisa, vida mía, / cuando en aqueste valle al fresco viento / andábamos cogiendo tiernas flores, / que había de ver con largo apartamiento / venir el triste y solitario día / que diese amargo fin a mis amores?* (Who would have told me, Elisa, my dear Life, / In the times when through this valley of cool wind / we gathered fragile flowers in our wandering, / that I would see, at my long seclusion's end, / the sad and solitary day arrive / that marks the bitter death of all my loving?) (Translated by William Ferguson)

actions as limited by the norms of a preordained and static social order. It is no accident that the play Luis rehearses with his students at the religious school is Calderón's *Great Theater of the World*.

In one scene where Luis brings Elisa to observe his class and to help him rehearse the play, Saura illuminates what has been up to this point the eccentric, seemingly cryptic nature of Luis's narration. As we observed in Saura's first use of the Calderonian allegory in *Ana and the Wolves*, the function of the auto sacramental is to teach its audience to submit to the positions it has been given in the world. But as Luis teaches the play to his class, and indirectly to Elisa, this conservative didacticism is rechanneled and ultimately subverted. Luis asks Elisa to read the lines indicated for the character called "World," as he reads the lines for the "Author." The class of young girls becomes an on-screen audience of this ironic rehearsal of the larger play of life. Everything is set up, in fact, for a self-conscious inter-rogation into the problematic issue of social identity and the positioning of the female subject to submit to preordained social roles.

For the free-thinking Luis, there is more than a bit of perversity in his selection of *Great Theater of the World* as the text for his class; for this work, it would seem, embodies everything he despises in the world that he re-jected twenty years earlier. We need to ask ourselves just why he has privi-leged such a work for his young wards and why he has insisted upon Elisa's participation in the rehearsal. There are clearly signs of Luis's premedita-tion in having assumed the role of *metteur-en-scène* in relation to the alle-gory. We need to recognize from the outset that he has lured Elisa into this position: first, in asking her to spend more time with him after the birthday party; then, in accompanying him to the school; now, finally, in rehearsing the scene with him before his class and thereby placing in the foreground for his daughter and his students the very self-consciousness of the struc-tures of constraint that have determined their social and personal identity.

Part of Luis's covert scheme seems to be to bring together a double au-dience in the classroom for whom he will offer a multiplicity of ironic read-ings of Calderón. For Elisa the act of rehearsal combines three simulta-neous perceptions of Luis: father, teacher, and performer of the role of the Calderonian Author. These are identities that in their redundancy begin to give her an illumination of the type of constraints, particularly by men, that have directed her life. The young girls who observe this double perfor-mance—the father and daughter and the religious allegory—have been given an illuminating distancing. What they are observing is both the re-hearsal of the didactic message of Calderón's theatrical work and the im-mediate transposition of that abstract message into the terms of their own social identities: their relation to their fathers and to the male figures who determine their identity. In the rehearsal, Luis's dramatic direction of Elisa mirrors the functions that he and she play in the narration of his memoirs. In creating his eccentric point of view in his autobiography, Luis constructs and projects a position of coherence that Elisa will eventually assume. But, as with his treatment of Calderón's play, his approach to his memoir is not aimed at didactically enforcing his point of view on his daughter, but rather at stimulating her to achieve her own self-distance and lucidity in relation to her life. This is a strategy that in substance as well as in form parallels the creative position of future distance on one's life that Saura constructs in *Cría!*

When, during Luis's final illness, Elisa assumes the role of director of the play, she appears to have completely absorbed her father's creative posture. We see her as director of the performance, but also as its spectator, exactly the dual role Luis held in his own narration. When she takes up her father's memoirs at the film's end, the audience finds itself replicating the very same roles. The final image of the film brings with it the recognition of our own revised perspective, just as Luis's instruction had worked to reposition his daughter's.

As the film insists, the individual's authentic sense of identity can only be achieved through a personal subversion of the collective norms that have shaped social consciousness. Luis's eccentric narrational strategy as the on-screen spectator-author-creator of his own life has dramatized the terms of regeneration that a father passes on to his daughter and a filmmaker may ideally pass on to his spectator.

Elisa, My Life was the official Spanish entry at the 1977 Cannes Festival. Though the foreign-press response to the film was cold, and even hostile, the festival jury gave Fernando Rey the festival award in the Best Actor category. Despite its complex narrational structure, *Elisa* had a respectable commercial run in Spain. Saura's rich experimentation in narrative and visual form seemed to find a more sympathetic audience at home among critics who could appreciate the film's rich cultural texture as well as its innovative cinematic form.

Political Theater

Though Saura's next film, *Los ojos vendados* (1978: Blindfolded Eyes), appears to be a kind of parenthesis in his exploration of the theme of female consciousness, there are a number of salient elements in this study of the effects of political violence that link it to the films that directly precede it. Similar to the conception of the political trilogy of the early seventies, the film owes its creation to the convergence of external events. The first was Saura's participation in May of 1977 in the Bertrand Russell Tribunal in

Madrid devoted to the documentation of political torture in South America and the moving statement made by one participant, a woman who related in a cold, emotionless voice the torture inflicted upon her by her military captors: "While I looked at that woman who was testifying about torture in that little Russell Tribunal, I asked myself if she weren't just playing the part assigned to her as a torture victim. And if I, myself, who formed part of the official panel—situated for that reason as her ideal spectator—wasn't forming part of that same theatrical work that was being presented and in which my role was that of spectator and actor at the same time" (Saura 1978, 20).

Shortly afterwards, and in an event quite unrelated to the tribunal, Saura's older son, Antonio, then sixteen, was beaten by right-wing youths in Madrid. Gradually, the idea came into focus of developing a script about the political intimidation to which individuals in a violent society are susceptible and the general passivity of the larger community in refusing to acknowledge even the existence of such intimidation. Certainly, the national mood in the immediate post-Franco period was fraught with tension as urban terrorism, particularly of right-wing inspiration, was on the rise. The early euphoria over the fledgling democracy quickly began to wane. "After Franco's death," Saura says, "there was for months an atmosphere of gestating terror, acts of violence perpetrated by the extreme right or by unspecified uncontrollable elements" (Gubern 1979, 44).

1977 is also the year of *Camada negra* (Black Brood), a film called the "most explicitly political film" made in Spain up to this point (Kinder 1983, 67). In it, Manuel Gutiérrez Aragón deals with the members of a family who perform in a church choir by day and are right-wing urban terrorists by night. In an essential way, this view of the relation of the family to terrorism sheds important light on the themes of *Blindfolded Eyes*.

The plot of Saura's film parallels his recent experience at the torture tribunal, with obvious dramatic and intellectual embellishments of some of the conceptual themes of *Elisa, My Life*. Luis (José Luis Gómez), the director of a drama school, becomes obsessed with the memory of the testimony given by Inés, an Argentine woman, at a public forum on political torture in South America. Dressed in a raincoat, kerchief, and reflecting sunglasses to protect her identity, she narrates in subdued, emotionless tones the story of her abduction and torture by political terrorists. As a member of the official tribunal convoked to hear the evidence of political torture, Luis finds Inés's story both arresting and, at the same time, disturbingly like a theatrical performance rendered by an actress who seems to know her part too well.

He forms the idea of producing a staged version of this tribunal and of Inés's story, as he sees it, to attack the problem of the ways in which human experience is betrayed by the social artifices within which those experiences are presented. But Luis also identifies intimately with the deeper spirit of Inés's story, her sense of defenselessness at the hands of anonymous aggressors. The motif of a theatrical staging, of course, suggests a connection with *Elisa* as well as with earlier films where the theatrical model was a ploy (*The Bunker*, *Garden of Delights*, and *Ana and the Wolves*). What clearly links *Blindfolded Eyes* more with *Elisa* than with his earlier work, however, is Luis's perception of ideological betrayal in the nature of theatrical representation, a problem the solution to which aligns the Gómez character with his namesake in *Elisa*. Yet, in Luis's choice of a restaging of the tribunal as a simulated true-life event, Saura returns in a way to his documentary roots, exploring again the possibilities of a form of representation potentially capable of inducing a heightened ethical identification in its audience.

In a move that some Spanish critics found forced, Saura introduces a parallel plot to Luis's story. Emilia, the wife of Luis's dentist and friend, Manuel (Xabier Elorriaga), asks Luis if she can join his acting classes. Again in a double role, Geraldine Chaplin plays the part of Emilia as well as that of Inés. As the dentist's wife, Emilia leads a confined existence and intuitively senses that Luis's acting school may afford her some outlet to her emotional problems. The friendship between Emilia and Luis quickly turns to love. When Manuel becomes violent with his wife, she leaves him and moves in with Luis. The director begins to see Emilia as the ideal actress to play the role of Inés in his play.

Marriage and family are once again seen as the source of the individual's repressive education. Here, however, Saura draws a narrative and thematic link between Emilia's marriage and the violence that will eventually erupt into political terrorism in much the same way that Gutiérrez Aragón makes explicit that same connection between the family and right-wing terrorism in *Black Brood*. As the rehearsals for the play progress, Luis begins to receive anonymous letters threatening him with reprisals if he does not abandon his project. Even after his studio is vandalized and he is beaten by thugs, he holds steadfastly to his idea of producing the play. He sees in the play a creative as well as an ethical act, one that affirms his identity both as a creative individual and as a member of a social community. In a curious way, this attitude echoes the position of Luis in *Elisa*, who saw the reaffirmation of his own creativity in the dramatic project of staging his Calderonian allegory. During the performance of Luis's play at the end of *Blindfolded Eyes*, a group of masked commandos armed with machine guns enters the theater and massacres the actors and audience just as Emilia is speaking Inés's lines from the beginning of the film.

The Spectator and the Author

In *Blindfolded Eyes*, the spectator is made the self-conscious focus of narrative order, and the spectatorial position is conspicuously inscribed into several key scenes. The film begins and ends in a theater. The first and last images are shots of the stage from the back of the theater, a vantage point recognizable as the site that a spectator would occupy in viewing a performance. A number of intervening scenes occur in this same theater, and, each time, Saura depicts the image or reflection of the on-screen spectators, thus relentlessly making the film's real audience aware of their position as viewers.

This bringing to the foreground of the spectatorial figure within the film's diegesis is modeled to some measure on the figure of Enrique in *The Hunt*, where the identity of the on-screen spectator was clearly tied to a question of ethical complicity born in one's having witnessed violence. In *Blindfolded Eyes* the intricate connection between bearing witness and the individual's ethical position is joined, tellingly, with a range of aesthetic and emotional issues as well. The fact that Luis, the theatrical director, is first introduced as a spectator establishes the film's premise of a critical linkage between ethical and aesthetic positions. His act of bearing witness to Inés's recitation motivates him to want to author a dramatic work in which he hopes others will recognize how their own passivity in the face of violence makes them accomplices to the reign of terrorism.

The narrative implicitly equates Luis's reassumption of his identity as author with his refusal to be the victim of intimidation, and this, in turn, leads to the emancipation of Emilia. Her transformation from a timid character brought to a new perspective on her own identity becomes, in the final scene of the film, the object of view of the real audience whose relation to the intimidating power of terrorism the film as a whole is attempting to define in activist terms. Thus, the chain of "effects" of Inés's story on her audiences implies the mobilization of on-screen spectators—Luis, Emilia, and potentially the real audience—who are moved to shed the mask of passivity of the spectator and to achieve the ethical and emotional liberation identified with the metaphor of the author.

The film's opening sequence explores Inés's presentation and establishes her relation to her on-screen audience at the tribunal hearing. We see her on the stage first from a long-shot taken from the back of the theater and then from a circular tracking that shows the audience rapt by her story. As she speaks, the camera cuts to a close-up frontal shot of Inés's face. She is wearing reflecting sunglasses so that, again, the audience's image is reflected in her image, thus reinforcing the film's point that the audience is always implicated in the tales of political torture they might otherwise prefer to disavow. Inés's story of abduction, brutalization, and torture by commandos will precipitate the identification that both Luis and Emilia make with their own experiences. But it is not so much the question of violence as such that appears to interest Saura here as it is its effect on a whole society that, immobilized by fear of that violence, unwittingly becomes its accomplice (Sánchez Vidal 1988, 132).

Though the details of her abduction are dramatic and emotional, Inés's delivery is intentionally cold and almost a monotone, giving the events an eeriness that seems only to intensify the impact of her words on her audience. She has, in effect, distanced herself from the events she describes, transforming the memory into the kind of theatrical performance that Saura himself experienced in the Russell Tribunal. The underlying force of Inés's story lies, however, in its power to evoke in her audience a form of identification that gradually comes to be recognized as what Luis will call "constructive imagination," an ability to stand back from oneself and imagine events in one's life as though they were theatrical, and thereby to gain some illumination of the experience.

In the action that follows the opening sequence, we find that Luis's own consciousness has been touched by Inés's appearance. He begins to discern the signs of menace and potential aggression against himself in a series of ordinary, everyday situations. After the tribunal scene, the action cuts to Luis's getting out of his car in an underground garage. He moves apprehensively as if sensing that someone is observing him, waiting to attack. The original shooting script called for Luis to encounter a woman and her young son in the garage structure, the latter carrying a toy machine gun.

Luis goes to Manuel's office and speaks to Emilia, who asks him about his acting classes. Emilia is wearing sunglasses and her appearance immediately triggers Luis's remembrance of Inés. Once in the office, Luis takes his position in the dentist's chair. But the drill and the light shining into his face again conjure in his mind the details of Inés's narrative. The sound of the drill evokes for him the story of political torture and makes the potential aggression of a seemingly innocent character such as Manuel seem immediately real and personal to Luis.

The experience of Inés's narration has obviously touched Luis in ways that strike to his very sense of identity. Returning to his studio after the visit to Manuel's office, he reflects on his life in a voice-over monologue that suggests that Inés's experiences have provoked a personal crisis for the theatrical director. He concludes his monologue in this manner: "I felt a chill, the chill of disaster, and for the first time in my life I had the sensation of having lived in vain, only touching the surface of things, without fully realizing the why and the wherefore of the things I had done. I found myself in the middle of things." Out of that self-revelation, triggered by

Inés, Luis begins both to compose the play based on her story and also to reshape his strategies as an acting teacher.

Through the dramatization of some of these classes, Saura articulates several of the key concepts through which his characters will define their strong sense of individuality and positive commitment to social groups. On the first day of classes, as Emilia merely observes the group, Luis leads his students in an exercise in which each is directed to "engage in a dialogue with an invisible antagonist." This exercise forces each actor to pick up on the idea of him or herself being spied on by someone whom they cannot see. Yet, instead of suggesting a paranoid perception by each student, the exercise reinforces in its participants a stronger sense of their own identity and movements. Tellingly, after witnessing this class, Emilia agrees to join the group, thus replicating the teacher/student relationship that was the thematic pivot of *Elisa, My Life* and out of which that film's heroine achieved her own liberation.

In one session, Luis speaks of the need for his students to develop a "constructive imagination" in their performances, not merely a mimetic illusion which will finally trap them. In this he means for them to move their own perceptual focus beyond the frame of representation, to understand that appearances and meaning in appearances are always somehow built upon the containment of the individual within visible illusions, packaged identities. Through Luis's words, Saura explains his own rejection of the aestheticizing social realism which, for decades, had held sway over Spanish cinema. As an outgrowth of the thinking that inspired Elisa's father, Luis's dramaturgy is really a strategy of spectatorship, a self-conscious standing back from the conditions of performance and representation and an interrogation of the individual's immobilization in illusion. While the film's didacticism appears explict and self-referential in these scenes, Saura's strategy of involving his spectator in this process is more subtle and much less self-contained than it might at first seem. Implicit in the process of self-illumination lies the question of the individual's distancing from his or her own life and a "standing back" process through which one comes to discern the terms of his or her confinement in the sentimental traps of marriage and family authenticated by society. That self-generating strategy of distancing, whose origin can be traced back to *Cousin Angelica*, is embedded in the radical juxtaposition of scenes that comprise the filmic text.

We see this in the scene of the first group class in which Emilia is present. The scene begins in the class, as Luis organizes the exercise around the notion of the dialogue with an invisible antagonist. It then abruptly cuts to the director's flashback memory of the circumstances under which he first met Manuel and Emilia. Driving on a lonely country road, he suddenly begins to feel chest pains. Stopping his car, he gets out and walks into the field at the roadside, then lies on the ground in what appears to be a spasm related to a heart attack. Manuel and Emilia, driving by, stop their car and offer to help. The scene then cuts back to the theater class which has now progressed to Luis's explanation of "constructive imagination." Later in the film Luis and Emilia will return to this same roadside spot and make love in the very field where Luis once lay prostrate. Significantly, this return to the field occurs as a cut away from a scene in which Emilia is rehearsing Inés's lines and having difficulty expressing the appropriate emotions. Luis tells her to read the lines as though she were repeating the details of some distant memory. The scene then cuts from the rehearsal studio to a reenactment of Inés's being pushed into a car by the masked assailants, finally, to Luis and Emilia driving along the country road.

Implicit in the sequencing of these juxtapositions of theatrical space and the spaces of love and death is the notion of a distanced place of interrogation from which to view one's own life. For Luis, the open field is defined as a creative, open space, a place that opposes the confined spaces of aggression and entrapment. The connotations that his own life brings to that otherwise barren field are of creativity and fertility through sexual union, analogous to the places of distanced, liberated perception to which the film alludes at various points. As with Luis's efforts to position Emilia so she may see and feel the terms of her own entrapment, Saura's process of radical juxtaposition among the three interwoven tales is designed to elicit from his spectator a similar sense of a distanced, illuminated position which both reveals the nature of containment and, more importantly, motivates that spectator toward transcending such structures of confinement.

Theatrical space at first holds a seemingly ambiguous function in all of these juxtapositions, certainly in relation to Saura's earlier use of theatrical motifs. As Luis directs his class to see, the theatrical experience for the actor is a form of confrontation, not of escape. In this the actor enables the audience to simulate an act of witnessing, thereby inciting a recognition of the individual's complicity in a social world. That initial confrontation between the theatrical and the social is underscored in the opening sequence: Inés's reflecting sunglasses mirroring the audience in her eyes while the impact of her narration prods Luis's recognition of his own vulnerability to violence.

As Saura conceptualizes it through his protagonist, theater is a powerful tool of confrontation with the forces that otherwise intimidate the individual. For that reason, the film's final scene, in one sense the closing of a circle of transformations of life into performances that incite other transformations, has the effect of suggesting a final confrontation between the real spectator and the intimidating power of political violence. In that last scene, Emilia has assumed the appearance and role of Inés and begins to

14. *Blindfolded Eyes* (*Los ojos vendados*, 1978)

speak Inés's lines before the audience. Visually, the scene is nearly identical to the opening sequence, except that now the spectator understands, as Luis had earlier sensed, that this is a theatrical performance. But all at once that performance is disrupted by the entrance of men in face masks who machine-gun both the actors and members of the audience. The final image of the film, shot from an empty seat in the back of the theater and framing the vacant stage, is a moment of distanced reflection for the real audience of the film, made to confront an empty space which is analogous to the open field earlier evoked by Luis. It is finally for the audience to confront the world blocked by mere theatrics and social positioning and to recognize that the view of their relation to the social world is limited by their own blindfolded eyes.

In its Madrid run, *Blindfolded Eyes* failed to impress either critics or the public. Commercially, the film was to prove the least successful of the Saura-Querejeta collaborations of the decade (Hernández Les 1986, *Singular*, 312). As Agustín Sánchez Vidal argues, by this point, with the dismantling of the censorship apparatus, audiences had begun to expect a more direct treatment of pressing social themes (Sánchez Vidal, 1989, 135).

Mamá cumple cien años (1979: Mama Turns One Hundred)

Saura confessed to interviewers that after *Cría!, Elisa, My Life*, and *Blind-folded Eyes* he felt exhausted, ". . . as if I were dried up. I saw the need to make a different kind of film, a film in a different tone. . . . The state of mind that seems to be at the root of *Mama Turns One Hundred* is that of a convulsion, almost a fury, a kind of catharsis" (Hidalgo 1979, 2). Indeed, in visual style and tone, *Mama* suggests a respite from if not an actual break with the films he had been making in recent years.

The film is conceived as a very loose continuation of the earlier *Ana and the Wolves*. Fifteen years or so have passed since the end of the previous film; Ana is married and has brought her husband, Antonio (Norman Brisky), to the house to help celebrate the matriarch's one-hundredth birthday for which a gala party is planned. Mama's children are vexed by her longevity and would prefer to see her expire quickly so that they can get on with the business of the future, which for them means selling her huge estate to land developers. They plan to precipitate her death by pro-voking one of her frequent epileptic seizures at her birthday party. Ana, again played by Geraldine Chaplin, is enlisted to protect the old lady by keeping Mama's medicine on hand at all times. In the twenty-four hours leading up to the festivities, we are shown just how much or how little everyone in the family has changed since audiences last viewed them. In one way or another, the image of the traditional Spanish family as the ideo-logical agency of cultural deformation has been the centerpiece of every Saura film since *Garden of Delights*. In *Mama Turns One Hundred* it first appears that Saura has reached a certain loving accommodation with the family, but that impression will be dispelled by the film's bittersweet end-ing.

Though seemingly a straightforward narrative, superficially not unlike the genre of forgettable *comedias españolas* of the sixties, a number of formal features indicate that a conceptual complexity belies the light surface of *Mama*. For one thing, the notion of the cinematic continuation of *Ana and the Wolves* should pose a basic problem for Saura's audience. At the end of the earlier film, it appeared that the three brothers attacked, raped, and murdered the governess. Even if one reads the final scene of *Ana* as a dream sequence, the nature of Ana's departure from the mansion would certainly preclude the kind of joyous return we note at the beginning of *Mama*. But such a discrepancy only points up Saura's carefree approach to the latter film: "Accepting the fact that Geraldine may have died does not seem a sufficient reason not to make a film where she is now alive" (Galán 1979, 48).

Another narrational "gap" in the film was created by the death of José

María Prada, the actor who played the authoritarian José in *Ana*. In a light-hearted homage to the actor, Saura incorporates Prada's death into the script by having Mama insist upon setting a place for her deceased son at the dinner table with a portrait of Prada on "his" dinner plate. These two intertextual elements which might otherwise be seen as disrupting the narrative coherence of *Mama* are flaunted conspicuously in such a way as to draw the audience's attention to a dimension of the film's historical thematics; for in order for the filmic narrative to operate smoothly, one needs to invoke a very selective memory, ignoring some facts from the fictional past and integrating others from the world outside the fiction. Retrospectively, the audience will come to recognize that these inconsistencies of historical treatment are perhaps like their own attitudes toward recent Spanish history. Indeed, the connection between the film's depicted attitudes toward the past and the spectator's forms the conceptual core of *Mama Turns One Hundred*.

Prada's death is flaunted from the very start as a way of focusing the film's temporal thematics. In the precredits we see Mama, flanked by her family and servants, contemplating José's grave. The camera then pans away in the credits to a view of a car approaching the front entrance of the huge and decaying country house. When the car draws up to the main entrance, Ana and Antonio get out and view the decrepit facade. Armed with a Polaroid camera, Ana takes shots of the building and the surrounding grounds. "*Madre mía*, how time passes!" she says with a sigh, as Antonio looks back furtively at the Madrid skyline, barely visible through the morning smog. With precise visual economy Saura uses the married couple to establish the thematic tension of the film as the convergence of two opposing historical perspectives: ingenuous nostalgia for an idealized past and a cynical view of the monstrous future that awaits the Spaniard.

Saura's self-reference to the earlier *Ana and the Wolves*, which is supposed to have preceded *Mama* by fifteen years but, in fact, was made only seven years earlier, alerts the audience to the fact that they are viewing the antics of the family members from a historicized perspective. This is a tamer version of the future frame in *Cría!* which similarly transformed contemporary Spain into the historical past and suggested to its audience a contemplative, distanced view of their own personal situation. Along with this lighthearted appropriation of *Ana and the Wolves*, Saura includes a series of other self-parodies of his filmography. For instance, the casting of Norman Brisky as Ana's unfaithful husband is a clear borrowing from the identical situation in *Elisa*, where he and Geraldine Chaplin last appeared together. Ana also appears in a scene of somnambulism in *Mama* that mirrors similar scenes in both *The Bunker* and *Elisa*. Even the use of photographs and the family-album motif, triggering connections with *Garden of Delights* and *Cousin Angelica*, leads Spanish audiences to an awareness of the director's self-reflection on his own recent past which will be paired eventually with the self-reflection Saura has prepared for his spectator.

A Conventional Audience

Despite the eccentricity of the temporal frame and the conspicuous self-referentiality of so much of the action, there appears little else in *Mama Turns One Hundred* to suggest the narrational complexity of some of Saura's recent films. But, finally, it is the film's very conventionality that proves to be its most extraordinary feature. The hoary genre plotting and the unproblematic visual composition of *Mama* seem designed to engage the very kind of audience in Spain that had long seen Saura as a hermetic, narrowly defined political filmmaker. It is not simply that he is here attempting to capture a larger market, although that is clearly one of the effects of the film. The pattern of narration and the treatment of plot center a tradition-bound Spanish audience not easily moved to recognize the dilemma of its own illusionist sight and beliefs. The seemingly reactionary cinematic narrative style of *Mama* again reflects Saura's pursuit of forms of representation that will both accommodate and engage particular audiences in reflection on their personal relation to the patterns of Spanish culture.

Once again Saura's ploy is a close scrutiny of a family plot, in this instance, literally the "plotting" of family members to hasten Mama's demise. Through such comic intrigues he weaves the threads of an interrogation of the underlying question of the individual poised on the edge of national history. Mama, who suffers from a series of ailments, including frequent epileptic seizures, is approaching her centennial birthday. Though her children seem at odds with one another on a number of petty points, they join together in their rejection of her unswerving belief in the integrity of the family. Her reverence for their huge mansion is symbolic of that belief in the family that it has housed.

But that family, as we discover, has been shattered by the advent of a concept of modernity that seems to challenge the ideals and even the identity of the old Spain. We see this crisis comically embodied in the activities of Mama's two surviving sons. Fernando, for instance, who once practiced religious meditation in order to achieve levitation, now attempts human flight by tying artificial wings to his arms and trying to fly like a bird. Frustrated with his sham marriage, Juan has simply run off with the maid.

As the film opens we discover that only Luchy (Charo Soriano), Juan's estranged wife, and his mystic brother, Fernando (Fernando Fernán Gómez), remain of Mama's progeny. Luchy is irked by Mama's steadfast refusal to die. In an effort to unburden herself of any memory of her failed marriage, she has devised a plan to sell the house and adjoining lands to condominium developers. To speed up the anxiously awaited demise of her mother-in-law, Luchy schemes to give Mama a placebo instead of her regular anti-seizure medicine during one of the matriarch's frequent epileptic attacks. But Mama catches on to Luchy's intentions and alerts Ana to give her a pill should the attack come, as Luchy hopes, during the excitement of the birthday festivities. As in *The Brothers Karamazov*, which one of the granddaughters is seen reading and which has more than a passing similarity to the plot, the party is going to be "an unfortunate gathering."

The energy of narration in *Mama* derives from the way the audience is made first to identify with and then become perspectivally and affectively detached from each character's situation. To this end the film continually stresses a series of long-shots, the distanced view of the house and characters as they are dwarfed first by their immediate landscape and then by the contemporary world emblemized by the distant and blurred image of Madrid which lies beyond the hills. This identification/distancing is further emphasized by the introduction of a dramatic technique of theatrical tableaux in which the sound of a helicopter is heard hovering over the house precisely at the moment of one of Mama's epileptic seizures. All the characters freeze, producing a *tableau vivant*, only to have the camera track away from them.

This device occurs twice, the first time when Luchy's husband, Juan, miraculously appears, returning for his mother's birthday; in that scene the family is gathered around the dinner table when one of the granddaughters asks Mama what will happen to the house after she dies. She answers emphatically that as long as she is alive the house will remain intact. There will be no nightmarish constructions of high-rise buildings on her land. At that very instant the sound of the helicopter is heard and all the characters freeze into a tableau. A mysterious wind sweeps into the room, and the camera tracks to the corridor where Juan makes his entrance. The action resumes. Upon seeing her prodigal son again, Mama immediately goes into her seizure. The second tableau scene occurs at the long-awaited birthday celebration and follows a similar pattern.

In both scenes Mama recovers, having had a momentary experience of her own death. The point of this illusion-breaking device seems to be to disengage the audience from the narrative intrigue, to make them stand back in much the same way that Ana (in *Cría!*) and Elisa do in the face of a death in their family. Here the audience is invited to contemplate the sense of an end and a beginning in the course of human action just as the characters in the film are doing. Tellingly, Saura makes both of these scenes moments of recovery and regeneration for the characters and implies a similar pensive position for his audience as well. These distancing techniques point up the obvious artifice of the entire plot as a mere pretext for contemplation of the past and reflection on the future.

Mama's second seizure, at the birthday party, is the film's conceptual and narrative climax. Just as it appears that she has finally died, she miraculously revives and tells the assembled guests that in one flashing instant she has seen her whole life rush by and she now knows it was all futility: "So many tears, so much strife, so much suffering . . ." Her words become inaudible as the film's theme music, a military march, is heard and the camera begins an accelerated tracking away from her, through the hall of the house, finally to the expanse of the front grounds, posing a view that necessarily dwarfs the house and its inhabitants. As the rhythmic strains of the military music become louder, the camera finally stops, providing a final distanced view which situates the world of the characters in recognizable relation to the audience, inviting us to ponder, along with the family, the questions of past and future.

From the contemporary vantage point of 1979, such a reflection reveals Spain in the throes of a crisis of identity and the traditional oligarchy of the Franco years, so consistently lampooned in Saura's films, in an economic crisis, as well. The family, which for so long had been the allegorical embodiment of values of the old order, now crystalizes the contradictions

15. *Mama Turns One Hundred* (*Mamá cumple cien años*, 1979)

between the Spain of tradition and the prospect of a total repudiation of those traditions in the name of financial, not patriotic or religious, pressures. Saura invites his audience, presumably one unaccustomed to reflect on such questions of historical direction, to consider not only the survival of traditions, but also, as Mama's final speech indicates, the cost of such a survival. Therein lies the black side of the comedy. Having depoliticized his symbolic family, Saura now reinvokes the aura of national history so that his audience can reflect upon the futility of the ideological and political baggage that has so deformed Spaniards.

There is no facile closure to the film. Rather, Saura moves his audience to assume all the specular positions that we now recognize to be the patterns of constructive imagination: distancing and disengagement from illusion; reflection on the past; finally, recognition of the perceptual snares that have situated the viewer within the confines of illusory representation. The final moments of *Mama Turns One Hundred* are really not unlike the structures that have informed all his films since *Cría!* The scene narrativizes a distanced place of perception beyond contemporary action and situates the contemporary moment within historicized consciousness for the spectator. As in the three preceding works, indeed, as in every Saura film up to this point, the ending brings the audience to a state of pensiveness and, with the perceptual knowledge it now has of its position in culture, invites reflection on the possibilities of a future distinct from the illusions of the past.

The popular commercial success of *Mama Turns One Hundred* in Spain was astounding. It ranked as the sixth in box-office receipts for 1979 and, with earnings of seventy million pesetas in its first year of distribution, became Saura's most commercially successful film up to this point (Hernández Les 1986, *Singular*, 312). Though it won an award at the 1979 San Sebastián festival and was nominated for an Oscar in the Best Foreign Film category, there was less enthusiasm for the film in critical circles both inside Spain and abroad. The view was widely held that Saura had moved away from the difficult themes of his most recent works and was merely pandering to an undemanding domestic audience. Such views failed to appreciate that with *Mama Turns One Hundred* Saura had, for the first time, made contact with a broad sector of the Spanish public to which, conceptually, his films had been directed for two decades.

VI

Generations

Generational Aesthetics

ON FEBRUARY 23, 1981, the attempted military coup headed by Colonel Antonio Tejero gave the nation breathtaking evidence of how fragile their recent experiment with democratic government was. Within eighteen months of the thwarted coup, however, orderly national elections produced the first socialist triumph on a national level in over forty years. Felipe González's electoral victory also evoked a sensation of déjà vu, for it brought back to many the stories of the ill-fated Second Republic of 1931 and the fears that the country might once again be on a course toward a schism similar to the one that had led to the Civil War. Even if the socialist victory and the coup attempt were inverted in sequence, the effect was still to induce in many Spaniards the sensation of a time warp.

The storming of the Chamber of Deputies was a far cry from the detailed planning of the July 18 coup of 1936, but the fact of the nation's continued vulnerability to the military's vision of Spain was a sobering lesson. Though the coup had failed and the socialists were seen not to be the red monsters of Francoist lore, the popular anxiety about these events clearly revealed that the mythologies that had shaped the collective consciousness about the left and the right—the rule of street mobs and the rule of armies—were still present in the thinking of many Spaniards. Neither event is the focus of a Saura film; yet the ever-present question of the Spaniard's identification with or disavowal of the ghosts of history is clearly the impetus for his principal work during the early eighties.

In 1979, after a twelve-year common-law marriage and close professional collaboration on eight films, Saura and Geraldine Chaplin separated. The break and Saura's subsequent involvement in a series of film projects seemingly unrelated to his previous films, led Spanish critics to hypothesize a "new" Carlos Saura, or various "new" Sauras. In truth, the prodigious variety of his films of the eighties, while clearly distinct in formulation and subject matter from the fourteen films that precede them, is still part of the conceptual canon begun over two decades earlier.

What is most distinctive about the four-year period beginning with the conclusion of *Mama Turns One Hundred* is the variety of projects in which Saura immerses himself: six films in a little over four years, some of which,

like *Bodas de sangre* (Blood Wedding) and *Deprisa, deprisa* (Hurry, Hurry!),
are practically simultaneous projects. Of these six films, the first two parts
of Saura's flamenco dance trilogy, *Blood Wedding* and *Carmen*, evolve
through the director's close collaboration with the noted Spanish choreographer and dancer Antonio Gades. Given the obvious unity of the dance
trilogy which sets it apart from the rest of Saura's work, these films will be
considered together in the next chapter. The four remaining films form
perhaps Saura's most fragile cluster of works; for the stylistic, thematic,
and production features of each at first suggest that they are isolated, even
random, works, not wholly consonant with the films that precede them.
No longer do there appear to be neat cleavages of period and style like
those that bracketed off the earlier trilogies. Instead, like Borges's vision of
Franz Kafka inventing his own precursors, each film in this cycle suggests
a move both backward to earlier Saura films and forward to new thematic
and cinematic experiments (Sánchez Vidal 1988, 145). We can see this
process clearly in the first of the major films of the eighties, *Hurry, Hurry!*
Though initially the film seems to be a radical shift from the introspective
works of the late seventies, the seeds of *Hurry, Hurry!* are firmly planted in
Mama Turns One Hundred, which was itself a self-referential tapestry of his
previous work.

In *Mama* the focus of action was the rift among the various generations
of the clan: rejecting the past, rushing into the future, or, as in Ana's case,
trying to find some point of accommodation between the two. But Mama's
family was situated in a physical setting which, as it looked out toward
Madrid, visually stated the gulf between classes and generations of Spaniards who still had the luxury of choosing their relation to history and
those, emblemized by the smog-laden skyline in the distance, who merely
lived the postmodern future as everyday reality. The fleeting images of Madrid that appear at the beginning and end of *Mama Turns One Hundred*
foretell the narrative of schism within Spanish culture as the separation of
generations, of spaces, but, most importantly, of cultural and aesthetic sensibilities.

In this sense, *Hurry, Hurry!* appears almost to be a reverse shot of the
view of urban blight that was pictured at the beginning of *Mama*, locating
its narrative and cultural perspective in the place of a *madrileño* youth gang
whose center of consciousness is devoid of all historical and temporal ref-
erents except the here and now. The coherence of this astounding film lies
in its absorption of the aesthetic values of the marginal youth culture which
had, by the end of the seventies, encroached upon the previously "safe"
space of Spanish bourgeois illusionism. The unspoken but ubiquitous
theme that dominates the film is that of generations of Spaniards separated
from each other by opposing aesthetics. The drug culture of *Hurry, Hurry!*,
like the nostalgia-ridden characters of earlier films, is only a symptomatic

mark of a more pervasive questioning that guides Saura's development through these years.

This same generational schism, a new perspective on the indiviudal's experience of history, marks his next three films: *Dulces horas* (1983: Sweet Hours), *Antonieta* (1984), and *Los zancos* (1984: Stilts), but each in a different way. In *Sweet Hours* (1983), Saura examines a character who appears to be a parody of Luis in *Cousin Angelica*, entrapped by the insistent memories of the Civil War and postwar period, but not due to anguish. Rather, he is a character who fetishizes the past, who suffers from the opposite malady of the characters in *Hurry, Hurry!*; he is burdened by history. In *Antonieta* (1983) the theme of a woman's identification with a historical personage raises a series of questions related to the issues of national cultural identity. A more modest, intimate film than any of the earlier ones, *Stilts* nonetheless raises the question of a more conventional generation gap through a story in which an old man's infatuation with a young woman provides a symbolic reawakening of his own creative instinct. In all three films, the central focus lies in a curious interrogation of the significance of historical generations and their metaphorical connection with the individual's creative re-generation. In this sense, Saura's thematic focus remains grounded in much the same personal and cultural framework earlier noted in *Elisa, My Life*. What is different, however, is the way in which this seemingly narrow range of questions has turned on a series of broader cultural themes and narrational strategies.

Deprisa, deprisa (1980: Hurry, Hurry!)

After completing work on *Mama Turns One Hundred*, Saura started on a script about urban youth gangs in the peripheral working-class communities that surround Madrid. In the summer of 1980, after a protracted period of revisions, he started shooting the film using a nonprofessional cast of actors from the Villaverde area just south of the city. Film reporters and interviewers were quick to assume that this new film was an updating of his first film, *Hooligans*. In repeated interviews Saura insisted that his earlier film, more often cited than actually seen, as he wryly noted, had nothing to do with his conception of *Deprisa*: "Spain has changed; Madrid has changed. It seems to me that this country has changed so much that the the two things have nothing to do with each other except the fact that I'm the author of both of them" (Hidalgo 1981, 22).

The changes of which Saura speaks account for the massive script revisions the film underwent prior to the actual shooting. He began writing a script based upon a file of newspaper clippings about juvenile delinquency he had been collecting over the years, particularly reports about robberies.

Dissatisfied with the result, he was convinced that his problem was that he was simply out of touch with both the characters and the milieu he was attempting to depict. So began an arduous period of research and interviews with youths in the working-class suburbs of Madrid, in search of the characters and situations that would emerge eventually in *Hurry, Hurry!*:

> It was surprising how little I knew a city in which I had spent the better part of my life, for the changes that had taken place during the last few years had completely modified its structure, even the language was different. In the outlying neighborhoods they spoke another way, with other trends. The result of this investigation was a new script that preserved some of the elements of the first and had many different scenes and dialogues. From the interviews we had with hundreds of kids, we selected some belonging to the same neighborhood, because I wanted them all to speak the same way, with the same slang in their speech, and that they be friends if possible.[1]

Saura describes the finished version of *Hurry, Hurry!* as a "romantic" film, in the historical sense of the word, as it expresses the outlook of the nineteenth-century rebel who stood outside society and who rejected social norms (Hidalgo 1981, 20). The film's four young protagonists are imbued with a spirit that, in its simplicity and rejection of the outward patterns of social behavior, harks back as much to the more historical romanticism of *Lament for a Bandit* as it does to *Hooligans*.

Pablo (José Antonio Valdelomar) and Meca (Jesús Arias Aranzeque), two urban youths, live from day to day by a series of robberies, mostly car thefts. After one such robbery, Pablo meets Angela (Berta Socuéllamos) and is instantly taken by her. They soon become lovers, promising to stay together always. Pablo teaches Angela to shoot a gun, and in a short time she is made a member of the gang, now consisting of four members: Pablo, Meca, Angela, and Sebastián or "Sebas" (José María Hervás Roldán). Sebas has joined the group to help in a series of more ambitious thefts, but he is initially unhappy with the presence of a female in the gang. Pablo assures him that Angela can hold her own.

In the first robbery, that of a factory office on the outskirts of Madrid, Angela, disguised as a boy with a moustache, serves as lookout. In the second holdup she kills one of the guards who has fired at the gang's car. At the conclusion of each of these robberies, Meca brings the robbery car, usually a stolen one, to a deserted area and sets it ablaze. He stands by the side of the fire and views the flames in an apparent pyromaniac trance.

Their share of the money from the two successful robberies enables Angela and Pablo to buy a new apartment on the outskirts of the city. It is

---

[1] From an unsigned interview published in English in the program notes for the National Film Theater of London's retrospective of Saura's films, September 1986.

from this location that the gang will plan a third robbery, the assault on a branch bank in one of the more congested middle-class neighborhoods of Madrid. During this robbery, Sebas kills one of the guards and, in turn, is gunned down outside the bank by a squad of police who have surrounded the area. Pablo, Meca, and Angela manage to make a getaway, but Pablo has been seriously wounded and is bleeding profusely.

Angela brings him back to the apartment to nurse him while Meca disposes of the getaway car in the usual manner. The black cloud of smoke attracts a police helicopter, and Meca is killed as he resists arrest. Understanding the seriousness of Pablo's wound, Angela calls a doctor who, upon arriving at the apartment, confirms the gravity of Pablo's condition. He has been shot in the liver and must be brought to a hospital if he is to survive. Refusing, she offers him a large bundle of cash if he will treat Pablo right there. Taking the money in his black satchel, the physician promises to return shortly with instruments for surgery. Hours pass, but he does not come back. Pablo, who remains unconscious, lies immobile on the bed. He stops breathing while Angela sits in the darkened room staring at him. When she realizes he is dead, she fills her own duffel bag with the remaining money from the robbery and walks out of the apartment. She disappears into the shadows of the approaching night as we hear the strains of "Me quedo contigo," (I'll Remain with You), the song earlier identified with the two lovers' promise of fidelity.

In returning to the lives of socially marginal characters, Saura emphasizes, in much the same manner as he did in *Hooligans*, his characters' impulse to spontaneity and improvised action. But unlike the earlier film, he now does not need to justify the robberies with any altruistic motivations as he was forced to do by the censors in 1959. As he explains, his characters live in the immediate present in which they don't have to think about what they plan to do five minutes from now: "One of these kids explained their philosophy of life to me very clearly: 'Look, in order for me to have a car I have to break my butt for a long time, and then I may not even be able to buy the car I like, which just happens to be parked right here. So, I take it and it's done.' These kids live completely in the present without thinking too much about the consequences of their actions, although they clearly assume the risks. They want everything and they want it fast" (Harguindey 1980, 17).

The youths of the story, rebelling against the constraints of social organization, are, in fact, products of the very system that they reject and that has rejected them. The Madrid of the eighties is the emblematic landscape that invites the Spaniard to live a new variation on the theme of false individualism. "From childhood, they have been bombarded by radio and television announcers telling them to buy and to desire the products that neither they nor their families can afford" (Harguindey 1980, 17).

At one ironic moment in the film, the gang members and their girl-friends sit on a hillside overlooking the massive tangle of the Madrid ex-pressway at dusk. They view the rush-hour traffic against a backdrop of the modern skyline which envelopes the newer areas of the city. Looking down from a distance at the fast-moving traffic below, Meca speaks mockingly to his friends: "Look at them, like madmen who finally go home. The guy's wife opens the door, gives him a kiss, and says, 'Hi, Juan. How was work?' The guy's all wet and sweaty. 'Fine, fine. I'm tired.' Then they switch on the TV. Then the kid comes in and gets shit. He gets a slap in the face."

Meca's little fiction poses in revealing terms the relation of these youths to the system of bourgeois order and incentives that surrounds them. Un-like Juan in *Hooligans*, who stood in a similarly contemplative situation before the image of the city, Meca's generation no longer possesses even the illusion of the possibility of material achievement. Instead, they have absorbed only the grotesque surface features of that illusion: an obsession with cars, and drugs. In a postmodern Spain bereft of history, where time is only the "nowness" of the moment, individuality is a continuing form of self-gratification. But in presenting that contemporary ahistorical circum-stance, Saura continually stresses the paradoxical ways in which these youths embody the rejection of middle-class norms and yet are caught up in the acquisitive activities that middle-class culture promotes.

He situates them within a landscape in which the desires of that new, dislocated generation are seen as a threat to, but also, paradoxically, the consequence of, the bourgeois social structures that produced them. Speaking of the intricate web of relations he has elaborated in *Hurry, Hurry!*, Saura says: "The contemporary world of juvenile delinquency is one which implicates youths in a social system . . . which shows its inability to solve its own problems. [It is] A system—and here we're not making reference to 'capitalism' but only to its basis in a peculiar conception of 'industrial progress'—that induces one to acquire things that are difficult to pay for, at the same time that it generates unemployment, and therefore delinquency; with a repressive apparatus—the police—catapulted by its own social dynamic and incapable of assuring public order without stifling individual freedom" (Harguindey 1980, 19).

Aggressors

This conflict between social classes and generations is narrativized in the relation of the characters to the middle-class ethos, implicating the bour-geois spectator within the fabric of the film. The first sequence following the credits establishes this paradigm. The camera begins by panning across the windshields of cars parked along a quiet, residential street. It pauses in front of a car in which Pablo and Meca are seated, Pablo furtively eyeing the surroundings, apparently as a lookout, as Meca fidgets with the ignition wires in an effort to start the engine. Sustaining the camera position from outside the car, with the reflection of trees and clouds on the windshield glass, Saura reminds us that we are on the outside of the enclosures that define the locus of action of the characters.

The camera cuts to a man and his family coming out of an apartment building near the car. In stunned surprise, the man realizes that the two youths are attempting to steal his car. He runs over and shouts for them to stop. Other passersby gather around the car; another car blocks the road so that the youths cannot drive away. The car owner shouts for someone to call the police. Pablo, in brazen contempt, pulls his gun out at the mention of the police and threatens to shoot the man. The group backs off. Meca finally gets the engine started and the car jets along the sidewalk as the youths make their getaway.

Interestingly, the discursive frame through which the narrative is initiated locates the spectator in the place of the bourgeois "victims" of urban crime, outside the car with the irate, middle-class witnesses. This strategy is quite similar to the precredit scene in *Hooligans* in which the blind lottery seller is assaulted. As in *Hooligans*, subsequent action will rebalance the equation by bringing the spectator into the minds of the aggressors and thereby opening up the notion of victimization to broader social and cultural questioning. It is Saura's specific intention in *Hurry, Hurry!* to humanize the youths who are traditionally portrayed in the news media as aggressors: "What is radically destroyed is that gross and repugnant newspaper concept, that way of stating that four robbers held up such and such a bank and never mention who those kids are in human terms" (Hidalgo 1981, 21).

Gradually, the narrative introduces characters who bear social and iconographic traits associated with the "victims" of the first sequence but who are made to appear as the real aggressors of the story. In an early scene, for instance, the youths visit the Sacred Heart of Jesus monument, just south of Madrid, that designates the geographic center of Spain with an imposing monument of Christ. When a National Police car approaches the monument, Pablo tells the girls to separate and remains with the boys for the expected police harassment. Their suspicion turns out to be correct, as the officers line them up against a wall and begin a body search. "Fine democracy we have here," Meca mumbles as as the police search him. He well understands the logic of the system. They have been stopped, not because of any particular wrongdoing, but simply because, as young people, they are assumed to be troublemakers. In this symbolic space, the geographic center of the old Catholic Spain, we see clearly the clash between two generational perspectives and the way in which the youths are viewed with suspicion and mistrust.

In the final scenes of *Hurry, Hurry!*, as Pablo lies prostrate in the apartment, Angela turns on the television for news of the robbery. The news coverage reinforces Saura's vision of the dehumanized treatment of the youths. We first hear the final words of the news anchor's report about the pope: "Even though the content of the papal message is secret, it is suggested that again he expressed his concern about the Catholic schools in Iran and the fate of the Catholic minority in that country." The contrast between the Church's concern for some and society's insensitivity toward others is the implicit message for the spectator of the report that follows. The announcer gives only scant details about Sebas, showing an identification photograph and merely naming him. The rest of the coverage emphasizes the bloody death of a woman who called the police from a telephone booth near the bank, and, ironically, became another victim of the indiscriminate crossfire that ensued.

The report concludes with footage of angry protests by citizens who demand better police protection and vengeance for the bloodbath. This image of middle-class Spaniards, framed by the television screen in Angela's apartment, connects with the opening scene of the first car theft. Saura has inverted the visual perspective, however, so that the deformed, caged creatures are not the robbers, but the respectable citizenry who appear as the real aggressors. Angela, who has been watching the program while waiting futilely for the doctor's return, gets up and turns the set off and sobs, "That son-of-a-bitch. What is he waiting for? He should be coming. He should be coming." The doctor, though absent, is also part of that chain of aggressors.

Another Landscape

While Saura's sympathies for his four protagonists is never really in question, *Hurry, Hurry!* is not a Spanish reworking of *Bonnie and Clyde*. As in so many of his earlier films, his approach is to understand and to illuminate the terms of the causes of that victimization. As in the obsessive linking of the family and the house in *Mama*, the questions of the individual and the social environment are thus inseparable in *Hurry, Hurry!* The strong identification between character and the mise-en-scène of the nightmarish Madrid of the eighties is one of the film's unspoken pivotal themes and, as well, a Saurian explanation of the characters' action and motivations.

Though the film begins in the type of quiet, middle-class neighborhood Spanish directors over the last twenty years have so often used as setting, the camera almost immediately moves us into what had been up to this point in Spanish film an unimaged dystopian view of Madrid as a kind of European Los Angeles.[2] In Pablo and Meca's getaway from the site of their car theft to the sprawling city expressway, lined with massive high-rise buildings, we are introduced to a space of action that both situates the characters and their story and also hypothesizes a relation between individuals and their environment.

In the recurrent motifs of dystopia—the monster of the city as viewed from various angles, the gang's passion for speed, their identification with cars and robberies, and the images of the debris that surrounds the urban jungle—we read a deeper scenario that connects the destiny of the aggressors and of their victims to the larger cultural scenario of the city. One of the earliest visual expressions of that scenario comes in the sequence that locates Paco's room in a small, older building in one of the blighted areas to the south of downtown Madrid. From a panoramic vista of urban sprawl, the camera cuts to a shot of an alley near one of the older buildings, then zooms to a window where a potted plant stands in solitary contrast to the inanimate and dehumanized environment that surrounds it. The window shade is lifted, and we cut to an interior shot of Angela watering the plant. Her identification with flowers and plants, both in Pablo's room and later in the couple's apartment, is a quiet statement of what must seem an incongruous aspect of Angela's nature. But it also brings to the foreground the pervasive pattern of encirclement of naturalness by sterile artifice.

This early-morning view of Pablo and Angela in their "home" environment will introduce a series of scenes in which dramatic action is secondary to the characterization of cultural spaces. These include the visit to the Sacred Heart of Jesus monument, a horseback-riding excursion that brings the group to a location where Pablo and Meca used to play as small boys, finally to the village where Pablo's grandmother now lives. Each of these scenes poses the essential questions of the individual's place and perspective within the fragmented metropolis as the gang members live out the fantasy of their own autonomy. During the visit to the Sacred Heart monument, for instance, the youths stand looking at the monument and question the source of the bullet marks that scar its surface. "Who did that?" Meca asks two elderly middle-class women who are nearby. "The Reds during the war," one woman answers, to which Meca queries, "Which war?" Not even the Civil War, which was the emblem of other decentered Spaniards, holds any meaning for this generation. Bereft of any form of

---

[2] Earlier in *Cría!* the shots of the city began to suggest the same urban nightmare. In José Luis Garci's thriller, *El Crack* (1981), we get a few shots of the smog-laden and traffic-clogged city, but nothing as panoramic or with the same critical intention as Saura poses here.

historical consciousness, they cannot identify with any of the cultural or historical forces that have given a center of coherence to the old Spain.

We gain a better sense of the coordinates of their generation's spatial and temporal consciousness in the next sequence, the horseback-riding excursion, which opens with a shot that appears to be taken right out of an American western: A bold-print sign reading "Kansas City" is seen as Pablo and Meca, mounted on horseback, ride into camera view. The group of five youths, the original gang members and Sebas's girlfriend, has come to a riding stable somewhere outside the city. To add to the chaotic juxtaposition of artificial landscapes, the party, all mounted precariously on their horses, proceeds outside the riding academy grounds toward the edge of a four-lane highway where trucks and cars have been stopped by a pedestrian cross light. The visual disorder is further heightened as the group crosses the highway and enters a dirt path across what appears to be an open field. As the five head toward a shady grove, the camera picks up a closer image of the field strewn with refuse and construction debris. Meca stops his horse to point out to his companions the place where he and Pablo used to play as children. "Of course, it was much cleaner then," he says, as the others laugh. The group dismounts and settles down to snort cocaine, all except Angela who retains her status as the outsider within the group; she neither drinks alcohol nor takes drugs.

The cinematic treatment of space as a chaotic continuum of radically juxtaposed artificial and contaminated environments emphasizes the lack of a cultural or historical coherence for these characters. We are witnessing, in effect, the results of the loss of a cultural or affective center for Spain. This is the logical destination of the cultural itinerary that the youths began at the monument to the Sacred Heart of Jesus. The identification of this landscape, contaminated by the refuse of a consumer society, as Meca's birthplace and the locus of his and Pablo's childhood experiences implicitly postulates the actions of these characters as additional "waste products" of this irrational postindustrial order.

In the very next scene, Pablo and Angela talk of what they hope to do with their share of the robbery money. Pablo wants a car; Angela wants to go to the sea and then to buy a new apartment for the two of them. Significantly, while rejecting the moral, religious, and political values of the dominant social order, these characters reaffirm the consumer society's acquisitive ethic. The deforming nature of that consumerism is pointedly demonstrated in the very next scene in which we see the couple arriving in a new red car at the home of Pablo's grandmother in a barren Castilian village. Pablo has come to fulfill his grandmother's fondest wish by bringing her a gift of a huge color television. The television set, which in subsequent scenes will be metamorphosed first into the bank surveillance system and then into the television screen on which Angela learns of Sebas's death, comes to symbolize the alienating relations that have shaped the social fabric of Spanish society over the recent decade. The center of gravity of Spain is no longer a religious monument, but a television monitor that shapes the desires, the identities, and the values of its audience.

If the landscape of this new Madrid is unfamiliar and deceptive, so too are its sounds. Perhaps the most striking textual element of *Hurry, Hurry!* is its use of a musical sound track with nearly a dozen different contemporary popular recordings by the Spanish rock group Los Chunguitos. From the start, Saura draws our attention to sound as the bearer of a more stable meaning than the visible world can provide characters or spectators. Rythmically, the pattern of the youths' impulsive action is coded by the sound track beginning with "Ay, que dolor" (Oh, What Pain!), the diegetically rooted title theme which Meca insists on playing on the radio tape decks of all the cars he steals.

The music that accompanies the car's trajectory from the middle-class neighborhood where the car was stolen to the expressway that situates them within the urban sprawl first appears to be conventional background music unmotivated by anything within the cinematic space. The first hint of the ambiental motivation that is progressively shaping the action of the characters comes as we discover that the music emanates from the stolen car's tape deck and that Meca insists that his actions be "orchestrated" by this same melody. Particular melodies appear to situate characters in a "mood," as suggested by Meca's playing the ballad "Erase una vez una mariposa blanca" (Once upon a Time There Was a White Butterfly) when Pablo first eyes Angela or the two discotheque scenes in which the gang members gather to get high on drugs. In other scenes, such as Pablo's and Angela's vow of eternal fidelity, we hear "Me quedo contigo" (I'll Stay With You), whose lyrics follow the romanticized theme of a lover's promise of fidelity and serve to underscore the clichés of the star-struck couple. At the film's end it functions in precise contrast to Angela's actions, suggesting that she has finally lost her romantic innocence.

Because so much of the music on the sound track is diegetically motivated, we begin to discern that at least some of the young gang's actions are not as spontaneous as they might at first appear, but are rather formed by the music they hear. The source of Saura's interest in the relation between music and character motivation goes back to the Aranjuez sequence in *Garden of Delights*, where Antonio Cano's wife tried to motivate his thoughts through background music by Rodrigo. The implicit message in that instance was that an unseen source could actively shape the thoughts and actions of the character. Saura returns to that same notion in *Hurry, Hurry!* to reveal a new dimension of the postmodern landscape. By focusing on the potential motivational conditioning of music on the characters, Saura gradually leads his audience to recognize the four gang members as performers within a social space. Their very improvisational status has been circumscribed by the patterns of a diffuse social apparatus which contains them within the illusion of their own freedom of movement. What at first appears to be the spontaneous action of the protagonists is gradually shown to be a set of conditioned responses which insistently emanate from the songs that fill their heads. This is most strikingly the case with Meca, but it also appears to shape the outlook and perspective of Pablo and Angela as well. In this respect, the personal milieu of the characters—drugs, music, cars—is at one with the larger postmodern mise-en-scène within which they move.

Angela Is the Protagonist

At the center of the action of *Hurry, Hurry!* stands the figure of Angela. Though apparently denied the kind of status as enunciative agency that might signal her centrality to the narrative, as was the case with other of Saura's female protagonists, such as Ana in *Cría!* and Elisa in *Elisa, My Life*, she nonetheless embodies the polemical force of Saura's argument. Her presence and, in particular, her piercing gaze, constitute a discursive resistance to the dominant forms of cultural coherence she observes. Through Angela's "look" and actions, Saura engages his audience in a reflection on their own position in relation to the culture of marginalization.

The film's action obviously begins before her first appearance, but it is Angela's presence that structures subsequent action. Tellingly, when Pablo first sees her in the bar, her image is accompanied by the jukebox melody "Once upon a Time There Was a White Butterfly," as if invoking the fictional story that will transform what might otherwise have been simply a documentary into a Saurian meditation on the status of individuality. Tellingly, what follows that first melodic/scopic fascination between Pablo and Angela is an adolescent love story: the female's fall from innocence (On the first night they spend together she tells Pablo that she is still a virgin); her education in the uses of firearms; the formation of the gang; and her transformation into a cold-blooded killer. To underscore her importance, Saura makes Angela the lone survivor of the ill-fated bank robbery. In the final scene, when she leaves with the duffel bag filled with money, we are brought to sense that with her disappearance into the black night of the city, we have also witnessed the birth of yet another generation of Spaniards, spawned by the intricate interplay of social and individual fantasies.

Angela embodies all the lessons Pablo and the others have taught her, as well as those that "society" in the persons of the chain of aggressors has provided. In a totally original way, *Hurry, Hurry!* repeats the basic postures of Saura's earlier films of repressive education, the shaping of the character's social identity by bringing him or her to internalize the system of values and motivations of the larger social community. Only here the formula is given more potency, for Angela's move back into the city in the final image disturbs the notion of a simple narrative closure to the film while forcing the audience to reflect on the monster of its own, that is to say, society's making. Saura's final provocative message is clear: Angela is the product of a form of negative creativity: the narcissistic creation of a new Spain which does not or cannot identify its own progeny. Her story is interwoven into a contemporary history in which the Spanish spectator is made to acknowledge his own complicity within the intricate "system" as Saura calls it.

Hurry, Hurry! proved to be a critical and financial success rivaling Saura's previous triumphs. Winner of the Golden Bear at the 1981 Berlin Film Festival, the film opened to excellent reviews in Madrid and proved to be Querejeta's largest-grossing production of the fifteen years of his collaboration with Saura. Yet the film was also ensnared in a curious and even ironic controversy. In France and West Germany there was talk of its being banned due to the view that Saura was glorifying violence and the drug culture. Eventually, however, it was released with restrictive classifications (over eighteen) in both countries.

Dulces horas (1982: Sweet Hours)

Buoyed by the critical triumph of *Hurry, Hurry!* at the Berlin festival, Saura began working on a new script which he described to one interviewer as ". . . the story of a man who simply takes refuge in the past. . . . He is an individual who realizes that the present is bad and so is the future, and he decides to return to the time when he was fifteen years old, the age when he was really happy. It's a reconstruction of those years" (Hidalgo 1981, 22). The project Saura described sounded to many like a return to the familiar ground he had covered in his films of the early seventies, especially *Cousin Angelica*. Yet, *Dulces horas* (1982: Sweet Hours) differs from those earlier films precisely in terms of the changes in Spaniards' attitudes toward the past during the intervening decade. Not only does the film play against the "cult of nostalgia" that emerged in Spain in the early eighties in many quarters, but Saura also conspicuously parodies his own earlier cinematic obsessions in the process.

Though this project had been in the planning stages for at least four years (Sánchez Vidal 1988, 165), *Sweet Hours* reveals a conceptual affinity to *Hurry, Hurry! Hurry, Hurry!* was a film about Spaniards bereft of history, who had been shaped in their outlook on the world in terms of an ahistorical consciousness. Now, mocking his protagonist's impulse to recede into a constructed illusion of his childhood, Saura depicts the opposite condition: the Spaniard's distorted idealization of the Civil War and postwar years as "the good old days." At the center of the plot is a series of remembrances, specifically the bombing of Madrid and the desperate winter of 1937. But while outwardly these appear similar to the earlier evocations of this period, Saura now deploys what he knows in 1982 to be the cliché of the war years in order to expose a new mythology that has reshaped the war into an aesthetic mold, transforming the national tragedy of death, destruction, and privation into an idealized golden age. Though clearly rooted in historical events, many of which were recorded in Saura's own brief memoir of the period (Saura 1978, *Recuerdos*), the implicit notion of history that informs *Sweet Hours* lies elsewhere, in what Fredric Jameson calls postmodernism's "cannibalization of historical images and styles" (Stephanson 1988, 19).

The fact that so much of *Sweet Hours* is recognizable as a Saurian self-parody begins to alert us to the film's vision of Spain: Old forms remain, but their meanings have changed radically (Hopewell 1986, 160). Even Saura's protagonist, Juan Sahagún (Iñaki Aierra), reminds us of Luis in *Cousin Angelica*, but, importantly, a Luis devoid of any tragic demeanor. He is a comic hero, a modern-day Oedipus, trapped somewhere between a parody of Freudian libidinal desire for the mother and a Sophoclean quest for the truth about his own origins. Indeed, nothing in Juan's words or memories can bring one to take seriously his emotional plight. He is clearly an amalgam of the tortured heroes of Saura's previous war films: He echoes Enrique's inquiries into the past, Antonio Cano's reveries, Luis's traumatic memories of bombings, and countless other Saurian remembrances of things past. Yet he lacks the kind of psychological energy that such a rich genealogy might suggest. Rather, he seems to function less as a psychologically motivated character than as a device to undo the effects of a deformed historical consciousness by using all the elements of that deformed consciousness to "reconquer some genuine historical sense" (Stephanson 1988, 19). Through Juan Sahagún's misguided infatuation with the past, Saura brings his audience to question the film's real theme of gravity: the roots of the contemporary Spaniard's misinterpretation of his past.

Saura makes Juan a writer, and this identity, combined with the cinematic self-reference to earlier Saura films and the confessed coincidences of some aspects of Saura's own childhood experiences with those of the protagonists, led Spanish critics to read the film as simply an embarrassingly autobiographical work that presented some of the most intimate episodes of the director's life. Yet, while some details of Saura's childhood are worked into the script, these coincidences operate to bring to the foreground the film's allegory of authorship, the suggestion that, like the Sahagún character, each spectator of *Sweet Hours* is also simultaneously the author, spectator, and performer in the drama of his own life. If the real-life Saura suggests a parallel to Sahagún, such a coincidence seems to work only to reinforce the invitation to the audience to consider their own relation to their memories in much the same way.

Displaced from what he had been taught to believe was his authentic past, Juan follows a retrogressive, romanticizing impulse and constructs his own "sweet hours." In the process, he is abetted by others who, like the actors he hires to rehearse the autobiographical play he has written, are similarly predisposed to cling to, even fetishize, a past that never was quite as attractive as they imagine it. In this regressive reverie, Saura focuses on what may well be the essence of that strikingly anachronistic impulse in Spanish culture: the urge to suppress within the weave of a familiar past the uncertainty of an uncharted present.

As a writer, Juan has come to adulthood harboring what his sister Marta (Isabel Mestres) feels is a dangerously false notion about their mother who committed suicide years earlier and whose memory Juan idolizes. In order to dispel her brother's errors, Marta gives him the correspondence between their parents written during the period in Juan's childhood when his father was in Argentina on business, eventually to take a lover there and abandon his family in Spain. Marta is certain that these letters will alter her brother's image of his saintly mother by revealing the domineering matriarch who, far from being a martyr, actually drove her husband to abandon her. Confirming Marta's view, the letters also trigger other memories for Juan and provide him with material for a theatrical reconstruction of key moments from his childhood.

He writes a play entitled *Sweet Hours*, the title taken from a popular Imperio Argentina song of the thirties, and hires actors, even a director, to stage the play for him in the very Madrid apartment where he lived as a child. Juan saves the central role of Juanico, aged ten, for himself, though he is now a man of forty. At prearranged times he goes to the apartment and "relives" his childhood with the help of the assembled cast of family members. The intimate autobiographical theater never really gets very far, for Juan quickly becomes enamored of Berta (Assumpta Serna), the young actress playing the role of his mother. He is so infatuated with her that, during moments of reverie induced by the theatrical vignettes that the group performs with him, Juan images Berta in the role of his mother in the recalled scenes from his childhood.

Outside the rehearsal periods, Juan explains his nostalgic dilemma to Berta: He loved his mother and has come to realize that without her the present and the future hold no interest for him. That is why he cherishes "las dulces horas de ayer," the sweet hours of yesterday, as mentioned in the Imperio Argentina lyric that haunts his memory. Eventually, Berta is able to get Juan to give up his belief in the power of the past as he recognizes that his loving mother was an egotistical woman who, as his sister said, manipulated his will even after her death.

The process of Juan's understanding of his misrecognition of the past is the pivot of the film's narrative trajectory. Harboring the false notion that he was somehow responsible for his mother's suicide, he recalls the day she received the letter from her husband telling her that he was leaving her for another woman. Teresa (played in all the retrospective scenes by Assumpta Serna) sent Juanico to the pharmacy to obtain the poison with which she was to take her life. The innocent ten-year-old stood by watching as his mother took the poison. That scene of his bearing witness to her death after having supplied the weapon tied the Gordian knot that would establish Juan's sense of guilt and complicity in his mother's death throughout his adult life. Only after his convoluted theatrical-oneiric peregrinations back to that moment does he understand that his "bearing witness" was only his mother's final cruel manipulation of him, which has bound him to a false notion of his own past ever since.

Constructed Nostalgia

Though the Civil War is an important historical intertext of the film, Saura's interest in the topic of the war are no longer political. Rather, he uses the imaging of the war to expose the more expansive aesthetic and emotional recoding of the past in popular cultural memory that has distorted the contemporary Spaniard's notion of national history. To underscore what might be called the false oral history that has contributed to this misrecognition of the past, Saura continually draws our attention to the evocative power of sounds and voices in general and to the music of the period in particular as the signifiers of constructed or distorted meanings.

The film's title, for instance, comes from a song, "Recordar" (Remember), by the popular singer and actress, Imperio Argentina.[3] The lyrics of "Recordar" fetishize the fond memories of a bygone love and a romantic past. But more importantly, Argentina was herself the popular symbol of that romanticized past. Unquestionably, the most popular film actress of the prewar years, in films like *Nobleza baturra* (1934: Rustic Nobility) and *Morena Clara* (1936: Clara, the Brunette), both directed by her husband, Florián Rey, she seemed to capture a notion of what Spaniards of all classes and political persuasions accepted as folkloric authenticity. With the out-

---

[3] Saura had already used several Imperio Argentina recordings in earlier films. "Rocío" (Dew drops) is an erotic leitmotif in several scenes in *Cousin Angelica*; "Ay, Mari Cruz" is played in *Cria!* as Ana's grandmother recalls her youth, and the same "Recordar" is heard as background music in the first sequence of *Garden of Delights*.

break of the war, Argentina, following her allegiance to the Nationalist cause, went to Berlin to make a number of Spanish films at UFA (Universarum Film A.G.), the most notable of which was *Carmen, la de Triana* (1937: Carmen, the Girl from Triana). Her voice and the repeated strains of *"Recordar"* in *Sweet Hours*, thus hold a double message: On one hand, they evoke the idealized past for Juan and the audience; on the other, they signify the ideological appropriation of that constructed cinematic illusion of a simpler, more folkloric Spain connected as it was historically to Nationalist cinema.

Though visually *Sweet Hours* ranks among Saura's most complex and labyrinthine plot structures, his narrative strategy is a relatively simple one: to dramatize the intricate process through which individuals have come to absorb as their own personal memories "constructed" or staged experiences of the past, at times internalizing experiences that are not even their own. As the plot suggests, the filter of those misrecognized memories is once again the family. As Saura has for so long insisted in his films, one learns to see the world through the images, words, and actions of one's family. For as much as we may believe that we have shed the outward marks of a previous generation's prejudices and foibles, the hidden legacy of the past reinserts itself through the sounds and images, often false ones, that we absorb and leave unquestioned.

To emphasize his thesis about generations and false consciousness, Saura includes a brief exchange between Juan and Marta in Marta's country house early in the film in which Juan's young nieces demonstrate the unchecked influence of former generations on individuals. The scene occurs on the terrace where, after the midday meal, Juan, Marta, and her husband are relaxing as Marta's two daughters, about ages seven or eight, are playing. Marta is in an advanced state of pregnancy and, in her nervousness about the conversation relating to her mother, she lights a cigarette. Her husband chides her for smoking while pregnant since it can have adverse effects on their unborn child. Marta ignores the comment. Meanwhile, her two daughters enter dressed up in their mother's clothing but with big pillows under their skirts, imitating their mother's pregnancy. The adults are amused by this improvised theatrical skit. The conversation then goes back to the theme of Juan and Marta's mother, and Juan makes a comment about Teresa's suicide. "Did Grandma commit suicide?" a questioning young voice from off-screen asks. Marta's husband again chides his wife, this time for mentioning the topic "in front of the children."

The entire sequence is constructed around the premise of the indirect influence of one generation upon another. The young girls' dress-up, for instance, introduces the idea of children's emulation of the adults' image and actions. More important, however, is the way Marta's daughter picks up the fact that her grandmother, whom she never knew, had committed suicide. The infomation enters her consciousness not as an experienced event, but as the result of an auditory influence that becomes part of a constructed impression of her own past even though she has not experienced it directly. Ironically, this scene in which we witness the creation of a new generation's memories of the past is also the beginning of Marta's demystification of Juan's notions of the past, as she gives him the letters that will eventually provide him with a revision of his childhood memories. The privileging of the auditory track throughout *Sweet Hours* finds its logical origins in this early scene in which the relation of sounds to memories is first dramatized.

Juan has been conditioned by his emotional bondage to his mother's memory to revere the past. That reverence is reinforced by a series of auditory cues, some of which, such as the Imperio Argentina melody, first heard on the sound track in the credit sequence, address the audience as well. As we witness Juan's extravagant reconstruction of his childhood, that auditory privilege gains even more prominence. His first visit to the Madrid apartment where the rehearsals of his memory play are performed is particularly revealing of his romantic bent toward the past. The sequence actually begins with a close-up of the letters written between his parents. As the camera scans the handwriting in close-up, the off-screen sounds of orchestral instruments begin to be heard. As they become louder, the images dissolve to a low-angle shot of bright, sun-filled sky broken only by the branches of trees. All at once we are in Retiro Park in the center of Madrid; the music becomes a lushly orchestrated Ravel waltz. Juan is located walking down the path toward the street which will lead him to his nearby apartment building. This use of discursive music is totally without precedent in Saura's films. We are situated in the recognizable Madrid of the contemporary period; yet that image, heavily coded by the convention of off-screen, cinematic music, connotes a romantic effect which appears to emanate from the character of Juan.

As Juan walks through the park he passes a small boy (Pablo Hernández) of about ten years of age coming down the path from the opposite direction who looks back at Juan as the two pass each other. We will later realize that this chance encounter was the inspiration for Juan's imaging himself as this very boy in his reverie of childhood. Just as the characters who populated Luis Cano's present in *Cousin Angelica* were transposed to his evocation of the past, so Juan Sahagún seems to be preparing for his memories by viewing people around him. The cardinal difference, however, is, as this moment suggests, that Juan seems to be consciously eyeing the "cast of characters" in the present for his memories.

When Juan enters the apartment, the maid informs him that his family is waiting for him in the living room and that they are angry because he is so late. We immediately grasp that, though an adult, Juan is being treated as though he were a small child of ten or eleven. He walks down a corridor reminiscent of similar scenes of nostalgic return in *Cría!* and *Elisa, My Life*, as strains of "Recordar" are once again heard. The Imperio Argentina melody, like the earlier waltz music, appears both to underscore Juan's reverie and to incite the real audience to a nostalgic regression as well. The ensuing sequence works on parallel levels of character and audience inducement to nostalgia through a series of dialogues and actions that involve a broad range of popular cultural references to the thirties and forties—the song, film titles, newspaper headlines. But as the scene quickly makes apparent, the inducement to nostalgia is boundless and uncontainable.

The actress playing the part of Juan's grandmother (Luisa Rodrigo) has trouble remembering her lines. Muddling through the dialogue, she often slips out of her role and reacts with her own recollections of the past. At one point, for instance, Juan explains that he was late because on his way home from school he went to the movies to see Rita Hayworth in *Gilda*. Instead of chiding him, the actress recalls having gone to see *Gilda* with her boyfriend when the film first opened in Madrid. Totally disruptive of the "effect" of Juan's reconstruction, the scene nonetheless dramatizes the force of identification with the past which holds sway over others besides Juan.

In a similar scene in the second rehearsal, the actor playing the role of Juan's uncle Angelito (Jacques Lelande), who was wounded at the Russian front as a member of the Spanish Blue Division, gets carried away with the discussion of his war wound and becomes delirious. He in fact has a small metal plate in his skull that is an injury totally unrelated to the conflict, but he is so befuddled that he imagines himself to have been wounded in the war. His antics disrupt the rehearsal, and the professional director who is also playing the role of Juan's uncle Pepe (Alvaro de Luna) suspends the session, lamenting that his actors keep confusing their own lives with art.

Sweet Hours, the play Juan has written for these hired actors to perform, and in which he is performer as well as spectator, is intended to have a similar triggering effect on Juan's memory. At key moments in the dialogue he will pause and go into a recollective ecstasy, visualizing scenes from his childhood that have been triggered by the words spoken by his actors. A case in point is when, according to the script, Uncle Pepe refers to *putas* (whores) in front of his grandmother and Juan remembers when his uncle took him for his sexual initiation at a Madrid brothel. In all these recollective scenes, it should be noted, the auditory power of the dialogue is the sole mechanism that triggers the evocation of Juan's memories. Those remembrances, however, are replete with misconstrued images. For instance, Juan imagines himself to be the boy he saw in Retiro Park in all these dreamed scenes, and his uncle Pepe in the brothel scene is imaged as the actor-director he hired for his play.

Most revealing of the transposition of characters from reality to staged memory is the imaging of Juan's mother. Teresa is evoked by his chance viewing of a young actress, Berta, on a Madrid street. Part of the reason he has concocted his elaborate private theater, we may deduce, is to be able to see her again. Berta's presence in the rehearsal contributes to one of the film's implicit gags: the depiction in Juan's reveries of what is assumed to be his confession of his incestuous desire for his mother as a small child. These "remembered" scenes of sexual desire between mother and son are evoked only when Juan is in close physical proximity to Berta during the rehearsal. But since the scenes this closeness triggers all include Juan's projection of Berta into the role of his mother, the audience's impression of a tale of Oedipal desire may well be only Juan's wishful fantasies about Berta in the present.

Cinema, History, Memory

The combination of staged and evoked memories of the past at first suggests a randomness to the film's recollective process. This impression is dispelled in the latter parts of the film as it becomes clear that the two prinicipal traumatic experiences of Juan's childhood are the Civil War aerial bombing of Madrid and his mother's suicide. The experiences are linked by Juan's status as involuntary and ingenuous witness to both and by the centrality of his mother's relation to him in each of these evocations. The link between the war and Juan's relation to his mother form a double myth of origin around which Saura establishes the interrogating energy of his film: the war, representing as it does in much current thought the origin of contemporary Spanish culture, and Juan's relation to his mother, the source from which his notions of himself have been stabilized in the present. At the source of those origins lies a vexing sense of the hero's complicity in his past that he cannot manage to disavow, just as he cannot seem to give up his sense of complicity in his mother's suicide.

We discover Saura's thinking in a critical two-part sequence which falls outside of Juan's little theater of life. The sequence begins when, between rehearsals, Berta invites Juan to watch her in her other job as a dubber for the Spanish-language version of American films. The stage is thereby set for yet another of Saura's simulations of the cinematic apparatus within the film, this time with particular focus on the synchronization of auditory and visual tracks. Juan sits in the back of a darkened auditorium and views the screen images while Berta and her co-worker read their script to coincide with the moving lips of the characters in the film being projected. The screen suddenly goes blank and a muffled shout is heard: *"¡Apaguen esa luz, apaguen esa luz!"* (Shut off that light! Shut off that light!) All at once the dubbing-room screen is filled with newsreel images of the German planes over Madrid, people running for cover in the streets, and then aerial bombings of the city.

The authentic newsreel footage elides into staged images of people fleeing a bombed-out building. Teresa and Juanico are identified among the survivors of the bombing. Juanico runs back into the smoke-filled building and returns cradling his dog in his arms. Later, when Juan has another remembrance of the blackest days of the war, he picks up the thread of this seemingly enigmatic memory, recalling his family sitting huddled in near-total darkness around a small table in their dining room during the terrible winter of 1937. Noises are heard from the animals in the nearby Retiro Park Zoo. Juan's mother explains that the animals have not been fed and are roaming loose in the park. Later in the scene, Juan is put to bed, but leaves a kerosene lamp burning in his room. An air-raid siren is heard and a voice calls out from the street below, "Shut off that light!" Juanico stares at the fluttering shadows on the darkened window in his room. Getting out of bed, he blows out the lamp and walks into the darkened hallway. The shrill sound of an approaching bomb is heard; then an explosion knocks the boy to the floor amidst smoke and debris.

Conceptually, this sequence parallels that of the school bombing in *Cousin Angelica*, a distanced re-viewing of a traumatic childhood memory of the horrors of the war in which the individual relives his vulnerability in the face of the ubiquitous, "off-screen" enemy. But here Saura has added a significant meta-cinematic dimension to the evocation of the past which implicates the real spectator in that revision process. Through the duplication of the material practices that produce the cinematic illusion—the synchronization of sounds with images as dramatized in the film-within-the-film—we observe the explicit strategy of constructed illusion as the source of the individual's positioning before and identification with images he has been made to see *as if* with his own eyes. By witnessing the act of dubbing a film, Juan is prompted to confront the source of multiple confusions related to the war years and emblemized in the off-screen call to "shut off that light."

The newsreels of the war hold a group of personal associations that relate to his family and the strong sense of loss and attack. In all these his mother appears as a central character. Importantly, through this set of mental associations triggered by the dubbing scene, he begins to locate the source of multiple personal confusions about the meaning of his own life as a conflation of external, collective history with the personal oral history supplied to him by his mother, which metonymically connects with the war and soon replaces it in Juan's mind. His move toward lucidity begins, ironically, with that off-screen call to "shut off that light," a pointed allusion to cinema as the locus of a chain of individual mystifications of personal and collective memories for the spectator. As Saura sees it, the subject, in culture as in cinema, has been immobilized by the weight of historical constructions: faulty memory, the voice of the family, and, finally, a naive acceptance of distorted forms of his personal history.

Illuminations

Within the plot of *Sweet Hours* Juan's relation with Berta seems like a personal escape from the cul de sac of his bondage with the past. She is, in a curious way, the figurative "voice of reason" who will dispel the distortions of his vision of the past, paralleling on the fictional level the function that Berta's literal voice serves for Juan in the dubbing scene, that is, as the demystifier of cultural representation. But Saura is aware that the idea of the cinematic "happy ending" is itself a mere cultural construction which has been taken as an illusory possibility in life. To draw attention to this cinematic effect on the audience's way of imaging their own past, he includes two impossible scenes of cinematic excess in the otherwise rational structure of *Sweet Hours*. These are two gaps in the text that cannot be naturalized within the illusion of Juan's staged or unstaged life, but instead, address the audience on the margins of their consciousness of the lure of their own seductively "sweet hours."

The first is a curious anti-memory occurring even before Juan is born, in which his father and then-pregnant mother are walking along the edge of the lake near the Crystal Palace in Retiro Park. They pause for a moment and Teresa, touching her abdomen, says that she is so happy that she wants the son she is carrying to always remember this place, this lake, these ducks. Her husband scoffs at his wife's incurable romanticism: "Tell him to pay close attention to everything he isn't seeing," he retorts, "this lake that's artificial, this crystal palace that is a bourgeois abomination, these ducks who are dying of hunger." "Yes," insists Teresa.

The scene is a curious and suggestive one on various levels. The formal question of whose recollection this could possibly be brings us to realize that all the other scenes have been either the script of Juan's play, or else his own memories. This scene, however, is discursively uncontainable by the yet-unborn Juan. So, addressed to the spectator as a gap in the text, it will become a key to our understanding of Teresa's transcending manipulation of her son, described by Marta as influencing Juan even after her death. Here, of course, the droll suggestion is that she started to control his memory even before his birth. The voice of Juan's father in this scene addresses the falsification that for him is synonymous with the bourgeois sweetness and bogus nature of such false memories. If Juanico remembers this moment, it is only because Teresa has described it to him in such detail that he imagines that it was really his own memory. In obvious ways the Crystal Palace scene connects with the earlier scene in which Marta, also pregnant, gave Juan the letters that motivated him to write his play. As in his brother-in-law's annoyance that the children had overheard the talk of their grandmother's suicide, we are once again reminded that memories are constructed by what one hears as well as by what one sees.

The final sequence of the film repeats the motif of the pregnant woman. The sequence begins with a scene in which Juan takes Berta for a picnic to a bucolic location that he remembers having visited with his parents as a small child. She gently mocks his persistent efforts to fill his life with the reconstructed memories of his childhood. Confessing her love for him, she tells him he must confront the past. He willingly reimages the crucial scene of the poisoning, but he now seems to understand that he had been manipulated by his mother at that decisive moment. That reimaging is a nearly exact replay of the original poisoning scene, but with a few changes of angle to suggest that, from Juan's contemporary perspective, he recognizes that his mother positioned him to view her as the martyr to his father's infidelity.

To signify Juan's reconciliation with the past, Saura has him embracing Berta as the off-screen music of the Imperio Argentina melody swells. The little phantom Juanico appears from behind a tree and joins the couple in their embrace, thus nearly replicating the scene of the original picnic years earlier with Juan and his parents. The music continues to swell, as in a clichéd final cinematic flourish the image cuts away from the trio in the woods to a shot of Berta, now also in an advanced state of pregnancy, doing a perfect lip synchronization with Imperio Argentina's voice as the latter once again sings "Recordar." To underscore the point that the film, not life, has written this happy ending, Berta faces the camera directly in the fashion of movie musicals of the thirties and continues to mouth the lyrics of the song. She then walks through the apartment to the bathroom where Juan is bathing. Pausing in her musical rapture, she kneels to play with Juan as though he were a little child. She then concludes her song in a close-up, once again facing directly into the camera.

The spectator is left to reflect with irony on how cinema has once again constructed a false image and a false story ending for Spaniards. Addressing the spectator directly while flaunting the material practices of voice-image synchronization, the final scene prods us to reflect upon the patterns of collective nostalgia which converge to falsify images and thereby to construct an erroneous notion of the individual's relation to his world and to his past. Saura would have us understand that such falsifications are no less debilitating for being sweet and apolitical.

Sweet Hours opened to the most devastating reviews of Saura's career, with Spanish critics charging that the time had long since past for this kind of film and mocking Saura's efforts to cover up what they viewed as his bankruptcy of imagination with self-parody. The hostility of the public reception so stung Saura that he broke with his long-held position of not accepting offers to film abroad and agreed to collaborate with Jean-Claude Carrière, for many years Luis Buñuel's scriptwriter, on a project that would bring him to film in Mexico and France. That decision apparently concluded Saura's collaborations with Elías Querejeta, his sole producer over the preceding seventeen years. Though the break was, to all appearances, a cordial one, motivated by the offer from abroad, Querejeta does not hide his feeling that *Sweet Hours* was a mistaken idea as a film project from which he had disengaged himself almost from the start: "Although," he hastens to add, "that was not the reason for not going back to work with Saura again" (Hernández Les 1986, *Singular,* 89).

Antonieta (1983)

Saura accepted the Carrière project based on an already completed script, although he was eventually to modify some of the film's dialogue during the shooting. On the surface, that script had nothing to do with any of the particularly Spanish themes of recent years, although there were certain obvious similarities between some of his earlier films and *Antonieta*'s treatment of the relation between individual action and the destiny of the nation. Carrière's project was to involve a multinational co-production among France, Spain, and Mexico. The actors included an international cast headed by Hanna Schygulla Isabelle Adjani, and the renowned Mexican actor Ignacio López Tarso. The technical crew included Spaniards in key positions (Teo Escamilla as cameraman and Pablo G. del Amo as editor), while all the shooting was done on location either in Paris or in Mexico.

Carrière's script for *Antonieta* (1983) details the life of María Antonieta Rivas (Isabelle Adjani), daughter of the Mexican architect who designed the famed monument to Mexican Independence, popularly called The Angel. Born in 1900, Antonieta seemed always to be in the vanguard of Mexican artistic and cultural life. Through her father's prestige and influence, she was at an early age thrown into contact with prominent artists and intellectuals. After the revolution and the failure of her marriage, she immersed herself in a continuous chain of projects to Europeanize Mexican culture. She helped to found a symphony orchestra and was patroness of the Teatro Ulisis, an influential avant-garde theater group in Mexico City which first performed the works of Kafka and Cocteau for Mexican audiences. By her mid-twenties, Antonieta was an accomplished translator who also performed in some of the plays she translated. But with the strident xenophobia of the postrevolutionary period and the rejection of European ideas and styles, her accomplishments were ridiculed.

During the 1920s, Antonieta met and fell in love with the Mexican intellectual-turned-politician, José Vasconcelos. As his supporter and eventually his lover, Antonieta involved herself in Vasconcelos's fruitless presidential candidacy in 1929 which ended in defeat, due in large measure to the falsified vote count of the official government party. Disillusioned by the results, Vasconcelos and Antonieta departed for France where, two years later, she committed suicide, shooting herself in the heart in the middle of the Cathedral of Notre Dame in Paris.

The story of Antonieta's life is told through a series of flashbacks inspired by the activities of a contemporary writer, Ana (Hanna Schygulla), who is conducting research for a book on twentieth-century women who have committed suicide. Intrigued by the story of Antonieta Rivas, Ana flies to Mexico to investigate for herself the reasons for her death. The inquiry into the motivation for a suicide which occurred so many decades earlier is one of the more conspicuous narrative points that links *Antonieta* to *Sweet Hours*. But whereas Juan Sahagún explored an intimate and familiar mise-en-scène, Ana's trip to Mexico brings her into a world that is as mysterious and exotic for her as it was for Saura. Indeed, much of the potential emotional force of *Antonieta* is dissipated by the Carrière script which transforms Ana's investigations into an elaborate form of travelogue. That pitfall derives, in part, from the explicitly intellectualized conception of the inquiry Carrière and Saura propose: a questioning of the linkage between Mexico and Antonieta's struggle to alter the primitive and folkloric aspects of Mexican cultural life and to bring that culture into closer contact with what she perceives as a sense of civilization.

The reasons for Ana's initial fascination with the theme of female suicides is never given any dramatic or psychological basis; she is simply a writer compiling information for a book. This omission limits the emotional importance of her search and her findings. Ana's research puts her into contact first with a poet, now an old man (Ignacio López Tarso), who knew Antonieta intimately, and then with a historian (Héctor Alterio), whom she chances to meet on her journey to a nothern Mexican city where Antonieta and Vasconcelos campaigned in 1929. But even these characters are merely colorful interviewees, never transcending as human beings their pragmatic functions in Carrière's plot. Finally convinced that she has found the answer to Antonieta's suicide in the Mexican cult of death, Ana returns to Paris, goes to Notre Dame, and imagines herself viewing Antonieta's act of suicide in the cathedral.

Speaking of his reasons for breaking his long-standing position of not accepting prescripted films, Saura recalls: ". . . the script was very close to me; Carrière had done me an enormous favor in providing me with something I might never have thought of doing. Suddenly, I found myself with a script I would like to have written. In that it seems fantastic because one of my dreams has been to find a script that I wouldn't have to write myself, because for me writing scripts is a tremendously boring task, and it's very laborious" (Ciompi 1982, 33).

A number of visual, narrative, and thematic features of *Antonieta* evoke Saura's filmic signature. The most prominent of these is the visual/narrative play between the present and the past as the on-screen spectator, Ana, listens to her informants and projects her own mind-screen re-creations of Antonieta's life. Yet, there is a detached, rhetorical quality to these flashbacks. They do not arise out of Ana's psyche as much as from the need to illustrate her informants' words. In the first of these, as Ana questions a woman historian about Antonieta's family, the image suddenly cuts to the elegant home and studio of Antonieta's father as the young girl poses for the monumental sculpture of the angel. A visit by the dictator Porfirio Díaz to examine the progress of the monument he has commissioned ends when rebels start shooting outside the house. A wounded soldier enters the courtyard with blood staining his shirt; the scene ends with a close-up of the child, Antonieta, her face expressing a combination of fright and fascination with the blood. In Ana's mind, such an incident appears significant as the possible source of Antonieta's fascination with the idea of death.

The narrational coherence of such a scene, its reason for being dramatized in such an elaborate and detailed fashion, depends on establishing an initial correspondence between Ana and Antonieta beyond the obvious pedantic ploy of a researcher's investigation. But unlike much of Saura's previous work along similar narrational lines, the psychological motivation for such a flashback is absent, and with that absence goes a lack of any deeper interest in the visual representation of the flashback. There are no flaws of memory or confusions of past and present characters, only the obviousness of the device of filling in Ana's and the audience's knowledge through dramatized history. At their best, such scenes provide folkloric color to the film and "explain" in a simplistic sense what Ana had initially perceived as the enigma at the root of Antonieta's life. At their worst, as in the background to the Cristero revolt of the 1920s, they become unmotivated illustrations of Mexican history.

Where the film comes closest to an authentic Saurian theme is in the one scene when Ana is in the northern Mexican city of San Luis Potosí, from where Antonieta wrote one of her many platonic love letters to a Mexican painter. While standing in the very bedroom in the hotel where the letter was written, Ana conjures up her own fantasies of the past. She hears a typewriter in the room next to hers. Entering the room, she sees Antonieta sitting at a desk and typing. This is the kind of waking flashback that brought so much richness to the conception of *Cousin Angelica* and *Cría!*

Here Ana tries to touch Antonieta's face but discovers that the woman is only a figment of her imagination. Ana now walks to the open window of the room which leads to a balcony from which Vasconcelos is delivering a political speech to the crowd in the plaza below. She looks back at Antonieta, who has now moved to another table and has taken a revolver in her hand. She plays with the revolver in the same manner in which a group of men earlier in the film had played a version of Russian Roulette. As Ana views Antonieta, the voice of Vasconcelos is heard from the balcony.

Imagining herself poised between Antonieta and Vasconcelos, Ana reads that conflict into the imagined moment when Antonieta might have flirted for the first time with her own suicide. The coincidence between Antonieta's flirtation with death and Vanconcelos's apparent success as an orator and politician suggests the problematic dichotomy of female sexual and social roles. This polarity between woman as individual and as a phallocentric construction, however, never really approximates the depth of insight with which that same theme was treated in *Cría!* and *Elisa, My Life*. Is Ana imagining that Antonieta saw her own identity as being diminished by her lover's career and so contemplated suicide? The forceful visual rendition of that question, however speculative its premise in historical fact, does give us a sense for the first time of the energy of an important idea motivating Ana, the investigator's search. For here Saura captures more explicitly than he was able to do in *Sweet Hours* the need for the individual to interrogate the past, not only as a personal pursuit of meaning, but also as a revelation of the reciprocity of individual and cultural identities.

Despite its dramatic shortcomings as a film, there are a number of noteworthy features in *Antonieta* that merit attention. Foremost among these is Saura's first characterization of a strong, unproblematic female in Ana. Her engagement in the illumination of historical events and simultaneously in the deciphering of female consciousness prefigures some of Saura's key moves in *Carmen* and *El Dorado*. Yet the problems of *Antonieta* seem to far overshadow the film's suggestive feminist project, with even Saura reluctantly concluding that the casting of Adjani, a French actress, in the role of the Mexican Antonieta was a mistake (Saura, 1989). Not surprisingly, the result is that *Antonieta* remains a film not well appreciated either in Spain or Mexico, and largely ignored everywhere else.

Los zancos (1984: Stilts)

After the completion of *Carmen* in 1983, and while awaiting final decisions on the international coproduction of his long-dreamed-of film spectacle, *El Dorado*, Saura made what he defined as a "minor" film, *Los zancos* (1983:

Stilts), based on a script coauthored with Fernando Fernán-Gómez, the actor-writer-director who had played the role of Fernando in *Ana and the Wolves* and *Mama Turns One Hundred*. Fernán-Gómez was a noted writer and director in his own right, and would play one of the lead roles in *Stilts*. With a very small cast, as on the scale of the Querejeta productions of the sixties, *Stilts* has much of the intimist feel and introspective style of those earlier films, with one critical difference: It reveals a visual complexity and richness quite distinct from the sixties films. This is in large measure the result of Saura's extensive directorial experience since then.

Following the suicide motif of his two most recent nonmusical films, *Stilts* begins and ends with the image of an old man, Angel (Fernando Fernán-Gómez), attempting suicide. Despondent over the recent death of his wife, the aging professor attempts to kill himself by opening the gas valves in the cellar of his house. He is saved by Teresa, his neighbor (Laura del Sol). Teresa and her husband, Alberto (Antonio Banderas), have moved to the country to get away from the noise and pollution of the city. She is a schoolteacher, he a musician who also stages children's plays with his theater troupe. The group performs these plays on stilts, hence the film's title. To thank Teresa for her help, and also to remain in touch with her, Angel writes a play for the theater company, *The Melancholy Gentleman*. Though she at first resists his sexual advances, Teresa eventually gives in, but she soon cools to Angel as it becomes obvious that his passion for her will lead to a reckless affair. When he sees her through the garden bushes embracing her husband, Angel attempts a second suicide, but can't go through with it. He sits on the steps of his house and broods.

In the development of the film's central character, Angel, *Stilts* reveals a number of stylistic and thematic affinities with earlier Saura films. Perhaps the most central of these is the subtle generational theme which Saura's script extracts from *Cousin Angelica*. In *Angelica*, López Vázquez's extraordinary portrayal of the little boy in the body of a man was intended to drive home the political theme of the generation of Spaniards who suffered inner exile by not being able to confront the specters of the Civil War. Here the perspective is reversed by presenting Angel as a man who rediscovers erotic desires and feels himself more and more the youthful lover trapped in the body of an old man. The sensation is a painful one; for, just like Luis, Angel is continually reminded by the visual evidence that surrounds him that there is an unbridgeable time gap that separates him from his adored Teresa. The point of his two suicide attempts is the bitter recognition of the passage of time which has left him stranded between generations.

To some degree, Angel is fashioned after the character of another Luis, the reclusive father in *Elisa, My Life*. Like Luis, Angel is a literature professor; he quotes Spanish Golden Age poetry to express his contemporary vision of the world. He is also moved by a spiritual kinship with younger generations. In this sense, Teresa, who is young enough to be his daughter, and the schoolchildren who are the audience of the play he has written seem to be a reworking of Elisa and the students in the earlier film. But whereas the conceptual design of *Elisa* was the revelation of regeneration, *Stilts* presents a much more somber and pessimistic vision of human generations. The integral use of video within the narrative symbolically states that idea of the generational gulf. The credit sequence, for instance, shows Angel caressing the image of Teresa in slow-motion close-up on a video monitor. Later in the film we discover that Angel has taken the video tapings of the theatrical rehearsals to replay them in the privacy of his house in an attempt to sustain the illusion of his possessing Teresa. The postmodern video image of Teresa which he can touch but cannot truly possess reveals to Angel the impossible schism that separates the two.

It is tempting to read a symbolic cultural narrative into this film, connecting the gulf between Teresa and Angel with the cultural schism between new and old Spaniards. Indeed, Angel seems to embody the culture and learning that are slowly fading from the essential culture of contemporary Spaniards. Even the stilts of the film's title, taken from a Goya painting, symbolize in this respect the visual distance between Angel and his love and, by analogy, the gap between the "melancholy gentleman of the past" and a more invigorated, extroverted generation that finds itself unshackled by the crippling attitudes that Angel embodies.

The script and style of dialogue in *Stilts* owe much to Fernán-Gómez's presence. Angel is a theatrical character much in the spirit of Fernán-Gómez's own film creations. His dialogues, however—at least those with his young neighbor—further remind us of Luis in *Elisa, My Life*. This is true because there is a despondency in Angel's tone that finds its most eloquent expression in Spanish Golden Age lyric poetry. He quotes Quevedo's melancholy verses on death and decay to Teresa, who is much more comfortable with the lilting poetry of Shakespeare's Juliet. The antidote to that brooding comes in his children's play which we see Alberto's theatrical troupe rehearse and finally perform.

The theatricality of the stilt-players is introduced in the film's very first sequence as Angel broods over his wife's death and begins to relive memories of their past together. At one point, the camera lingers on the image of the garden wall as seen from the interior of the house. On the other side of the wall we see actors, obviously on stilts, walking past the house. The image is a surreal one, not clearly differentiated from Angel's melancholic reverie, nor illuminated yet by the details of Alberto's theater project. That image lingers to draw our attention to the world of fantasy that is metaphorically on the other side of the wall of Angel's life.

The theatrical motif, here the medieval fairy-tale productions that stilt-players performed, is quite unlike Saura's previous treatments of a play-

16. *Stilts* (*Los zancos*, 1984)

within-the-film. It is the ambiguous lure that moves Angel beyond his closed world, but eventually reveals to him that he has deceived himself. Theatricality, the use of play rehearsals and costumes, imparts a complex visual and thematic texture to *Stilts* that works in tandem with the self-conscious use of video. Through the pretext of the theater troupe's activities, two otherwise isolated individuals, Angel and Teresa, are brought together. His writing the play to be performed for small children at first suggests that theater can bridge the gulf separating individuals as well as generations. But as Angel's efforts to possess Teresa move her further and further away from him, the break between the generations appears visually restated in the stilts that Teresa and Alberto wear during the performance, for they dwarf Angel. The medieval music and pageantry of the performance, earlier read as a historical "bridge" that brings young and old together, becomes in retrospect the mark of the illusion that has led Angel into the garden of his own self-deception.

While every bit the "minor" film Saura described it as, *Stilts* is, nonetheless, a film that illuminates the darker sides of Saura's vision of the widening gap among generations of Spaniards in the eighties. Considerably more modest a production than *Antonieta*, as well as conceptually clearer and more accessible to Spanish audiences, *Stilts* still failed to elicit more than faint praise from critics when it was shown at the Venice Film Festival and, much like *Antonieta*, disappeared after a brief run in Spain.

Though radically different in focus, narrative style, and apparent subject matter, *Antonieta* and *Stilts* share a curiously similar attitude toward the theme of personal and cultural regeneration. The narrational focus in each film lies with the questioning of the tension between a sensitive, artistically creative figure and the social milieu from which she or he feels alienated. Each film thus seems a logical thematic extension of the cycle that began with *Hurry, Hurry!* and *Sweet Hours*. Though devoid of the obvious social referentiality of either of the two earlier films, *Antonieta* and *Stilts* still situate themselves within a spiritual landscape quite similar to the one that motivated those earlier works. Tellingly, in each of these minor films, the character's contemplation of death serves thematically to bring to the foreground the gulf that separates and finally robs him or her of the possibility of his or her own creative identity. In this, both films may serve as brief meditations on the larger Saurian theme of the individual's creative status within a radically changing world that has redefined the social and cultural centers of coherence for Spaniards. In all, the "reasoned optimism" in the individual's potential for liberating consciousness that had marked Saura's films of the late seventies has apparently shifted to a more pessimistic view of the isolating confinement of social and spiritual generations.

VII

Performers

A Flamenco Trilogy

UNLIKE any of Saura's previous projects, the three "flamenco dance films," *Bodas de sangre* (1980: Blood Wedding), *Carmen* (1983), and *El amor brujo* (1986: Love, the Magician) form a discrete unity set off from the rest of his filmography. Though certain of their themes and visual strategies clearly derive from his other films, the centrality of the dance element in these works and the appearance of members of the Antonio Gades dance company in the principal dramatic roles bracket these films off from the larger corpus of Saura's films of the eighties. The production of the three works covers a six-year period from 1980 through late 1985, a period punctuated by three other films: *Sweet Hours, Antonieta*, and *Stilts*. Yet despite their separation in time and their heterogeneous inspiration, the dance films constitute a unified and structurally organic whole.

The essence of that unity lies in Saura's inquiry into one of the most universalized and mythified expressions of Spanishness, the *españoladas*—the Andalusian folk and gypsy tradition glorified in the works of nineteenth-century romantic writers and painters, and exported abroad in theatrical, pictorial, and cinematic renditions. The sources of these mythic images of Spain are many and varied. They cover different genres and periods and focus on different aspects of Andalusian culture and folklore. Yet, unmistakably, the different strains of Andalusianism constitute an easily identifiable, perhaps to foreign audiences *the* privileged, iconography associated with Spain. This is the material Saura treated much earlier in *Lament for a Bandit* for which he based his research on Doré's illustrations of Andalusian customs and on the Prosper Mérimée travel diaries.

The principal focus of *Lament* had been the falsely seductive representations of Spain purveyed by foreign artists. Exoticized impressions of folkloric types were, in turn, cultivated by Spaniards in musical and pictorial forms over the next century, but never more energetically than under Franco's Ministry of Information and Tourism during the sixties. In the dance trilogy, there is no such simple focus sustaining all three films. Saura's attitude toward his sources varies from film to film, yet in all of them the specter of the falsifications to which the notion of Spain has been submitted by foreigners and by Spaniards alike remains present.

Equally constant, too, is the centrality of flamenco dance as performed by the Antonio Gades company and that of Gades himself as the protagonist of all three films. Part of the great originality of the flamenco trilogy lies in Saura's refusal to use the cinematic medium merely to record the performance of a dance company. Rather, he inverts the formula of the traditional dance film, exploiting its conventions to explore the formal problems of such representations as both staged and filmed events. The most insistent and indeed the most critical aspect of that problematic issue comes in the recurrent interplay of cinematic realism with the staged illusion in which the thematic clichés of the españolada fold back upon themselves and bring the spectator to question the various constructions of exotic or picturesque Spanishness.

Ultimately, it is not the outward, clichéd trappings of Andalusianism that we come to see as the unifying element of the trilogy, but rather Saura's characteristic impulse toward a lucidity about the familiar cultural artifacts that construct social and personal identity. For that reason, the centerpiece of all three films is the figure of *performance*: dancers playing the part of fictional characters who are bound inextricably to fatalistic scenarios; individuals whose identity as dancers is itself the result of a willed submission to a cluster of artistic and social mythologies; finally, the figure of the Spaniard as performer of a cultural ethos to which his own identity appears irrevocably bound.

This notion of the Spaniard as a performer of culture is in no way original with Saura. In 1927 José Ortega y Gasset, in a speculative essay on the Andalusian character, appropriately entitled "Theory of Andalusia," spoke of this same performative feature of Spanishness: "This propensity of the Andalusians to play act and mimic themselves reveals a surprising collective narcissism. The only people who can imitate themselves are those who are capable of becoming spectators of themselves, of contemplating and delighting at their figure and being" (Ortega 1961, 112). In Saura's collaboration with Gades, the Ortegan vision is expanded to embrace a broader notion of Spanishness, but its focus on the problematic nature of performance in culture remains curiously akin to Ortega's description nearly sixty years earlier.

Blood Wedding: Another Story of a Story

Saura's decision to make a film version of Federico García Lorca's folk tragedy, *Bodas de sangre* (Blood Wedding), thus seeming to break his long-standing resolution not to adapt works from other genres, was prompted by the insistence of his friend and sometime distributor of his films, Emiliano Piedra. While still preparing the script for *Hurry, Hurry!*, Saura at-

tended a private performance of the Gades company's ballet adaptation of
the Lorca play. From the start, Saura understood that Piedra was attempting to interest him in doing a film version of the Gades production, and so
he approached the invitation with considerable trepidation and pessimism
about the artistic possibilities of the performance, expecting to see a ballet
danced by stereotypical gypsies. What he discovered was, instead, quite the
opposite:

> Gades had prepared a "general rehearsal" just for me. For the occasion he only
> directed the performance and the part he normally would dance in the work was
> performed by another dancer. In the huge hall of the old building [of the Na-
> tional Ballet] redesigned for the ballet—an entire wall covered with mirrors, im-
> mense, elongated windows and high ceilings—the rehearsal of "Blood Wedding"
> was transformed into an unforgettable spectacle. For me it was a revelation. Ga-
> des had achieved what I had imagined was impossible to capture in Lorca's the-
> ater; and it all seemed so easy: He maintained the popular spirit of Lorca in the
> most profound sense of that word; there was a prodigious, rigorous integration
> of the story, the austere, tight ballet, and the music with its popular flavor. (Saura
> 1984, 49–50)

Saura readily agreed to a collaboration with Gades and Piedra on a filming of the ballet but had to postpone the project until the completion of
Hurry, Hurry! One of the problems that the three had to confront was the
question of the length of the proposed film. The Gades ballet ran barely an
hour and so had to be expanded in some way to bring it up to a duration
sufficient for commercial distribution. The idea was proposed to add a prologue of sorts as an approximation of the rehearsal Saura had witnessed.
This prologue would include members of the Gades company who would
be seen arriving at the rehearsal hall, preparing their makeup, and working
out in preparation for a dress rehearsal.

While adding a decisive "documentary" focus to the film, this prologue
was entirely consistent with Saura's conception of the rehearsal format as a
way of breaking through the clichés of the españoladas. It also enabled him
to draw from his earliest professional experience as a photographer spe-
cializing in photographs of dancers:

> Of the dance rehearsals what I most admired was the iron discipline, the preci-
> sion of movements, the grace acquired at times by continuous work, and, above
> all, the physical exercise, the sweat on the skin of the women who, on the day of
> the performance would dance as though they were some ethereal, pure maidens.
> Here in the rehearsals, though, everything seemed so prosaic: the sweat was
> sweat and the straining could be seen without any effort to disguise it. And that
> was what I liked. The ballet became something closer to me; it was humanized.
> The girls ceased to be inaccessible, transforming themselves into human beings

who got hot and sweaty as they covered their bodies in rehearsal with wool costumes. (Saura 1984, 50)

Thus the initial impetus of demystifying the Andalusian theme is immediately joined to the parallel theme of demystifying the dance and the dancers.

As Saura conceived it, *Blood Wedding* was to be the story of the dancers who, as members of the Gades troupe, are rehearsing a ballet adaptation of the Lorca text. Their story, in effect, frames the ballet and so shifts attention from a primary consideration of the folkloric narrative to a contemplation of the process of transformation of the dancers as individuals into members of an ensemble company, then into characters assigned to them in the dance narrative. The austere rehearsal hall setting, the suppression of dialogue, and, lastly, the camera's probing of the sweating bodies of the dancers in the rehearsal atmosphere all work to focus the spectator's attention on the multiple and parallel levels of performance operating within the film.

Though obviously filming a documentary of the rehearsal process, Saura would later admit that his approach was to treat the film as if it were a fictional one: "I said to myself from the first day: This is not a documentary. This is a fiction film and I have to handle it as such: with plot, a resolution, and an ending" (Chijona 1983, 39).

Lorca's Story and Its Transformation

Lorca's *Blood Wedding* plot is based on newspaper accounts and the widely circulated stories of a murder in the region of Níjar during the summer of 1928, which involved adultery and a family feud.[1] In Lorca's adaptation of the original newspaper report, there was an effort to cleanse the material of its original exploitative details and to situate the events within a more timeless traditional Andalusian culture without the usual folkloric trappings. In his version, a young woman, referred to only as the "fiancée," has had a liaison with Leonardo, who has abandoned her to marry her cousin, according to rural custom, for financial gain. As the play opens the fiancée is about to enter into an arranged marriage with the last of the clan that has been wiped out in a feud with Leonardo's family. The preparations for the wedding are clouded with ominous premonitions and foreboding, as characters are reminded of the fiancée's background and the tragic history of her bridegroom's family. These foreshadowings are realized in the play's

---

[1] See "La novia de 'Bodas de sangre' falleció ayer in Níjar" (*El País*, July 10, 1987: 30), which reports the death of the woman who was reputed to have been Lorca's inspiration for the tragic heroine of *Blood Wedding*.

swift action: Leonardo appears at the wedding festivities; he flees with the fiancée and is pursued by the groom and guests; the groom finds the couple, and the two men struggle in a knife fight—finally killing each other. At the end of the play three women: the fiancée, the bridegroom's mother, and Leonardo's widow, express hatred, sorrow, and loneliness, as a chorus of villagers laments the tragic events.

Lorca's text of *Blood Wedding* reflects the playwright's effort to transform what might otherwise have been a folkloric melodrama into an authentic folk tragedy. The essence of that narrative lies in its treatment of the codes of honor and revenge which, as part of a Mediterranean and more specifically Spanish cultural tradition, define social action in terms of primitive instincts. In the years since its first staging, that material has been progressively deformed in much the way Saura feared Gades's production would be—that is, with clichés of the españoladas which have arisen out of the pandering of Spanish companies to the foreigner's notion of Spanish culture. The Gades adaptation, already highly successful in performances in Spain and France, carefully avoids most of these pitfalls. If anything, Gades has intensified the theme of submission to social constraints and the instinctual rebellion of the individual by depleting the libretto of its verbal narrative and by focusing on the centrality of the human body as the locus of the drama.

Standing back from the Lorca script with its embrace of a classical tragic style, even from Gades's refinement of it, and looking for a way to circumscribe the story of the performance of that story into a film, Saura focuses on the body as the site of an institutional suppression of instinctual identity. While adhering to the spirit of Lorca and also of Gades, he introduces his own theme into the film: the questioning of the meaning of social performance and its relation to the ideology of artistic form that shapes performance as well as performers.

He does this by focusing on the figure of Gades throughout, first as the choreographer who directs his company in the preparations for a rehearsal of the Lorca play, then as Leonardo, the central figure in that play in rehearsal. Gades is thus at once both a spectator-in-the-text by virtue of his status as company director and also a metteur-en-scène, a choreographer-director. The audience is inevitably drawn to him as both the principal object of the narrative, and also as the locus of a number of crucial positions of meaning in both the fictional representation and within the theatrical space of the rehearsal hall.

As the bearer of an authoritative glance that controls the dancers' movements, Gades is implicitly figured as a dramatized authorial figure within the narrative, but one, ironically, whose authority is abridged by the fact that, as choreographer, he has internalized in a totally unself-conscious way the theatrical conventions that have stabilized the relationship of spectator to performance. This is, in effect, the meaning of his artistic identity as choreographer, and it will serve within *Blood Wedding* to shed light on the Lorquian world as well as the broader question of cultural performance. What is, at first, striking and perhaps paradoxical about this shaping of the Gades figure is the apparent contradiction between the perspective of the spectator and that of the performer. Standing metaphorically between the two, Gades leads us to recognize that there is indeed a conflict between these positions that has been resolved symbolically by an aesthetic masking of the institutional constraints on the dancers' bodies in the name of art. That resolution is, however, put under intense scrutiny by the film's structural transposition of the world of the dancers into the world of the characters they portray in the Lorca play.

A Transparent Mise-en-Scène

The film is divided into two major sections: The first is the arrival of the members of the dance company at the hall and their preparation for the rehearsal; the second is an uninterrupted run-through of the entire ballet performed without the aid of realistic settings, only the backdrop of the bare studio walls. Far from being merely the filler Piedra has asked Saura to supply, the first part of the film serves to bring into focus the process of transformation of the dancers that the film will ultimately chronicle.

The first shot after the credits is of the empty dressing room as viewed by a stagehand. We hear the approaching sounds of human voices as the dancers enter the studio in groups of two and three, moving to their makeup tables and beginning their preparation for the warm-up exercises. The scene runs about two minutes but establishes an important visual paradigm that will structure many of the scenes to follow: the filling of "empty" space with human activity and the transformation of that space into the site of isolated dramatic scenes.

In the second scene, the camera pans the makeup mirrors, presenting the first of the mini-transformations of characters as framed reflections, as viewed from behind each dancer's shoulder. The third scene focuses on Gades, who until this moment has not been clearly distinguished from the other members of the company. He sits and stares at himself in the mirror and begins to apply makeup as he gazes into the camera which, as in earlier Saura films, occupies the place of the mirror. A voice-over monologue by Gades provides autobiographical information about the dancer's childhood, detailing his moves from an early interest in dancing for his own amusement to his subsequent professional training and his contact with a number of noted Flamenco dancers. This individuation of Gades from the other dancers parallels Lorca's similar individuation of Leonardo, the role

Gades will perform, as the only character in *Blood Wedding* identified with a name. Saura's effort is clearly to establish through this device a suggestive "mirroring" effect between the world of the dancers and the roles they assume in *Blood Wedding*.

The fourth scene takes place in the stark rehearsal hall, directly adjacent to the dressing room of the first three brief scenes. There is a wall-length mirror on one side of the room from the direction of which much of the action of the warm-up and rehearsal will be shot. A direct extension of the dressing-room mirrors, this mirror will be treated self-consciously by the dancers from the moment they enter the rehearsing space. Looking at it, they are aware of their own image, thereby acknowledging for the spectator the sense of performance that surrounds all actions and character motivation in the film. Along another wall there are three sets of French doors, the windows of which are illuminated from behind by the strong sunlight pouring in. Stark and unadorned, as is the entire mise-en-scène, these doors serve a double function that is both visual and conceptual. The harsh and glaring light from behind will flatten and denaturalize the image of the dancers, giving their skin at times a waxlike quality and their features the look of mannequins. By shooting a number of scenes from the opposite wall, Saura will use the doors as a frame for his characters, suggesting the symbolic containment of individuals by transparent patterns of thought and social grouping. If the space of the dressing room established the paradigm of individuals filling in empty space, the rehearsal hall proper reveals the film's other major visual paradigm: that of individuals made aware of the constraining structures that entrap and denaturalize.

The significance of this mise-en-scène begins to gain prominence in the spectator's mind as Gades runs his dancers through some of their exercises, intended to limber up the group for the strenuous performance to follow. These exercises serve to orient the audience toward the process of transformation that the dance medium effects upon the dancers. Gradually shedding their individual identities, the dancers assume through the synchronization of their body movements with other dancers a new identity as members of an ensemble. In this sense, the first dance movements of the film, those simple warm-up movements of a *pasodoble*, performed by the dancers under the watchful eye of the choreographer, mark the exact moment when the dancers begin to submit their bodies to the conventions and discipline of dance.

Their submission to that series of conventions is occasioned by the presence of Gades as spectator of the dance; he is the ideal and ubiquitous audience whose very presence seems to give order to the dancers' bodies. But Gades is not the sole embodiment of an ideal spectator in the rehearsal room. Saura notes the importance of the dance mirror which serves a similar function: "This seems more like theory than anything else, and theory bothers me a lot, but the truth is that in ballet there is a very cinematic invention. The dancers don't know how to do anything without a mirror, and in function of that reflection, they do their exercises. When they become professionals, they spend hours on end trying to perfect themselves. They don't even need anyone to teach them. . . . We [the spectators] are always either a mirror in front of which they are rehearsing, or else an audience which is for them a kind of imaginary mirror" (Chijona 1983, 40–41).

The mirror is, as Saura understands it, a socially regulating apparatus for the dancer, facilitating movements and gestures by always implying the offstage presence of a social community which will valorize those movements and gestures. The deciphering of that figure of the apparatus in the mirror helps us to recognize the ironic similarity in structure, although as "mirrored" reversed reflections, of the dancers' submission to socially regulated movement of their bodies and the performance of the drama of characters who rebel against that socially regulated behavior.

Dance of Submission

The emphasis on the idea of a rehearsal rather than the completed public performance brings to the foreground the fact that the individual's submission to social regulation is not a spontaneous but rather a learned concept that must be rehearsed and perfected. This is an idea whose roots go back to the notion of the rehearsal in *Ana and the Wolves*. Here, of course, the theme of submission is further connected to the operation of an ideology of artistic form. We understand the individual dancer's desire to submit to the discipline of the dance as a positive cultural motivation, the popular notion of artistic creation masking the symbolic social significance of that submission. But the ironic paralleling of the artistic submission of the dancers to the fight against submission on the part of the fictional lovers they portray unmasks the register of scenarios of individual action shaped by social and cultural institutions.

The ballet adaptation of Lorca's play consists of six scenes that follow with remarkable fidelity the details of his original script. The work begins as the bridegoom's mother is helping her son dress for his wedding day. She discovers that he is carrying a knife and quickly disarms him. In the second scene, Leonardo's wife awaits her husband's return as she serenades their infant child. The only spoken words are the lullaby sung by Marisol which comes directly from Lorca's text. When Leonardo (Antonio Gades) arrives, the couple quarrels. Alone, Leonardo imagines the fiancée (Cristina Hoyos) preparing for her wedding day and dreams of making love with her. Gades underscores individual instinct as the source of motivation for the subsequent rebellious action of his two principal characters through a series of shots, first of each of the dancers separately as they dream about the other, then together as their dreams of carnal union "mirror" each other.

In filming this critical scene, Saura emphasizes the centrality of the body as the battleground on which the struggle between instinct and conformity to social regulation will be played out. Focusing on the individual bodies of the two dancers as they simulate lovemaking and embrace each other, the camera shows us at once the results of the dancers' submission to the discipline of the dance which, ironically, has enabled them to perform the fictionalized rebellion of instincts against the social regulation of that same body.

In the fourth scene, Leonardo arrives at the fiancée's house just as the wedding festivities commence. This is the longest and most elaborate scene of the ballet, involving not only the Gades troupe, but also a group of traditional Andalusian singers and musicians. The musicians play a paso-doble in honor of the newlyweds, and each guest pairs off with a partner. Leonardo arrives and eyes the fiancée with her new husband. The other couples dance around the room, while Leonardo cautiously circles the group in an apparent effort to approach the fiancée. She has taken note of his presence and her eyes remain fixed on him. At one point, the bride-groom initiates the gesture of changing partners and hands the fiancée to another guest to dance with. Seeing his opportunity to reunite with his former lover, Leonardo interrupts the pair and couples off with the fiancée. The two embrace passionately amidst the festivities.

This scene is a key moment in both the Lorca story and Saura's narra-tion. Within the Gades staging of Lorca's scenario, the dance of the wed-ding couples embodies the obstacles the community erects to constrain renegade desire. Leonardo's circling movement underscores that commu-nal interdiction. In order to achieve his union with his lover he must there-fore somehow disrupt the conventions of the dance. Saura underscores the importance of this crucial moment by means of a series of shots of Leo-nardo carefully circling the dancing couples. Taken from across the room, these shots place the couples in the foreground and Leonardo in the back-ground. In this way Saura is able to emphasize the symbolic truth that remains invisible to fictional characters and to Gades's company of players as well: Dance is a simulation of the process of containment and social subjugation of individual bodies and individual actions.

In the fifth scene, the bridegroom leads a group of men in pursuit of the fleeing lovers. During the rivals' struggle, the two enact a dance of death in slow motion. As they stab each other, the fiancée, her arms outstretched, appears behind them as though embracing the two bodies that symbolize what were once her two opposite destinies. Each man succumbs to the other's attack and both bodies slump to the floor. The camera cuts to a close-up of Leonardo's agonized face, then to the bridegroom's face, finally to a full shot of the scene showing the men's bodies now prostrate and immobile on the floor as the fiancée walks between them toward the wall-length mirror. She stares directly into the mirror and pauses. We can now discern the two bloodstains on her white dress, symbolically inscribing on her body the two alternate destinies that might have been hers.

This final image of the dance thus produces a logical point of closure to the story. But, importantly, it is an aesthetic rather than a psychological closure, affirming the values of tragedy and dance as artistic forms rather than the psychological reality of the doomed lovers or the adulterous triangle. As if to underscore that point, Saura inserts a final coda to the ballet: a group portrait of the Gades company in an ensemble photograph. That same group photograph has appeared twice before in the film: once as the background to the credits; then in the wedding reception scene. In the photograph, each character holds a stilted pose and acknowledges the way traditional ceremonial photography inscribes the presence of the camera in the very posture of the photographic subjects. During the reception scene, of course, these pronounced gestures were a way to simulate the act of taking a wedding photograph within the dance. But now, dislodged from that context, we can see how the photographic tableau reiterates Saura's underlying theme of the imposition of the collective norm upon the individual's body and mind.

But more than merely a repetition of those earlier thematic points, the photographic figuration of the dancers reinscribes the ideological effect of artistic forms in valorizing the social submission of the indiviudal as a positive, creative activity. Art, namely the dance, affirms as positive what might otherwise be read as the negative social regulation of the body which Lorca's tragedy chronicles. This naturalization of the social within an aesthetic design, and its consequent aggrandizement as "art," is the underlying constant of Saura's treatment of his source material. Like the strategies of lucidity, of standing back from one's life and viewing it as historical, the filming of the dance rehearsal opens up a similar margin of interrogation of the relation of aesthetic forms to the larger social fabric of Spanish culture.

In the terseness of Saura's film, however, these conceptual questions seem overshadowed by the impact of the dance narrative. *Blood Wedding* opened to excellent reviews in Spain and abroad, winning a special prize at the 1981 Cannes festival. Its commercial success, particularly in the U.S., where it was billed as a "dance film," led Emiliano Piedra to propose a second collaboration between Saura and Gades which, within two years, would yield Saura's most commercially successful film to date and one of the major artistic triumphs of his entire career: *Carmen*.

The Story of Saura's *Carmen*

When Piedra brought Saura and Gades together to consider a second collaboration, the three agreed on some variation on the Carmen theme as an appropriate vehicle. Earlier, Emilio Sanz de Soto, Saura's longtime friend and the artistic director of a number of his films including the recent *Sweet Hours*, had given him a copy of the Prosper Mérimée tale of *Carmen* with the urging that he read it. In late 1981, Saura was approached by the French production company Gaumont and asked to consider a number of projects, one of which was a film version of the Bizet opera to be made in France with a maximum of fidelity to the original text. Saura was not at all interested in the idea and chose instead to direct the Carrière script of *Antonieta* as his first non-Spanish assignment.

When subsequently returning to the discussion of a second collaboration with Gades, Saura proposed to Piedra that the new project be a modern variation of the Carmen theme but, ". . . with the direction and atmosphere of the characters of *Hurry, Hurry!*, especially in respect to the relationship between the strong, dominant woman and the jealous lover" (Saura 1984, 46). For his part, Gades had favored the choice of *Carmen*, since he had already been considering such a project even before the occasion arose for a collaboration with Saura. By the time he had finished filming *Antonieta* in Mexico and France, Saura was willing and available to start work on the Carmen project. But it wasn't until January of 1983 when Gades, now freed from other dance commitments, could devote himself in earnest to the project. That collaboration, which Saura calls "a continuation of the joint work done in *Blood Wedding*" (Saura 1984, 51), produced a film that bears many of the unmistakable marks of Saura's highly distinctive thinking on the cultural politics of "Spanishness."

Where *Blood Wedding* posed a muted, some might argue a tangential, critique of the extravagant españoladas, *Carmen* makes those points of critique explicit. While there is a gap of twenty years between *Carmen* and Saura's last treatment of the foreigners' "vogue of Spain," the common roots of the two films are irrefutable:

> It's worth remembering that in the tail end of Romanticism, Spain was transformed into the goal of a lot of would-be adventurers fleeing from the mist of the north in search of sun and exoticism. German, French and English travelers were interested in our country. Russian and French composers would avail themselves of our popular tunes for inspiration. Painters and illustrators turned their heads in this direction. Anyone who's read Baron de Davillier's book of his travels through Spain illustrated by Gustave Doré in the middle of the 1800s will note the fascination that the people and landscapes of Spain incited in foreigners. In the splendid etchings that Doré made to illustrate *Travels Through Spain* there

is more documentation about our country than you can find in any other medium of information. And even though it is true that in some of the landscapes, those dedicated to Andalusia, the illustrator's unbridled fantasies go overboard, and he exaggerates dress and costume looking for a scenic Romanticism with theatrical touches, the precision of the illustrations always shows us unforgettable faces, streets and landscapes. (Saura, 1984, 53–54)

The narrative materials out of which the *Carmen* story is shaped pose for Saura an even clearer-cut dichotomy between authenticity and the romantic falsification of cultural images. The earliest of the *Carmen* sources, the Prosper Mérimée *nouvelle*, represents not only a worthy treatment of customs, as Saura points out, but also a knowledge of Spain much greater than that of the majority of Spanish authorities who have attacked the French writer's work. In his comments on his published script of the film, Saura even admits that the Mérimée text contained for him ". . . unforgettable passages that connected at times with childhood memories, vague desires and very strong, persistent images" (Saura 1984, 52).

But if the Mérimée *Carmen* appears to capture positive values for Saura, he views the Bizet opera, based upon Mérimée's work, as a betrayal of that ethos. The españoladas derive not from Mérimée, but from Bizet, Saura argues, and perhaps even from his scenarists, Meilhac and Halevy, the authors of the operatic text of the story. The principal brunt of that falsified image of Spain appears to be the creation of the "toreador" Escamillo who does not even exist in the nouvelle. The pairing of the gypsy girl with the bullfighter is, in fact, the kind of universal stereotype of violent and exotic Spain that fuels the Carmen myth well into the present century and intermingles with other exaggerated expressions of the perpetually romanticized attitudes foreigners, especially writers and artists, still hold about Spain.

The plot Saura and Gades constructed revolves around two opposing ideas of Carmen: the more or less authentic Carmen who, tied to some historically and culturally acceptable notion of the nineteenth-century characters and milieu, has been largely blocked and displaced by the more exuberant cliché of the gypsy girl who emerges from the later Bizet-Meilhac-Halevy collaboration. The essential point of Saura's archeological recouping of the sources of the Carmen myth is a very contemporary one: Spaniards, having come under the spell of the foreign, imposter impressions of Spain, find themselves seduced by this falsification of their own cultural past. The creative artist, bereft of any authentic tradition with which to identify, and situated within an artistic milieu he does not even discern as colonized by a specious foreign mentality toward Spain, only repeats the models of that fraudulent Spanishness in his own works and perceptions.

Though that is obviously too heady and abstract a theme to posit within the second dance film, Saura and Gades, nonetheless, remain faithful to that vision of an impostor Spanishness by developing a script in which the key dramatic problem is explicitly one concerning the ways the individual artist has learned to "image" the icons of his own culture. They even carry that critique of the falsified Carmen to the point of posing a parody of Bizet's stereotypes by the members of the dance company within the film.

Staging the Story

In Mérimée's 1845 nouvelle, the story of José's love for Carmen is re-counted in the third of four chapters. Curiously forgotten in subsequent renditions are the two pivotal chapters that precede the story and consti-tute the framing tale about a pedantic French scholar. Lured by the attrac-tion of an exotic Andalusia, this unnamed narrator tells how he befriends the brigand José and later meets Carmen, José's gypsy lover. It is here, in the elaborate frame story, where the ideological investment the foreign ro-mantic makes in the myth of exotic Spanishness is most cogently expressed. Having heard the stories of daring thieves and bandits, Mérimée's narrator is beguiled by the notorious highwayman and even aids him in escaping from the authorities. José represents what his narrator calls "a domesti-cated danger" (Saura 1984, 10), and one gradually comes to realize that Mérimée's interest lies at least as much in this drama of the domestication of perceived cultural danger as in the erotic personage of the title character.

An implicit system of exchange between the narrator and the characters underlies the form as well as the content of this deceptively simple narra-tive. The storyteller is undeterred, for instance, when Carmen steals his pocket watch. So enchanted is he by the spirit of freedom and daring these marginalized characters embody that he willingly trades his possessions and comfort for an intimate glimpse of their exotic world. By the time this unnamed narrator reencounters José in jail awaiting execution, it seems only fitting that José should repay the Frenchman's past favors by telling him the story of his life with Carmen. Bizet's 1875 opera entirely drops this framing story of Spanishness bartered to the foreign tourist, and José's recitation becomes the narration that future generations identify with Mé-rimée's title.

From Saura's perspective, the relation of the frame to the story is the conceptual key to the Carmen myth, for Mérimée has clearly woven two interconnected stories into a single narrative design which Saura's film will reiterate. The better known of the two is the tale of primitive instincts and passions of individuals who, as outcasts, live on the margins of established society. The other is the dramatized narration of that tale for the foreigner whose naive fascination with these exotic characters leads him through a chain of "exchanges," trade-offs, and barterings which finally culminate in José's recitation. In giving narrative prominence to the modern-day story of a Spanish choreographer, Antonio (Antonio Gades), who attempts to "stage" José's narration, Saura is able to recapture something of the cultural conception at the root of Mérimée's original "contract narrative."[2]

Returning to the theme of the ideological underpinnings of artistic form that were present in a muted form in *Blood Wedding*, Saura makes the choreographer in his *Carmen* an incurable romantic of the order of Mérimée's framing-tale narrator. As such, he possesses a contradictory amalgam of traits that define the narrational and conceptual project of Saura's film: an impulse to attain authenticity, and a counter-desire to "stage" that authenticity. Though a Spaniard, Antonio embodies an attitude toward the lived experience of Spanish popular culture that is perilously close to the foreign artist's construction of Spanishness. Like Mérimée's narrator, he is as much a foil to the *Carmen* story as José, the character he will play in the ballet, is for the seductive lure of the gypsy girl. This ironic construction enables Saura to interrogate the problematic issue of Antonio's Spanishness, bound up as it is in the colonizing aesthetics of foreign perceptions of Spain. Ultimately, the domestication of marginal culture through the intervention of art becomes the conceptual focus of Saura's *Carmen* and the figure of Antonio the key to that conception.

From the start, Antonio has internalized contradictory identities. He is a performer in a cultural spectacle of imposture, but, as choreographer, he is also the ideal spectator of that spectacle, attempting through dance to subordinate the impressions of the world he sees around him into a stylized and controlled artistic effect. This is explicitly depicted in the striking precredit sequence of the film beginning with a high-angle shot of Antonio in his studio conducting auditions for the lead dancer's role in his flamenco ballet of the Mérimée story. He stands with his back to the wall-length mirror which reflects the image of a dozen or so young women who have come to audition. Gradually, the camera comes down to the level of the dancers and stops with a medium close-up of Antonio, thus showing, in a single frame, the intensity of his "look" and the reflection of the dancers at whom he is looking. He breaks his gaze in order to show the dancers another step which he performs as though part of the ensemble. The full-wall mirror comes into view as we understand that in this theatrical space Antonio is both performer and spectator. He moves away from the dancers

---

[2] Saura reads Mérimée in much the same way that Roland Barthes read Balzac, and his conclusion dramatizes the Barthesian hypothesis about the social usage of narrative in Balzac: "One does not narrate to 'amuse' or 'instruct,' or to satisfy a certain anthropological function of meaning; one narrates in order to obtain by exchanging; and it is this exchange that is represented in the narrative itself" (89).

and turns around, his back once again to the mirror, in order to observe each dancer directly. Through the agency of his gaze an initial position for the real spectator is stabilized by and identified with the studio mirror.

The mirror as the apparatus of perception is thus equated with the fictional character from the very outset. Though the mirror-camera-spectator chain is common to a number of earlier films, it should be noted that here the process of spectatorial alignment takes place under a mark of ambiguity. The dance mirror, which in the precredits is established as the film's principal agency of narrative enunciation, functions ironically in later scenes as the signifier of the spectacle of imposture to which Antonio is bound.

At the end of this sequence, the camera cuts to the credits which reveal the precise artistic canon to which Antonio is committed. They are shot against the backdrop of the Spanish sketches of Gustave Doré, as the Bizet score of the opera *Carmen* is heard. In short, Antonio's experiences will be mediated by the logic of a foreign art that has codified Spain and Spanishness into specific artistic conventions of imageability. In this he is less an individual character than the figuration of a kind of social mentality: the artist in a colonized culture who, though inspired by a creative impulse and an awareness of the history of cultural imposture, is unable to live his lucidity either in his artistic identity or in his personal life.

His dilemma is dramatized pointedly in the first full narrative sequence after the credits in which Antonio listens intently to the Bizet score as his flamenco ensemble attempts to compose a *cante jondo* equivalent to the melody. When Paco (Paco de Lucía) explains that a flamenco imitation of the Bizet melody will be impossible to dance to, Antonio is not deterred; he even demonstrates a dance step with his co-choreographer, Cristina (Cristina Hoyos), to show that it can be done. The struggle of the singers, musicians, and dancers to adapt to Bizet's music points to the troublesome status of the Spanish folk arts of song and dance which serve in Antonio's mind as illustrations to the Bizet score. Later, when he discovers the ideal woman to play his Carmen (Laura del Sol) in a flamenco dance school, Antonio's reaction is to recite the words spoken by Mérimée's José when he views Carmen for the first time: "I looked up and saw her. It was Friday and I'll never forget it. At first, I didn't much like her and I returned to my work, but following the habits of women and cats, who won't come when you call them, and come when you don't, she stood before me and spoke" (Saura 1984, 73).

His words betray his profound submission to art as his intuitive response to his personal experience. Subsequent plot elements reinforce this paradigm of Antonio's efforts to impose upon his own experiences the coherence of an external artistic model. Though he may appear to stand back from his craft as if struggling to achieve some diagnostic truth about his art and his Spanishness, he nonetheless reveals himself to be the product of a colonized consciousness.

There is, for instance, a telling moment when Carmen, having made love with Antonio in his studio-apartment one night, suddenly departs without explanation. Bewildered by her action, Antonio returns to the rehearsal room and dances before the wall-length mirror. At once, as in some hallucination, Carmen appears before his eyes in the mirror. She is wearing the conventional mantilla and carrying a fan, just as in the most absurdly clichéd versions of the French opera. She even has a rose in her hair. "Why not?" he asks himself. "Why not all the trite commonplaces?"

In Antonio's words of submission to the hoary clichés, there is an implied recognition that he has succumbed not simply to the individual trap, but to the process of historical imposture. His words signify the painful knowledge that he cannot live the intellectual notion of himself and his art. Verbalizing his recognition of the "absent causes" of cultural colonization of Spain which have thwarted his efforts to create and possess his own Spanish Carmen, his words trigger a self-conscious moment of lucidity for the real spectator who, up to this moment, has followed the simple and direct logic of Antonio's narrational point of view. Tellingly, the site of the choreographer's submission to the imposter art that has created this hal-

17. *Carmen* (1983)

lucination of Carmen is the illusory mirror which has come to embody his way of seeing and being seen in the world.

A key phase of the film thus ends here. Clearly rhyming with the pre-credit sequence in which the spectator assumed a visual and narrational identification with Antonio, this scene displaces our sight from his; so distanced, we are now able to theorize Antonio's perceptual subjectivity. In other words, having seen through his eyes, we now also see him and his relation to the foreign scenarios of Spanishness that mediate his experience of himself and his art. Though in the action that follows Saura includes a number of scenes that appear to blur the lines between Antonio's conscious and hallucinatory perceptions, they seem to follow the logic of the choreographer's personal and artistic dilemma as defined in the first part of *Carmen*.

Symbolic Displacements

Conceptually, the roots of *Carmen* lie in *Blood Wedding*, specifically in the notion of the dancer's willing submission to the aesthetic apparatus that regulates the illusion of artistic order in the eyes of the other. Antonio's cultural confusions in *Carmen* clearly derive from his subservience to the condition of otherness which is implied in his identity as dancer-choreographer. From the very beginning of the film, he sees the dancers, including himself, as "others," objects in the eyes of an unseen spectator. Not only does he serve as the agency of the real spectator's sight through much of the film, but he is also the mediator of an artistic convention that stabilizes and orders images into theatrical performance.

We come to recognize that, for Saura, performance has become the allegorical key to reading Spanish culture. The specularization of the dancer by means of the ubiquitous mirror replicates on the level of aesthetic performance the cultural ideology of Spanishness which, as Ortega had pointed out, was itself performance and spectacle in which individual Spaniards willingly participated. This allegorical register, which was latent in *Blood Wedding*, comes to dominate the narrative of *Carmen*. The artistic mise-en-scène of Antonio's studio becomes a symbolic displacement of a social-historical mise-en-scène in which Spain, like Carmen, is a highly stylized performer who, precisely as an outcast from the norms defined by foreign culture, is transformed into the object of desire.

From the moment Antonio offers Carmen the lead in his dance production and tells her to "learn the role," we sense the shaping of the individual drama into a cultural allegory. In their own interactions with each other, the characters will involuntarily act out the very moves through which they will unwittingly valorize the foreign artists' notion of the "Spanish picturesque," transforming their own experiences into predetermined theatrical clichés. Tellingly, the process of Carmen's "learning" parallels Antonio's essential retreat from contemporary social reality and his repudiation of his original impulse toward authenticity in his art. In the elaborate tobacco-factory dance sequence in which, according to Mérimée's text, José first meets the gypsy girl, Saura reveals to just what degree Antonio's perception of his own experiences has been subsumed by the logic and theatricality of a foreign art.

For the factory sequence, Antonio has charged Cristina with training Carmen, but, from the start, frictions erupt between the two women. As the aging dancer who is the epitome of the artistry of flamenco dance, Cristina feels hurt by having been passed over for the lead role in the ballet for the younger and clearly less talented dancer. We view the tension grow as they rehearse before a studio mirror. Through the transparency of this mirror we and Antonio view the erupting rivalry. An assistant calls Cristina to Antonio's office, which is on the other side of the rehearsal mirror. As he asks Cristina for a truce with the younger dancer, Antonio's conversation with her is viewed against the backdrop of the office window-mirror through which the unsuspecting Carmen is being viewed in her dance movements. The mirror as the constant artifice informing the life and actions of the various characters is brilliantly demonstrated here, as the framed image of Carmen prefigures the dancer's future transformation into the fictional gypsy girl.

In the next scene, Antonio has a private rehearsal with Carmen to go over her part in the tobacco-factory number. The sequence in question dramatizes the furious rivalry between the fictional Carmen and Micaela, another factory worker. Cristina is to play the part of Micaela in the first of a series of suggestive parallels between the theatrical and the world outside it. Antonio explains to Carmen that she needs to put more passion into her role, to give it more fire. "You can't let Cristina eat you up; you must devour her!" he tells her. His advice seems sufficient stimulus for Carmen to transpose her real-life animosity against Cristina into the theatrical role she is playing, for, as she goes through her steps with Antonio, it is apparent that she has become surer and more convincing in her movements. Unwittingly, the younger dancer is learning to channel her instinctive energy into the constructive design of a theatrical figure, staging her anger in much the same way that Antonio has staged his life.

The simulated dress rehearsal of the tobacco-factory sequence, in which Carmen murders Micaela and is taken off to prison by José, works as an artistic resolution of the personal conflicts among the three dancers. Antonio symbolically displaces Cristina, who is the interloper in his love relation with Carmen, and thereby positions himself to possess the young firebrand just as his character, José, imagines he will possess his gypsy girl.

18. *Carmen* (1983)

Ironically, Antonio's admonition to Carmen to "devour" Cristina serves as a perfect metaphor for the artistic cannibalization which by this point has taken over the entire cinematic narrative.

In this way the dance fiction comes into focus as the medium through which Antonio will resolve the series of conflicts and contradictions that plague him in the world outside the dance. A precise trajectory has been completed here in which Antonio has moved from one side of the dance mirror to the other, situating himself within the artistic illusion of the ballet, but also regressing haplessly into the other artistic order of the historical-literary character he is portraying—whose destiny is determined by the cultural politics of Spanishness. "Being" and "seeing" merge here and the condition of "being looked at" becomes vertiginous expressions of characters' personal and social identity.

At the start, the artifice of the mirror was clearly distinguishable from the figures reflected in it. Now, the mirror has devoured the dancer as the tobacco-factory sequence ends with Antonio's staring into the mirror, returning the spectator to an awareness of the fictional frame which has entrapped the character on multiple planes. This sequence underscores the self-authenticating illusion of the individual transfixed by the seductive "effect" which binds him as an observer of art to a false mode of consciousness with which he intimately identifies.

Beyond Performance

The allure that has defined Carmen for Antonio is a relentless spectacle which, by the film's finale, has taken over his whole being. That she is the embodiment of an instinct and naturalness that are the antithesis of the rehearsed and the performed is only a reiteration of the cultural allegory interwoven into the drama of the choreographer and the dancer. Indeed, his tumultuous relationship with Carmen is a series of struggles to transform her spontaneity into the patterns of a familiar artistic model and thereby to domesticate her within the clichéd identity to which he has already submitted. Running parallel to this allegory of two forms of Spanish identity—the spontaneous and the rehearsed—is the literal representation of sexual politics in the film. Not only Carmen, but all women, appear under Antonio's, that is to say, the male's authenticating, gaze as objects to be molded by him into artistic forms. Carmen's evasiveness to Antonio, her infidelities, finally, her open rebellion against him, may all be read on the realistic plane of the modern Spanish woman's assertion of an individualistic identity that traditional phallocentric culture has so long denied her.

The weight of all of these struggles defines the conflict that sets the stage for the film's final scene. The sequence is introduced by Antonio's inevitable discovery of his lover's infidelity. After the rehearsal of the card game and duel scene, when it appears that finally Antonio has eliminated all possible rivals, he discovers Carmen making love with one of the other dancers in the wardrobe room. He throws the two out, but the scene then cuts rapidly to a shot of various dancers silently donning costumes for another dance sequence. The linkage between these two scenes poses a suggestive causality, as we once again sense that what appears to be a forward jump in the action may only be the fanciful invention of Antonio's mind in which he resolves his emotional conflict once again through a choreographed resolution.

An elaborate dance scene begins to take shape as a crowd of dancers and musicians enters the studio, simulating the stylized sights and sounds of a popular Andalusian dance hall. Strains of a pasodoble are heard, and the dancers divide into couples. Carmen and Antonio are recognized among the assembled crowd. Carmen leaves Antonio's side to flirt with a torero dressed in his corrida costume. A dance duel ensues between the two men that threatens to end in a knife fight. In certain ways this scene parallels the earlier tobacco-factory sequence, also the site of a violent struggle before a crowd of dancers in which a rivalry is resolved symbolically as the community views the displacement of Antonio's rival. As in the factory scene, the logic of this encounter appears to coincide with the choreographer's need to stage a public, albeit symbolic and theatrical, resolution of the emotional conflicts revolving around his relationship with Carmen. But just as there appears to be a standoff between José and the torero, Carmen walks out of the rehearsal, and, when Antonio tries to stop her, she tells him that things are over between them. Her phrase, suggestively ambiguous, works well in both the theatrical and the real-life relations between Carmen and Antonio. In her refusal to participate in Antonio's performance, whether in the rehearsal hall or in their private relations, Carmen has effectively denied Antonio the critical condition of spectacle so central to his identity. Her action thus precipitates a profound crisis for him which leads to the inevitable replication of the tragic murder scene with which both Mérimée and Bizet end their versions of the *Carmen* story.

Antonio follows Carmen to the dressing room as the strains of Bizet's somber finale music are heard. We see a partial shot of Antonio struggling with Carmen at the door of the dressing room; then he pulls a knife from his pocket and stabs her to death. Having followed the couple, the camera now slowly pans away to reveal a near-empty rehearsal hall, as if the dance sequence that preceded this moment had not taken place. The film's final, lingering image is a distanced shot of two members of the dance troupe seated at a table chatting, unaware of the murder which may well not have taken place, except in Antonio's mind.

What is distinctive about the final sequence is not its ambiguity as narrative, but its cinematic reflexivity. The dramatic crisis provoked by Carmen's denial of spectacle has been transposed to the level of enunciation in which the audience is led to confront its own relation to the process of spectation dramatized in the text. This is, tellingly, the only scene in which characters refuse to "look" and where performance, in the negative sense that Saura equates it with contrived Spanishness, has ended. We are finally shown the on-screen figures of spectators unbound by performance. Sunlight streams into the dance studio, and we are left with the final image of dancers indifferent to what appears to have transpired near them.

In striking contrast to nearly every other scene that precedes it, this is the space of a truly ordinary world without spectacle, without the compulsion to bind oneself to representation or performance. What has really been at stake in *Carmen*, as we may now understand, has been the unmasking of the ideology of an artistic form which, within the historical context of a deformed and misrecognized Spanishness, constructs and determines subject positions within and beyond cultural performance.

Such a moment in which Spaniards might become self-consciously aware of the patterns and history of imposture which have formed their identity in culture is one that recurs in a score of Saura's films over the years. As in those earlier works, Saura's self-awareness of the volume of deforming cultural weight that has shaped the Spaniard's image of himself in the world will not allow him to posit a simplistic narrative utopia. Instead, the image of the bare rehearsal hall lingers, prodding the audience to reflect upon the ambiguity of a cultural narrative without performance or closure and its implications for Spaniards, who, by this point in the eighties, are beginning to sense that their destiny is not already written in their past.

El amor brujo (1986: Love, the Magician)

Carmen enjoyed immense popularity in Spain and abroad, and, with adept promotion, it became the largest grossing Spanish film in U.S. history. It was nominated in the Best Foreign Film category for the 1984 Oscars, Saura's second nomination. This artistic and commercial success made it inevitable that Piedra would urge a continuation of the Saura-Gades collaboration. The artistic partnership between the filmmaker and the choreographer had begun very modestly, with the limited task of filming Gades's ballet version of Lorca's play. There had not been any discussion of a more ambitious structure to their work. But by the time conversations began on a third film project, it was obvious that a set of common themes informed and unified these collaborations. While *Blood Wedding* was motivated by an effort to demystify the false Andalusianism of the españoladas, *Carmen* focused more emphatically on the foreign impostures of Spanishness that had clouded the Spaniard's image of his world. In the third installment, *El amor brujo* (1986: Love, the Magician), a film adaptation of a flamenco ballet by the famed Spanish composer Manuel de Falla, Saura and Gades give flamenco culture a more central and positive place than it had in either of the preceding works.

Flamenco is not necessarily the core of Spanish culture, but its significance as a cultural institution does give it a peculiar artistic privilege. Saura explains: "Flamenco is nothing more than one of many kinds of dance that exist in this country, although it has come to be considered *the* Spanish dance by definition, perhaps because it is sufficiently flexible to be adapted to varied dramatic and expressive interpretations" (Saura 1984, 51).

Blood Wedding had contained an element of artistic challenge for Saura in its focus on dance as narration. Once the rehearsal begins, there is no spoken dialogue to narrate the story. *Carmen* posed a similar set of challenges. It depended on a certain amount of improvisation of dialogue and gestures by the actors, and then a more intense use of dance numbers to dramatize the emotional states of the two protagonists. But *Love, the Magician* was to be the most ambitious of the three films in its emphasis on the storytelling register of flamenco. As Saura notes, the de Falla work was, to a large measure, unfinished, filled with musical and narrative digressions, in which even the relation between musical numbers and the plot were at times ambiguous (Saura 1986, 217). Thus, he and Gades had to reconstruct and, at times, even create the choreographic and cinematic structures through which to tell a filmic story through dance. As a result, *Love, the Magician* uses a more highly developed narrational register than was even the case in *Blood Wedding*. To this area of experimentation, Saura added his own insistence that in all ways this new version of *Love, the Magician* be a work of decidedly popular flavor while maintaining maximum fidelty to de Falla's original work (Saura, 1986, 218). To achieve that goal, he refrained from using a classical concert soloist to sing the de Falla songs and instead chose the popular flamenco singer Rocío Jurado.

Similar to *Blood Wedding*, the film is also based on a previously choreographed Spanish ballet, de Falla's 1915 two-act ballet of the same name, one of three in which de Falla took his inspiration from Andalusian cultural and musical traditions. Commissioned as a vehicle for Pastora Imperio, a well-known flamenco dancer of the early decades of this century, the work boasts a scenario by the playwright Gregorio Martínez Sierra, based on a story told by the dancer's mother, "an old gypsy versed in the lore of her race" (Chase 1959, 189). To highlight Imperio's talents as a singer as well as a dancer, *El amor brujo* contained a hybrid score that included authentic gypsy songs as well as the de Falla melodies which were of a decided oriental rhythm, attesting to the long-held belief of the Moorish origins of Spanish gypsy culture. Though premiered in Madrid in 1915, it was not until 1928—when Antonia Mercé, "La Argentina," and Vicente Escudero performed the ballet at the Opera Comique in Paris—that *El amor brujo* became accepted into the standard repertory of international dance companies.

The artistic distinction of de Falla's work is its embrace of authentic Spanish cultural tradition—gypsy culture which itself combines oriental, Byzantine musical tropes with other less popular folk strains—and an aesthetic stylization that seeks to universalize what even for Spaniards has been the marginal culture of the gypsies. This same effort to stage authentically Spanish cultural figures and traditions within a more universal aesthetic comes to characterize the third Saura-Gades-Piedra collaboration. Again, as in *Blood Wedding*, the actual duration of the ballet was too short for normal commercial distribution—only twenty-seven minutes. But instead of seeking a behind-the-scenes frame for the story, Saura and Gades chose to follow the cue of the original Imperio production and combine authentic gypsy songs with the de Falla score.

Optimistic that Saura and Gades would repeat the popular and commercial success they had had with *Carmen*, Piedra made no attempt to limit the production costs of this new film, but, instead, conceived of the work precisely as the kind of cinematic spectacle that would be both necessarily and inevitably exportable. In fact, the distribution rights to *Love, The Magician* were sold to U.S., French, Italian, and British companies a full two months before actual shooting began, a procedure rare for Spanish films, even films that boasted Saura's name.

A Different Kind of Spanishness

Following de Falla's strategy of expanding the gypsy and folkloric elements both in dance and in the ballads, Saura chooses to underscore the element of a more or less authentic Spanishness. It is as if *Love, The Magician* were intended to be read as a demonstrable solution to the problem of creativity within the range of authentic Spanish culture, which had been the cultural conflict at the heart of *Carmen*. The new production fashions elements of popular gypsy culture into a sustained narrative form as had seldom been done before in a Spanish film, suggesting in the process the director and choreographer's desire to experiment with those creative possibilities they had so closely scrutinized in their preceding collaborations. The most striking aspects of their experimentation were to come in the areas of filmic narration and cinematic mise-en-scène. In terms of narration, we note that the film relies much more heavily than in the earlier collaborations on the emotive powers of the dancers to tell the story. Although there is connective dialogue between scenes, much of the filmic narration is conveyed through elaborate dances. The majority of these are artistically choreographed sequences that illustrate the de Falla score. But these numbers are punctuated by some of the traditonal gypsy or flamenco dances which are not tied to any specific narrative thread. The resulting dance trajectory thereby situates these popular dances within a more universal narrative context. This is the case, for instance, in the elaborate rendition of *La mosca*, part of the wedding scene as performed in the film by a gypsy group from the caves of Sacromonte in Granada.

The second critical feature is the deft use of mise-en-scène. Shot entirely in the old Samuel Bronston studio in Madrid, the film continually flaunts its status as a stage representation. Yet through Gerardo Vera's imaginative set design, which approximates the environs of a gypsy ghetto on the outskirts of an unnamed city, and Teo Escamilla's camera work, the film creates the curious effect of realism within the confines of its own artificial space. This strategy involves a necessary flaunting of the staginess of the setting in the early parts of the film, followed by a progression of moves to suppress that theatricality, such as a windstorm and a sequence involving torrential rain. The artifice of the mise-en-scène circumscribes the characters and actions in much the same way that the traditional españoladas, through their artificiality, frame flamenco cultural reality.

This elaborate mise-en-scène harmonizes with the narrative theme of external social reality's framing of the magical human dimension of gypsy culture. The original gypsy legend, as told by Pastora Imperio's mother and later formalized into Martínez Sierra's poetic scenario, is followed in the film script with a number of adjustments to extend the story's duration and provide a showcase for Gades, Cristina Hoyos, and Laura del Sol, the three principals from the earlier *Carmen*.

The story begins in a gypsy shantytown on the outskirts of the city. Two men enter into a pact of friendship in which they promise the marriage of their respective son and daughter when the two children have grown up. Years pass and the betrothal promise is fulfilled as Candela (Cristina Hoyos) marries José (Juan Antonio Jiménez) in an elaborate ceremony involving the entire gypsy community. But even amidst the wedding festivities, impending tragedy is foreshadowed. Carmelo (Antonio Gades) has always secretly loved Candela and witnesses the ceremony with frustration and grief at the loss of his beloved. For his part, José seems uninterested in giving up his former lover, Lucía (Laura del Sol), and even jokes with her on his wedding day about a future liaison.

After José is killed in a knife fight, Carmelo is unjustly accused of the murder and imprisoned for four years. When he returns seeking Candela, whom he now hopes to marry, he discovers that she is haunted by the ghost of her deceased husband. Every night she goes to a deserted field and calls his name. She imagines that he appears and dances with her. Others look on with consternation, for they only see Candela dancing alone, embracing the air as if holding José's body. Carmelo brings Candela to Tía Rosa (Emma Penella), the village sorceress, who tells the couple that the only way to rid Candela of José's ghost is through a fire dance. But José's hold on his widow is stronger than the magical spell of fire. Carmelo decides to use his own strategy to liberate Candela. He convinces Lucía to participate in a call to José to appear; when Candela invokes the ghost, Lucía, José's former lover, dances with him. The two adulterers disappear into the air, leaving Carmelo and Candela united in the morning light.

Enclosures and Liberations

The pivot of the plot of *Love, The Magician* is the supernatural bond that love is said to form between individuals that can only be broken by the *hechicería*, the magic, of another, stronger love. In Gades and Saura's version of the story, dance is interwoven into the leitmotif of magic. According to the gypsy legend around which the story evolves, love can be a destructive as well as a positive force for, while it unites two lovers, it also holds its victim in a state of perpetual bondage, as the work's title suggests with appropriate ambiguity. In the Martínez Sierra and Gades reworkings of the legend, dance is similarly given positive and negative meanings: Candela's bondage to the specter of José is forged in the dance. Conversely, we see her liberation from his ghost effected through Carmelo's strategy of manipulating the dance.

The mise-en-scène, which both flaunts its own artificiality and incites its spectator to accept the power of illusion as real, thematizes that same duality of entrapment/liberation. We readily discern this paradigm in the pre-credit sequence. The film begins within what will shortly be recognized as a cavernous studio with a shot of a shadowy space broken by the light streaming in from a door opening to the street. The door is closed with a resounding echo, which is synchronized with the first chord of the de Falla overture. At the same instant, the screen is plunged into near-total darkness, and the camera begins a high-angle tracking movement through the backstage of the studio, moving past rows of massive stage curtains that form circular columns. From what is retrospectively understood as the physical reality of the outside world, only fleetingly glimpsed through the stage door, we move now to the behind-the-scenes images of a staged reality. The camera moves out of the shadows into the brilliant artificial stage light, revealing the main plaza of an elaborately constructed gypsy shantytown.

Two men sit at a table drinking. In a very crude, blunt tone, one offers his daughter, Candela, in marriage to the other's son. In a similarly drunken stupor, the other man accepts. The future bride and groom, each about ten years of age, are summoned. "You, José, will marry Candela. Isn't that right?" the father asks. The boy answers with a halting affirmative. The same question is put to the little girl, who gives a similar acquiescent answer. "Let's settle this marriage with a pact," one father tells the other. They clasp hands and pour wine over their entwined arms, symbolizing the union of the two families. The camera then cuts away to the image of a third boy who has viewed the marriage pact from afar. This is Carmelo; the camera lingers on his face in an intense close-up as the off-screen strains of the de Falla overture continue.

The image of Carmelo is transformed into a freeze-frame over which the title and credits are superimposed. With each dissolve of a title, the image of the boy's face becomes a bit more blurred and then, through a lap-over dissolve, is replaced by the freeze-frame image of Antonio Gades, who plays the role of Carmelo as a grown man. At the end of the credit sequence, the image of Carmelo still staring directly into the camera comes to life as we see him, with a grim expression, staring into a mirror as he dresses for the celebration of José and Candela's marriage.

This masterful sequence cleverly aligns the artifices of cinematic and stage illusion, highlighting the idea of creative as well as destructive enclosures. The closing of the studio door, locking out everyday reality, is the visual overture to the audience's magical entrance into the world of liberating make-believe in which the artistic always overpowers the prosaic. The film's first expansive traveling shot crystalizes this move, from the door, through the rows of curtains, to the reconstructed shantytown plaza. But at the exact point at which the camera liberates the audience's imagination by bringing them into this fictional world, the narrative introduces the motif of enclosure and entrapment with the custom of the arranged marriage between José and Candela.

Against the backdrop of a liberating artistic imagination, Saura juxtaposes the confining strictures of community tradition that seek to control the destinies of each successive generation. Standing apart from the two fathers and the betrothed children is Carmelo, his distanced placement in the scene and his cold, piercing eyes emphasizing the pattern of enclosure to which he is bearing witness. By means of the series of lap-over dissolves of the young Carmelo's face, we, the extra-textual audience of the drama, bear witness to the "magic" of cinematic imagination that produces the effect of a miraculous passage of time. This counterpoint of cultural and artistic forces will continue to reenforce the two major structural gestures out of which the dramatic and thematic form of *Love, the Magician* is forged. The story that follows skillfully juxtaposes the ritual patterns of this stereotypical tale of gypsy passion in a world steeped in magic with the figure of the individual who is liberated from the confines of that closed world of predetermined love and death. Though the film initially appears to establish its coherence around the impression of an authenticity in cultural customs, as the precredits suggest, the concept of the community tradition will be viewed as the critical obstacle to individual fulfillment.

The Community Embodied in Dance

Love, the Magician mixes traditional flamenco songs and dances with the artistically created simulations of flamenco dance to convey the story of Candela, José, and Carmelo's impossible triangle. To underscore Saura's thematic premise, the film adds a number of specific variations to the original scenario. Of these the most significant is the inclusion of several ensemble dances that celebrate the values of the community and its continuance over time. Simulating traditional folkloric dances, these ensemble numbers comprise the community's ritual of identity: the elaborate wedding ceremony and celebration; the gypsy Christmas dance; and finally, the fire dance that Tía Rosario calls upon the group to perform in an effort to ward off the ghost of the deceased José. As can be readily noted by their mere enumeration, these traditional numbers, involving the dance ensemble as community, reaffirm the cyclical pattern of collective renewal and communal solidarity.

In the wedding sequence, for example, there are actually four phases of dance. The first is the betrothal dance in which the ensemble breaks into two groups, each holding one of the wedding pair on their shoulders. To the accompaniment of a traditional gypsy song, the groups dance in a movement which symbolically states the merging of the two individuals into a single couple. The embrace of the wedding couple becomes inseparable from the merging of the two groups into a single community. During this dance number, Carmelo stands on the side and only looks on as the dance of union is performed, repeating in his placement and perspective the same relation he had assumed to the marriage pact in the precredits. His self-isolating position in both sequences places the subsequent narrative within the larger cultural tension of individual desires in conflict with the patterns and desires of the community.

The second part of the sequence details the festivities in which the group calls for Carmelo to perform a flamenco dance with the bride. At first he is reluctant to approach the woman whom he cannot have, but prodded by the animated calls of the revelers, he agrees. Now paralleling the previous dance of union of José and Candela, this dance suggests that Carmelo and Candela make a more desirable couple than the betrothed. Not only is the dance performed with traditional flamenco steps, but the community also shows its stronger appreciation of this couple by their effusive response. Throughout this number, José is absent; he has gone in pursuit of his former lover, Lucía.

The third part of the sequence is the dance of the older women (gypsies from the caves of Sacromonte), who have formed a circle around Candela and Carmelo and now are given the space in which to perform the gestures of traditional *sevillanas*. Each woman is given a solo and reveals the agility of her body as well as her zeal in sharing in the communal celebration of conjugal union. Importantly, this particular phase of the dance sequence highlights the participation of all generations in the cycle of love and marriage that began with the pact of the two fathers in the precredits. The dance of the old women is finally upstaged by two youthful rock singers bellowing out the popular contemporary lyric "¿Qué quieres de mí? (What Do You Want from Me?), a song that ironically echoes Lucía's earlier words to José. As the song ends, José, in fact, has just returned from his encounter with Lucía and breaks into the dance begun by Carmelo and Candela. Particularly striking in this sequence are the parallel strains of traditional dance and the interwoven artistic dances that effectively join the scenario of the larger life cycle of the community with the individual tale of marriage and betrayal.

In the equally elaborate *Nochebuena gitana* (Gypsy Christmas Eve) the notion of the community's engagement in collective, cyclical behavior is again juxtaposed against the individualized story. The scene is introduced with a close-up of a crèche and the sounds of tambourines playing a gypsy version of a traditional Spanish Christmas carol. The camera tracks away to reveal Candela now seated in a circle of singers who are apparently celebrating the Christmas season. A second group of singers passes by heading toward another clearing where Lucía and Carmelo are dancing. José appears and breaks into the dance with Lucía. A group forms around this new couple as the circle of observers clap their hands rhythmically to the stomping cadence of the dancers' feet.

The image cuts abruptly to a simultaneous action: a close-up of Candela sitting among the carolers. All at once she stops. The others in the ensemble assume a tableau posture as Candela rises and performs what is the first of her dream dances, expressing her intuition of her husband's infidelity. Candela's solo has the curious effect of shattering the *verismo* effect of the choreography and mise-en-scène of this scene. The tableau freize of characters and symbolic dance representation of Candela's inner thoughts effectively highlights for the spectator the sense of artifice of the staged setting, while juxtaposing that contrivance with the theme of the tormented individual. In structure, this is identical to the narrative formula of the precredits in which the child Carmelo was featured.

Candela's dance ends with a close-up of her anguished face. The camera then cuts back to the location where José and Lucía have been dancing. Members of a rival gang appear and a fight-dance ensues in which José is stabbed to death. Candela and Carmelo rush to the fallen body as the crowd disperses. Police sirens are heard as Candela grasps her dead husband's body. A strong spotlight appears on the pair to suggest the arrival of the police, thus bringing to an end the first act of the original de Falla ballet.

Within this first part of both the ballet and the film, we note how dance has embodied the community's values on a number of levels. As in *Blood Wedding*, the control and domestication of the individual's body is effected through a series of public dances in which the community participates and bears witness. Regulating the erotic body of individuals, the community thus controls the definition of individuality. What we see in a more elaborate form in *Love, the Magician* is the tension between collective, institutional submission and the emergence in two characters, Candela and Carmelo, of a contrary notion of individuality. This is not the Lorquian rebellion of the individual who cannot submit to the collective design. Rather, as Saura stresses, we are witnessing the development of two obedient characters who have followed the dictates of the group and have attempted to suppress their instinct, conforming to communal rituals, only to be led gradually to a union that is validated within the terms of the

19. *Love, the Magician* (*El amor brujo*, 1986)

community. The vicissitudes of their search for union is chronicled in the second part of the libretto and film which detail actions occurring four years after José's murder for which Carmelo has been charged and imprisoned.

Love Is Magic

The visual register of verismo overpowers much of the first part of the film, as does the theme of the community. With Carmelo's return and his discovery of Candela's hallucinatory state, the motifs of bewitchment dominate both the story and its telling, as the power of the two individuals gains more and more prominence. There are only two ensemble dances in the second part of the film: the washerwomen's sequence in which Candela learns that Lucía had been José's lover even during their brief marriage; and the spectacular fire dance ordered by Tía Rosario as the only way to expel José's ghost. Contrasting with the scale of these two ensemble numbers are a few more modest dances which center on Carmelo and Candela and the latter's bondage in the shadow of her husband's ghost.

The most important of these are the scenes in which Candela evokes José's spirit and dances with him. The first is actually a kind of prologue to the second part of the film and begins with Candela in bed. We see her awaken, as if a somnambulist, and dress. Because her departure from the house is shot from within the cabin, her receding image is framed by the doorway, thus reinscribing the visual motif of entrapment and enclosure with which Carmelo had earlier been identified. Once in the clearing near the dump, she calls José's name, and he magically appears. The couple dances a sensuous series of movements. Suddenly, José disappears and Candela is left standing alone. She walks back to her cabin still in a dream-like state.

This same dance is repeated in a new context when Carmelo returns, hoping now to marry Candela. He learns from a friend that, in her hallu-cinations, José's widow has imagined the return of her deceased husband and each night has gone out to the dump where she imagines she is danc-ing with him. Carmelo follows her to the site one night and watches as she calls to José's ghost. While the spectator sees José's appearance and his repetition of the erotic dance movement with Candela, all that Carmelo sees from his vantage point behind an abandoned car is Candela dancing alone, embracing the air in a series of solo movements.

This depiction is, of course, a simple matter of cinematic cross-cutting, but, importantly, the second scene operates to present Candela's halluci-nation as an alignment of dance and cinematic sight as expressions of in-dividual imagination. The story has moved us progressively further away from the romanticized world of the clichéd gypsy passion and communal rites. Though the aura of magic still obviously pervades the film, it is the power of individual imagination rather than the mysterious force of gypsy spells that characterizes the latter parts of the action. Indeed, Tía Rosario's claim that only fire can expel José's ghost proves false. Only the power of individual love—José's irresistible passion for Lucía and Carmelo's con-stancy for Candela—can bring the story to a reasonable closure.

In the final sequence, Carmelo persuades Lucía to join him and Candela in a call to José. At first reluctant to join in what she thinks is foolishness, Lucía finally agrees. When José's ghost appears, the couple dances as in Candela's earlier hallucinations, only this time, Carmelo is able to see José. At one point in the dance, José eyes Lucía and, as in his previous life, shuns his wife for the charms of his lover. Carmelo then joins in the dance with Candela as José and Lucía disappear. The film's final scene shows Candela and Carmelo embracing as the sun rises on the fantasy backdrop against which all of these dreams have been performed. The camera moves away from the lovers who are at last able to realize their love without the com-munity or personal obstacles which had for so long frustrated them.

This denouement self-consciously highlights the dance medium in a way that returns us to the question of the ideological underpinning of artistic form that was at the heart of the earlier parts of the flamenco trilogy. Car-melo uses dance as a means through which to free his lover from her emo-tional bondage with the past, thereby recalling a situation in *Carmen* in which Antonio similarly attempted to mobilize dance as a symbolic resolution of personal problems. In the earlier film, however, Saura was able to draw our attention, often in a self-conscious manner, to the ways that the artistic effects of dance masked the underlying logic of the individual's submission to patterns of social order. That critique of the aesthetic effect is not only absent in *Love, the Magician*, but the filmic narrative appears to valorize the protagonists' submission to social order at the expense of their own individuality.

As in the earlier flamenco films, the plot of *Love, the Magician* hinges on the scenario of individual rebellion against the dictates of a constraining social order. Leonardo and the fiancée in *Blood Wedding* as well as the defiant gypsy girl and her contemporary double in *Carmen* had all been figures who stood in defiance of social norms. But now José and Lucía, the adulterous lovers, while sustaining that motif of rebellion, are really not the center of the film's action. Instead, and perhaps to the detriment of the audience's emotional engagement with the film, that center is occupied by Carmelo and Candela, two acquiescent protagonists who become the embodiments of the very ideology of conformism to socially constructed identities that was the brunt of Saura's critique of action in the two preceding films. The manner of their union at the film's end seems to subvert the thematics of the earlier parts of the trilogy, for the conflict between the individual and the social is now resolved in behalf of the latter and the power of dance is once again viewed as a means of holding instinctual rebellion in check.

In part, this apparent conceptual reversal is the result of Saura and Gades's pledged fidelity to the original Martínez Sierra libretto. But it is also the unavoidable consequence of Saura's own decision to use flamenco dance as a mode of narration; for the dance medium, as we earlier noted in *Blood Wedding*, continually reaffirms the theme of submission. Unlike the earlier installments, there are no breaks or fissures in the aesthetic texture here within which to posit the kind of critique of artistic form that was an essential part of the earlier flamenco films. The result is thus a film that, conceptually at least, appears to contradict the meditations on the theme of individuality that had characterized the two preceding parts of the trilogy.

This apparent shift in focus away from the critique of constructed social identity gives *Love, the Magician* the feel of an anticlimax in comparison to the two earlier dance films (Sánchez Vidal 1989, 196). While recognizing the film's artistic merit, Spanish reviewers were somewhat subdued in their praise of Saura. Despite that coolness, *Love, the Magician* received an enthusiastic response from the Spanish public. It became the eighth highest grossing Spanish film of 1986 (Llinas 1987, 99), a particularly noteworthy achievement given the very fickle nature of the Spanish reception to a number of Saura's more recent films. Abroad, the film did equally well. Foreign critics and audiences, especially in the U.S. and France, were enthusiastic in their praise of the work. The nature of the artistic and cultural experiment presumed by *Love, the Magician*—a film that sets out to demonstrate the expressive range of flamenco dance and utilizes dance as its primary mode of narration—prefigured a rather limited audience appeal. Yet, curiously, despite the demands that the film places on its viewer, *Love, the Magician* managed to garner an impressive worldwide audience. It was shown as the final screening of the 1986 Cannes Festival and opened the Munich Film Festival. When the film was shown at the Montreal Film Festival, along with *Blood Wedding* and *Carmen*, Saura was awarded a special jury prize for the entire trilogy.

Afterword

Looking Back

Historical Fictions

By the late 1980s, Spain had achieved conspicuous marks of cultural and political maturity. Increasing economic development, characterized by massive foreign investment in the country, was matched by an internal spirit of cultural tolerance and, importantly, signs of political stability as a genuine democracy. These achievements, read from the perspective of outside observers as the repudiation of the country's often violent past, made it increasingly less fashionable for artists to harp on the historical differences that had traditionally separated the dominant cultural and intellectual spirit of Spain from that of the rest of Europe. Yet, in such a climate, precisely at the moment when, from all appearances, the liberal and pluralistic notions of Spain were realizable for the Spaniard, Saura returned to the past to reflect upon the constructions of the narrow historical discourse of Spanishness in two films: *El Dorado* (1988) and *La noche oscura* (1989: The Dark Night).[1]

These are not only historical films, but also very narrowly conceived *Spanish* historical films, each focusing on political rebels of the sixteenth century. *El Dorado* details the adventures of the allegedly mad conquistador, Lope de Aguirre, whose insurrection against both the Spanish crown and the expedition in search of El Dorado had earlier been the subject of Werner Herzog's 1972 film, *Aguirre: The Wrath of God*. *The Dark Night* recounts events in the life of the Spanish mystic poet, Saint John of the Cross, whose work as a reformer of the Carmelite Order led to his imprisonment by defiant members of that sect who saw in the priest's activities the erosion of their position of authority in the imperial Spain of Philip II.

---

[1] The conception of both films actually dates back at least a decade. The idea for *El Dorado* came originally from Saura's fascination with the character of Lope de Aguirre when he read Ramón Sender's novel about the failed expedition sent in search of El Dorado, *La aventura equinoccial de Lope de Aguirre*. Later, when he viewed Herzog's film about the expedition, he was struck by the historical inaccuracies in Herzog's script and what he felt were Klaus Kinski's dramatic excesses in the leading role. He began to explore the possibilities for a film on the subject in the late seventies, but was unable to find a producer interested in the project until 1986 (Sánchez Vidal 206).

The original inspiration for a film about St. John of the Cross came while filming *Ana and the Wolves*, in which Fernando Fernán-Gómez's role as the ascetic mystic is based on St. John (Sánchez Vidal 215).

20. Carlos Saura on location in Costa Rica (1987)

Saura's films of the eighties had been marked by an increasing thematic focus on social rebellion, with characters who, like the protagonists of *Hurry, Hurry!* or the instinctual rebels of the flamenco trilogy, stood in defiance of established social order and normality. *El Dorado* and *The Dark Night* accentuate that line of development, but locate it, importantly, within the context of questions of history. The action of each film is situated at a moment in which the relation of individuals to the cluster of precepts we have identified with Spanishness has not yet been stabilized. These are films, therefore, about the discursive origins of the construction of Spanishness, and Saura uses such a historical context to theorize a moment when it might have been possible to imagine a cultural tradition for Spain quite antithetical to the repressive legacy thus far chronicled in his films.

The idea of history has, of course, long been at the core of Saura's work, particularly in the expression of personal memory as a parallel to national history. But, unlike the situation of his "contemporary" protagonists, the narrative destiny of each of these historical characters brings into focus the gaps and ruptures in the seeming coherence of the dominant discourse of Spanishness. Both films are laden with a series of contemporary analogies to historical events, as was the case in *Lament for a Bandit*; yet each film avoids the simplistic inducements for the spectator merely to read the present into the past. For what is really in question here is not so much history in the form of some eternal return for the Spaniard, but the patterns of popular historicism, nurtured, no doubt, by forty years of Francoism. As Saura showed us in *Lament* and again in *Garden of Delights*, the old regime's privileging of certain historical events served to emphasize the individual's submission to the various institutions that reinforced and replicated Spanishness: the family, the community, and or the Church. In choosing sixteenth-century iconoclastic figures, he now focuses on what are apparently for him exemplary events in national history out of which a counter-tradition might be formed: the ideological struggle between the liberal and humanistic ideal of individuality and its antithesis in the conservative ideology identified with imperialism and later with Spanish fascism. Such a development serves, in a sense, as a conceptual framing device to Saura's cinema in that it situates the struggles that characterize nearly all his films within the broader tensions that define Spanish cultural tradition.

Though we have concentrated in previous pages on the textual moves that promote the spectator's historical reflexivity within individual films, the project is much more far-reaching than any one analysis up to this point might suggest. We may begin to get a sense of its scope as we realize that, though largely intuitive, Saura's preferential emphasis within so much of his film work has been on three decisive periods of Spanish cultural history: the Civil War and the immediate postwar period; the early nineteenth century, and, finally, the sixteenth and seventeenth centuries, often called the Age of the Spanish Empire or the Age of Philip II. Fixing our attention on those moments when the liberalizing spirit finds itself in a symbolic struggle against the forces of a repressive orthodoxy, Saura's films have appeared on the whole to gravitate toward the questioning of the discursive production of a history of Spain that asserts as dominant the submission of the Spaniard to the orthodoxy identified with that narrow vision of Spanishness.

The Civil War is the most easily identifiable of the periods of inquiry, serving as a backdrop for *The Hunt, Garden of Delights, Cousin Angelica, Sweet Hours* and the recent *Ay, Carmela* (1990). In these films, the war is the occasion in which the idea of Spain is made the focus of contention. It is a decisive moment, as Saura perceives it, when the liberal ideal is vanquished and Spain closes in on itself.[2] But the Civil War is also the culmination of a longer struggle that for centuries has pitted the liberal ideal of a humanistic culture against the intolerant impulse of religious and political conservatism. In Saura's reading of his nation's history, one telling antecedent to that scenario of conflict comes with the failure of liberalism in the early nineteenth century. After Spain broke with the rest of Europe, what followed was both a period of national self-estrangement and distancing from intellectual and cultural currents from the outside world. Ironically, as a result of that isolation, foreign artists began to cultivate their own romanticized notion of Spanish themes, the españoladas, of a folkloric and picturesque image of Spanishness. *Lament for a Bandit* treated this material in terms of both the historical forces that shaped this isolation and the romantic imaging of the "vogue of Spain." The later flamenco trilogy focused on the aesthetic spectacle to which the ideological construction of picturesque Spanishness has bound Spaniards.

The more distant, sixteenth- and seventeenth-century material appears less conspicuous in that, until *El Dorado* and *The Dark Night*, it had only been incorporated as textual allusions to a Counterreformation aesthetic and theological forms which, for Saura, expressed the triumph of conservative ideology. In the 1970s his films exploited Calderonian themes in an effort to ground notions of constrained contemporary action within the framework of historically defined cultural positionalities. In *Garden of Delights, Ana and the Wolves,* and *Elisa, My Life* he dramatized individual characters in the throes of their submission to the social apparatus of the family and other social institutions that reproduce the ideology of the state. By inserting the Calderonian intertext in these works, Saura drew an analogy between contemporary events and the repressive cultural traditions that historically forged the Spaniard's notion of him or herself in the world. In *Elisa, My Life,* for the first time, he began actively to explore the heterogeneity of Spanish cultural tradition in an apparent effort to counterbalance the distorted view of Counterreformation conservative ideology.

Contemporary consciousness, as all of these films insistently suggest, is built not only on a system of societal constraints on individual action and

---

[2] Saura, personal interview.

identity, but also on a long historical legacy of social attitudes that arise out of Spain's culture of isolation. While, technically, the age of Philip II (1556–1598) is distinct from the period of Calderón's theatrical production by more than three decades, Calderonian theology derives its conceptual logic from Counterreformation attitudes in general and the political and cultural ideology of Philip's notion of Spain in particular. That ideology, which systematically moved the nation away from liberal and humanistic currents of thought, is so pervasive in subsequent periods of Spain's authoritarian culture that Saura is led to see Francoism as its ideological continuation (Saura 1989, interview).

Tellingly, in both *El Dorado* and *The Dark Night* the image of Philip II frames narration, situating the stories of the rebels against the orthodoxy that Philip's empire embodied. *El Dorado* begins with a credit scene that shows a full shot of Antonio Moro's well-known portrait of Philip II, followed in successive frames with close-up details of the painting. Throughout the subsequent action, constant reference will be made to Philip, in whose name the expedition headed by Pedro de Ursúa set out in September of 1560 in search of El Dorado. The shadow of the ascetic monarch, in effect, transforms the story from an isolated historical chronicle of greed and violence into an exemplary tale of Spaniards and the forging of the Spanish nation. As Saura implies, at the historical moment when it might have been possible to universalize an enlightened Spanish humanistic tradition, Philip projected a notion of Spanishness shaped out of his own sense of Catholicism as a bellicose orthodoxy, thereby dooming the empire and leaving the nation a legacy of cultural intolerance and marginalization in the world. The action of *The Dark Night* is set in roughly the same historical period, situating the abduction and captivity of Juan de Yepes, Saint John of the Cross, against the backdrop of what amounts to a religious civil war between opposing factions within Philip's Spanish Catholic empire.

The underlying tension of both films derives from placing into question the dominance and homogeneity of the historical discourse of that Spanish orthodoxy. *El Dorado* and *The Dark Night* each construct a historically coherent text and then inscribe the places of contemporary interrogation on the margins of narration from which the spectator observes and questions the "historical fiction" of a discursive formation of Spanishness that will be absorbed by future generations as their cultural heritage. The focus of these historical fictions is the problematic status of the individual who rebels against that orthodoxy and, in Saura's view, thereby becomes figurative author of a countercultural tradition. That is to say, by their affirmation of their own individuality, Aguirre and Saint John of the Cross put into cultural circulation the idea of the Spaniard as an authentic individual, making possible the eventual discourse of individuality that will oppose and disrupt the orthodoxy of conservative Spanishness throughout much of modern Spanish history.

Saura's seemingly radical reading of these two "historical" figures appears to be intentionally provocative, inviting the audience's active reconceptualization of their own cultural tradition. At the root of such a strategy lies Saura's conviction, inscribed into the textual order of so many of his films, that history, in the sense of historical reflexivity, is not merely a reconstruction of earlier events. Rather, it lies outside the field of textual representation in the space of interrogation between the spectator and the film. The question becomes one of the contemporary viewing subject's recouping the absent causes of cultural tradition, to use Jameson's terms, so as to grasp the discursive practices that a seemingly neutral process of cultural archeology has constructed for them. In particular, the return to the distant period of Spanish imperial power in these two films serves as an invitation to the spectator to confront the historical origins of Spanishness in light of contemporary notions of individual identity and self-expression.

El Dorado (1988)

El Dorado, the costliest production in Spanish film history, is also an ambitious project of historical imagination. In it Saura attempts not only to redefine the character of the historical Lope de Aguirre as a resistance fighter to Castilian imperialist ideology, but also to involve his contemporary audience in questioning the institutional processes through which the image of Aguirre has been appropriated into a distorted discourse of Spanishness. Thus the critical tension of the film operates on two interrelated planes: the narrative of Aguirre's pursuit of his own dream of Utopia; and the chronicling of his quest by participants in his ill-fated expedition.

The action unfolds through a series of sequences depicting key moments in the thirteen-month expedition that set out in 1560 under the orders of Pedro de Ursúa (Lambert Wilson) from Santa Cruz de Capovocar, Peru, when Lope de Aguirre (Omero Antoniutti) was still only an obscure foot soldier. As a rebel, Aguirre becomes the historical expression of Saura's contemporary view of the politics of personal consciousness, his rejection of Philip II's narrow vision of Spain constituting a defiant act of disavowal of the dominant power structure that has marginalized individuals. The crux of Saura's conception of Lope de Aguirre comes from his interpretation of Aguirre's defiant cry of *"Viva la libertad!"* after his participation in the assassination of Ursúa. The chronicles of the period and later histories read that cry as a confirmation of Aguirre's madness, though Saura prefers to see him in Foucauldian terms, his madness simply constituting a deviation from the norm of subservient Spanishness. "Either Aguirre was a lu-

21. *El Dorado* (1988)

natic," Saura says, "or [his words] were the unequivocal sign that the most powerful empire on the earth was beginning to fall apart" (Saura 1987, 184). It is, of course, the latter notion that moves Saura to transform Aguirre into the precursor if not the frustrated author of American independence in the sense of being the originator of the discourse of liberation.

His rebellion against the Spanish crown, his rejection of both the Church and the clergy, finally, his opposition to slavery are all expressions of Aguirre's liberating imagination. It is not by accident that Saura underscores these attitudes, for they clearly prefigure by three centuries the positions espoused by prominent nineteenth-century Creole leaders of the revolt against the Spanish empire in America, thus reaffirming the notion of Aguirre as the precursor of American independence. But Aguirre's authorship of American independence is, by Saura's design, enigmatic. His character and, indeed, the whole of *El Dorado* function to raise for a contemporary spectatorship the questioning, not only of the fate of the character, but also of the ideal of freedom that his rebellion signified. "What interests me is the anarchist in Lope de Aguirre," Saura admits, "the fight for power, the exacerbated hatred of his country of origin, the desire for independence, the zeal for liberty. Aguirre is representative of many of our features, of our eternal chaos" (Boyero 1988, 32).

The telling irony of Aguirre's historical position, as Saura portrays it, is that he is able to sense the destructive force of the orthodoxy of Spanishness as he observes it around himself, yet is not sufficiently lucid to realize his own entrapment in the cult of a false individualism. Aguirre's first appearance in the film establishes this psychological tension between individual status and the collective order around which his tragic story will unfold. Ursúa has gathered the members of the expedition at the river's edge to witness the launching of the boats that will take them on their voyage to the golden land. Standing on a platform above the assembled soldiers and Indians, flanked by his mistress, Doña Inés (Gabriela Roel), and his captains, Ursúa proudly christens the first boats. Only after several panoramic shots of the assembled group are we able to locate Aguirre, dressed in his armor and mounted on a horse. He, too, is flanked on either side by his close comrades. One makes a comment in low voice about Ursúa's "whore," Doña Inés; the men laugh, but Aguirre does not say a word. He simply looks with piercing eyes at the spectacle before him. His facial grimace reveals obvious disdain. To the roll of drums, two boats are launched, but with the same rapidity with which they enter the water, they break apart and sink. The tropical moisture has obviously rotted the wood. The camera cuts back to Ursúa and the other dignitaries, and then to Aguirre who again remains silent.

As observer-witness, Aguirre assumes a curiously ambivalent position in this scene. He is at once the self-distanced spectator, bearing witness to both Ursúa's humiliation and the derailment of the heroic pretensions of the empire. But he is also a member of that group, placed within the crowd he would inwardly prefer to disown. His efforts at self-distancing from and disavowal of the Spanish cause will ultimately fail because he cannot fully disengage himself from the very ideology of false individualism that the enterprise of the empire has nurtured in Spaniards. Tellingly, Saura gives us no close-ups of Aguirre in this scene. We only view him in shots that situate him within the larger group, thereby highlighting as a spectatorial problem the question of Aguirre's status as an individual, the very problem that will in subsequent scenes motivate his ruthless and violent actions. In later action, when Saura does privilege his protagonist with close-ups, it is to underscore Aguirre's obsession with his own individual will. Consumed as much by the desire for liberation from the oppression of crown as by the need to affirm his own individuality, Aguirre is gradually metamorphosed into the author of his own self-destruction.

Voice-over narration by his comrade and subsequently the secretary of the expedition, Pedrarias (Paxti Bisquert), chronicles Aguirre's trajectory from the margins of action through a period of conspiracy first against Ursúa, then against his replacement, Pedro de Guzmán (Eusebio Poncela), finally to his assumption of a cruel and despotic leadership and apparent madness. As one critic rightly suggests, this narrational strategy recalls the logic of *tableaux vivants* (Heredero 1988, 26). Pedrarias's narration represents a filmic approximation to what might be termed the "official" story of the expedition and Lope's fortunes. This official history is interrupted at various points by the opposing narration of Aguirre's adolescent daughter, Elvira (Inés Sastre). To the crescendo of bloody, violent male rituals of conquest and annihilation narrated by Pedrarias, Elvira provides a counterpoint in an intimate narrative that gives centrality to the female perspective as it conspicuously centers on the theme of family and the shaping of each new generation's perception of its predecessors.

Elvira is attracted to Doña Inés and, through her, begins to question her own father's sanity. Her way of seeing, interrogating, and finally disavowing the world she witnesses ultimately constitutes a subversion of the bellicose, official view of Spanishness embodied by the conquest.

Elvira's enunciative centrality is enforced by key dream scenes at the beginning and end of *El Dorado*. The first of these, immediately following the credits, dramatizes one of the legends of the golden land of which she had heard the Indians speak. That dream, however, only serves as the basis of her interrogation of those around her about the plausibility of the expedition. At the film's end, when Aguirre is felled by fever, he, in turn, has a hallucinatory dream of killing his daughter in the jungle with his own sword. The dream is, in fact, a premonition of his murder of Elvira shortly thereafter. The significance of these two dream scenes involving Elvira is primarily to undercut the apparent linearity of Pedraria's external "historical" narration of the legendary avarice of the Spaniards, juxtaposing it with a more intimate one. In the process, however, these scenes frame the entire film and give a certain centrality to the female figure as a discursive "counter-historical" voice and perspective. Obviously motivated by her emotional identification with her father, Elvira struggles to understand the violent events in which he is involved and to comprehend the terrible things she hears about her father's actions.

Elvira is the extension of a number of Saura's female characters over the years, most importantly, Ana in *Cría!* and Angela in *Hurry, Hurry!* Standing back from events, she silently assesses the world around her, struggling to find a point of identification first with her father, then with the doomed Inés. Emotionally, she is drawn precisely to the two figures of cultural marginalization in the film who have sought to defy the orthodoxy: Inés, the mestiza by her manipulation of the leaders of the expedition; Aguirre by his desire to achieve his own status in the New World. She is, from our contemporary perspective, the witness of the destiny of doomed individuality. Elvira's way of seeing continually reminds us that the price of the dream of empire, of which the pursuit of El Dorado seems only a striking aberrational example, is the continual submission and marginalization of Spaniards to the ideal.

The film ends with an image of the water of the seemingly endless river as Pedraria's off-screen voice, recounting the "official" chronicle of the expedition, tells of Aguirre's savage act of murdering his daughter. That dramatization of Elvira's murder as a premonitory dream, coupled with the voice of history, functions as a bitter epilogue to the film. Saura here juxtaposes the two discourses around Elvira's death and thereby underscores for his audience the centrality of her destiny as victim even more than Lope's. In the official chronicling of the empire, the fate of rebels has been largely suppressed by the voice of official history which, in Pedrarias's telling of the fate of the madman, Aguirre, seems to be admonishing its audience against the excesses of heretical individualism. The chronicler's voice reconstructs the untroubled, homogenous discourse of official history that, from the problematic perspective of the contemporary audience, is seen as patently false.

La noche oscura (1989: The Dark Night)

Fewer than twenty years separate the action of *The Dark Night* from the period of Aguirre's struggle for political independence. While on the surface, the convent in Toledo where St. John of the Cross was held captive would seem totally removed from the Amazon jungles of Aguirre's insurrection, the two films share a common feature in their depiction of the stifling atmosphere created by the orthodoxy of late-sixteenth-century Spain under Philip (Saura 1989, *La noche*). The excess embodied in the expedition in search of a golden land parallels in intensity the excesses of the domestic crusades in Spain against all forms of heterodoxy (Elliott 1963, 243–244). As Saura says, the 1560s and 1570s are an age of ideological civil war within Spain[3] against the threat of real and perceived Protestant intellectual currents, among various religious orders, finally, even within particular orders, as was the case with the Augustinians as well as the Carmelites. J. H. Elliott contends that these feuds were in reality a reflection of the continuing struggle between Renaissance and anti-Renaissance, between those who accepted elements of the humanistic tradition and those who did not (244).

Saura transposes the battle from the exterior world to the mind and spirit of one exemplary combatant, the physically frail but defiant priest, Juan de Yepes (Juan Diego), who, because of his participation in ecclesiastical reforms, was kidnapped and imprisoned for nine months by mem-

---

[3] Speaking of the period of St. John's captivity, Saura says: "Civil War is a terrible theme, and the most terrible part of it is that, as we probe deeper into Spain's past, civil war continually reappears. A fight between brothers, always that duality, that confrontation, that manner of looking at things from two different ways . . . and it has always been imposed by the most reactionary forces. . . . What happens to St. John is like a tiny civil war, a war between brothers, the discalced and the sandeled Carmelites" (Plaza 16).

bers of his own order. *The Dark Night* chronicles the period beginning in December of 1577 when Yepes was sequestered by members of the Carmelite establishment who, in an attempt to force him to recant his statements of belief, incarcerated him in a convent in Toledo. Subjected to systematic torture and deprived of all food apart from bread and water, Juan defied his captors with his display of spiritual resistance. His resolute nature soon touched his jailer (Fernando Guillén), who agreed to provide his prisoner with pen and ink with which to write his poems. During the nine months of his captivity, Juan experienced a number of apparitions, each of which is represented in the body of a woman (Julie Delpy) who appears first in the guise of the Virgin Mary, then as a temptress, and finally as a nun. Resisting all these, and led as if by divine inspiration, Juan de Yepes composed his lyrical poem, "The Dark Night."[4] In August of 1578, with the tacit cooperation of his jailer, he managed to escape from the convent.

The political conflict that frames the action of *The Dark Night* centers on St. John's leadership of the reform of the Carmelite Order, a movement aimed at returning to the austerities of a more primitive religion. Because this movement espoused dispensing with the pomp and ceremony of ecclesiastical intermediaries, seeking instead individual communion with God, Spanish mystics like St. John were considered every bit as ideologically dangerous as the Protestant heretics (Green 1965, 165). Saura's contemporary reading of these events casts St. John's heresy as an implicit affirmation of the autonomy of the individual against the imposition of the collective order of the Church. This provides him the occasion to posit what is finally the motivating question at the root of all his inquiries into Spanishness: the status of the individual within the cultural and political traditions of Spain.

As in *El Dorado*, the affirmation of individuality is situated within a political landscape that bears a striking similarity to Spain in the twentieth century. That analogue to the Civil War is buttressed by visual and narrative markers that place the viewer in the realm of a specific ideological scenario. In the opening scenes, for instance, we see the priest delivered blindfolded to his captors and offered the opportunity to recant his opposition before the Carmelite leadership. Forcing Juan to discard his ragged clothes and to don the white robes, the traditional tunic of the order, the abbot of

[4] One of the essential ingredients in Saura's symbolic rendering of St. John's captivity is the relation between his spiritual liberation from the outside world and the composition of his most famous lyric poem, "La noche oscura," the "Dark Night" of the film's title. Saura is apparently aware that the historical St. John did not actually compose the poem until months after his escape from the convent. Thus, the claim for a historical correction as the basis of the film, as was the case for *El Dorado*, is not at all justified. Rather, it might be argued, in *The Dark Night* Saura seeks to address the deeper significances of historical tradition upon the contemporary audience.

the convent mocks the reformer's resistance: "You see how little effort it takes to obey," he scoffs. His words appear to foreshadow the ensuing struggle which will not be between armies but attitudes, with the battle being waged to break the priest's will and his individualistic spirit. In this, Saura's St. John bears a striking likeness to the protagonist-victims of the earlier political triptych (*Garden of Delights*, *Ana and the Wolves*, and *Cousin Angelica*), except that here Juan's resistance is aligned with the theme of creative authorship, imbuing the historical St. John with a decided contemporary—and, for Saura, autobiographical—resonance.[5]

"What really enthralled me," says Saura, "was what happened in the nine months when St. John was shut up in that foul hole of a prison cell. He came to regard himself as God's messenger, writing poetry at God's dictate, an intermediary between God and the earth. I was fascinated by St. John's conception that the author of his verses was not himself but God, the 'supreme author' to borrow from the words from Calderón" (Saura Medrano 1989). But while St. John may insist upon his authorship in the Calderonian sense of man as the "divine scribe," Saura's spectator is gradually moved to understand that figure of the author in a more suggestive, metaphoric light as a subjective positionality within culture, which enables one to transcend the confining limits and constraints that would otherwise block that individual's self-realization. As in *Elisa, My Life*, authorship is the metaphor for the assumption of an independent, creative position in culture, embracing heterogenous traditions and plural ways of seeing.

Indeed, metaphoric and allegorical allusions abound in *The Dark Night*, transposing the otherwise austere tale of the priest's captivity into a number of significant contemporary contexts. Perhaps the most immediately notable are those that reinscribe the cinematic situation of spectatorship, sight, and the cinematic apparatus into the narrative of St. John's captivity. We begin to sense this in the ways in which Saura shapes the jailer into the figure of an on-screen spectator. Following that now well-established specular strategy within his films, Saura positions the jailer in relation to the drama unfolding before his eyes in much the same way that in *Elisa, My Life* Luis positioned his daughter and his students to grasp the message of their own social and sexual confinement in Calderón's *Great Theater of the World*. This deconstructive specular ritual is restaged in *The Dark Night* as the jailer is drawn first by compassion and then by intense curiosity to observe the various phases of Juan's struggle against bodily and spiritual temptations. He begins to discern the lessons of a forceful individual faith that implicitly challenges the prescribed obedience and submission that his

---

[5] The shift from an external conflict to an ideological coercion of the priest begins to suggest rich parallels with Saura's own spiritual captivity under the dictatorship. His experiences with the censors, which led him to develop symbolic and allegorical modes of communication, mirror St. John's spiritual captivity and creative strategies.

Carmelite brothers have taught him. The jailer's "spectatorship" as a framing device for Juan's story parallels Saura's earlier use of Elvira as an enunciative agent whose presence effectively also "staged" the struggle of the
film's protagonist for a contemporary audience.

The mise-en-scène of Juan's confinement subtly reinscribes the Saurian
motif of the ideological captivity and the liberating practice of seeing, for
gradually, as Juan adjusts to this confinement, he passes through stages of
resistance to spiritual and physical temptation that will enable him to
"shed" the habits of superficial viewing and discover the inner vision that
will lead to his liberation. The priest's cell becomes the symbolic space of
specular captivity, akin to Plato's cave or the mythic site of Baudry's cinematic apparatus. In such a charged space, liberation comes from the beam
of light emanating from the window which sustains the captive's hope of
a world beyond his confinement. That light, suggesting the impermanence
of the cell, reinscribes for Saura's audience a meta-cinematic trope. Cinema, conventional filmmaking, and the cult of realism, are all merely deceptive visual surfaces, confining the spirit if not the body of the viewing
subject. The spark of light, "*esa luz*" ("that light"), as Saura called it in
Sweet Hours, invites the spectator to attempt an act of specular liberation.

The stages of Juan's various temptations and spiritual triumph coincide
with the change of seasons: the moments of deepest despair and greatest
temptation coming in the bitter winter; spiritual emancipation corre-
sponding to the onset of spring. During the latter stage, the jailer brings

22. *The Dark Night* (*La noche oscura*, 1989)

Juan paper and ink and the priest begins composing his poem, "The Dark
Night," which mirrors the stages of his own liberation from worldly concerns and his mystical union with God. Like Juan's spiritual struggle, his
creative act is a protracted effort. Saura stages the completion of the poem
so that it suggests to its audience a cinematic equivalent to the kind of
allegorical ambiguities that have made St. John's mystical poem so powerful. Saura has his protagonist seated at the table in his cell staring into
the light of the candle as he begins to recite verses of his poem. The image
of his face dissolves into that of a woman (Julie Delpy), the same one who
had previously played the various temptresses and devils. Symbolizing the
soul's liberation from the body and its mystical union with God, Juan's
poem recounts how the individual, portrayed by Delpy, has left her house
under cover of night and come to the woods where a man, played by Juan
Diego, embraces her. The scene then dissolves back to Juan's cell as he
recites the final verses of the poem. A sudden lightning bolt shakes him
from his poetic ecstasy as a wind tosses his papers around the room.

Saura attempts to mirror St. John's allegorical style by having Juan Diego and Julie Delpy in the dramatized roles of the soul and God. The result
is a richly ambiguous dramatization of the poetic "dark night" as the individual's deliverance from spiritual and perhaps sexual isolation. Importantly, in this scene, the candle is situated in the foreground in the cell,
further intensifying allegorical alignments between the light of the poet's
creative inspiration and his sensation of divine or erotic union. The scene
is masterfully constructed to designate the moment of Juan's poetic and
mystical rapture as the point of allegorical "contagion," the textual juncture
at which the spectator is made aware of the transposition of actions and
images from one plane of meaning to another: from spiritual to sexual
struggles; from profane to divine spheres; finally, from historical to contemporary contexts. Like the scene of Juan's poetic composition, the film
as a whole invites its audience to read into the priest's struggle a meditation
upon the possibility of their own liberation from physical, ideological, and
spiritual confinement.

Standing outside the frame of the poet's reverie, the jailer views and is
himself transformed by what he sees. In an ironic reversal of his social identity, triggered by his condition of spectatorship, the jailer becomes the captive's liberator, thus opening the film up to another metaphoric intertext,
namely the idea of spectatorship as dual identities of imprisonment and
liberation. Gradually, we discern that within that duality lies the possibility
of the spectator's scopic as well as ideological liberation. That possibility is
symbolically stated in the final scene, when St. John, having been tacitly
aided by the jailer, is at last able to make his escape from the convent. He
ties together his sheets and even his tunic to make a rope from which he
can descend the convent walls. The camera then situates the audience out-

side the convent on one of the hillsides overlooking Toledo. We see the frail priest, naked to the world, descend the wall and begin to walk through the dawn light down the hillside. Having born witness to St. John's spiritual liberation, the spectator is now transposed to the site of his physical liberation.

Throughout the film, Juan's captors attempt to enact their battle on his body through imprisonment and torture. Saura gradually shows us that the real struggle has not been physical, but rather ideological, in the way one sees oneself and, in turn, the way one is led to see the world. The strategy of the film, indeed, the strategy of all Saura's films, has been to dislodge the audience from the throes of that physicality and to reposition them to a place from which they may explore the inner register of meanings, challenging them to free themselves from the shackles of a cultural and spiritual captivity. The image of St. John's descent into the world as though it were a rebirth in the symbolic space of a Castilian dawn affirms the possibility of the triumph of a defiant way of seeing. The allegorical contagion continues as Saura brings his audience to witness that dawn as the moment of spiritual and specular regeneration.

Works Cited

Items listed here are referred to in the text only by the author's name and year of publication, unless further data is needed to distinguish the publication from others by the same author. All translations from the Spanish are my own, except where indicated.

Alonso, Maximiliano. 1968, "Entrevista con Carlos Saura." *Joven Crítica Cinematográfica* (Circular ordinaria) 13 (June 1968): 1–10.

Aranda, J. Francisco. 1969. *Luis Buñuel: biografía crítica*. Barcelona: Editorial Lumen.

Barthes, Roland. 1974. *S/Z*. Translated by Richard Miller. New York: Hill and Wang.

Bartholomew, Gail. 1983. "The Development of Carlos Saura." *Journal of the University Film and Video Association* 35.3: 15–33.

Baudry, Jean-Louis. 1975. "Le Dispositif," *Communications* 23: 56–72. Translated in *Camera Obscura* 1 (1976): 104–28.

Benjamin, Walter. 1969. *Illuminations*. New York: Schocken.

Boyero, Carlos. 1988. "Carlos Saura: Aguirre es el caos español," *El Independiente* (April 9, 1988): 29, 32.

Brasó, Enrique. 1974. *Carlos Saura: introducción incompleta*. Madrid: Taller de Ediciones Josefina Betantor.

———. 1977. "Entretien avec Carlos Saura (Sur *Cría cuervos* et *Elisa, vida mía*)." *Positif* 194 (June 1977): 3–8.

Bratton, Jean. 1967. "The Stress Is on Geraldine Chaplin." *New York Times*, November 21, 1967: D13.

Braucourt, Guy. 1974. "Un Cinéaste-Témoin." *L'Avant-Scène du Cinéma* 152 (November 1974): 4–5.

Brenan, Gerald. 1957. *The Literature of the Spanish People*. New York: Meridian Books.

Browne, Nick. 1981. "The Spectator-in-the-Text: The Rhetoric of *Stagecoach*." In Caughie 1981, 251–60.

Carr, Raymond, and Juan Pablo Fusi. 1981. *Spain: Dictatorship to Democracy*, 2d ed. London: George Allen & Unwin.

Castellet, José María. 1957. *La hora del lector*. Barcelona: Seix Barral.

Castro, Antonio. 1974. *El cine español en el banquillo*. Valencia: Fernando Torres Editor.

Chase, Gilbert. 1959. *The Music of Spain*. 2d rev. ed. New York: Dover Publications.

Chijona, Gerardo. 1983. "La cámara detrás del espejo: Entrevista con Carlos Saura sobre *Bodas de sangre*." *Cine Cubano* 104: 37–42.

Ciompi, Valeria. 1982. "Entrevista con Saura sobre *Antonieta*." *Papeles de Casablanca* 21 (September 1982): 32–34.

Cobos, Juan. 1963. "Entrevista con Carlos Saura." *Film Ideal* 124 (July 15, 1963): 413–17.

Cohn, Bernard. 1969. "Entretien avec Carlos Saura." *Positif* 110 (November 1969): 27–33.

Egea, José Luis, and Santiago San Miguel. 1962. "Entrevista con Carlos Saura." *Nuestro Cine* 15 (December 1962): 33–35.

———. 1964. "Llanto por un bandido." *Nuestro Cine* 34 (October 1964): 58–62.

Elliott, J. H. 1963. *Imperial Spain: 1469–1716*. New York: Mentor.

Fiddian, Robin, and Peter W. Evans. 1988. *Challenges to Authority: Fiction and Film in Contemporary Spain*. London: Tamesis Books Limited.

Font, Domènec. 1976. *Del azul al verde: El cine español durante el franquismo*. Barcelona: Editorial Avance.

Foucault, Michel. 1972. *The Archeology of Knowledge*. Translated by A. M. Sheridan Smith. New York: Pantheon Books.

———. 1977. "What Is an Author?" *Language, Counter-Memory, Practice*. Ithaca: Cornell University Press, 113–38.

Fuentes, Inmaculada, de la. 1981. "Pasarlo bien es bueno para todos: Entrevista con Elías Querejeta." *El País Semanal* 244 (December 13, 1981): 12.

Fusi, Juan Pablo. 1985. *Franco: autoritarismo y poder personal*. Madrid: Ediciones El País.

Galán, Diego. 1975. "El cine político." In Lara, 87–107.

———. 1979. "La libertad de Carlos Saura." *Triunfo* 872 (October 13, 1979): 48–50.

———. 1974. *Venturas y desventuras de La prima Angélica*. Valencia: Fernando Torres Editor.

Green, Otis H. 1965. *Spain and the Western Tradition: The Castilian Mind in Literature from El Cid to Calderón*. Madison and Milwaukee: University of Wisconsin Press.

Gubern, Román. 1979. *Carlos Saura*. Huelva: Festival de Cine Iberoamericano.

———. 1981. *La censura: función política y ordenamiento jurídico bajo el franquismo (1936–1975)*. Barcelona: Editorial Península.

———. 1973. *Cine contemporáneo*. Barcelona: Editorial Salvat.

———. 1974. "La oscuridad del cine." *Cuadernos para el diálogo*. Número Extraordinario 42 (August 1974): 294–96.

———. 1977. *Raza: un ensueño del general Franco*. Madrid: Ediciones 99.

———, and Domènec Font. 1976. *Un cine para el cadalso: 40 años de censura cinematográfica en España*. Barcelona: Editorial Euros.

Harguindey, Angel S. 1980. "Berlanga y Saura atacan de nuevo." *El País Semanal* 180 (September 21, 1980): 14–19.

———. 1975. "Entrevista con Carlos Saura." *Cría cuervos*. Madrid: Ediciones Elías Querejeta: 117–130.

Heath, Stephen. 1981. "Comments on the Idea of Authorship." In Caughie 1981, 214–20.

———. 1972. *The Nouveau Roman*. Philadelphia: Temple University Press.

Heredero, Carlos. 1988. "*El Dorado*: el envoltorio de la tragedia." *Dirigido Por* 156 (March 1988): 22–29.

Hernández Les, Juan. 1986. "El cine de Elías Querejeta: un productor con persona-lidad." *Reseña* 167 (September–October 1986): 2–5.

———. 1986. *El cine de Elías Querejeta: un productor singular*. Bilbao: Editorial Mensajero.

Hidalgo, Manuel. 1981. "Carlos Saura: el oro de Berlín." *Fotogramas* 1648 (March 11, 1981): 20–22.

———. 1979. "Saura cumple veinte años." *Fotogramas* 1610 (September 7, 1979): 2–5.

Higginbotham, Virginia. 1988. *Spanish Film under Franco*. Austin: University of Texas Press.

Hopewell, John. 1986. *Out of the Past: Spanish Cinema After Franco*. London: BFI Books.

Ilie, Paul. 1980. *Literature and Inner Exile: Authoritarian Spain 1939–1975*. Balti-more: Johns Hopkins University Press.

Jameson, Frederick. 1981. *The Political Unconscious: Narrative as a Socially Symbolic Act*. Ithaca, New York: Cornell University Press.

Kinder, Marsha. 1983. "The Children of Franco." *Quarterly Review of Film Studies* 8.2: 57–76.

Kovacs, Katherine S. 1984. "José Luis Borau Retrospective." *The USC Spectator* 3.2: 1–2.

———. 1981. "Loss and Recuperation in *The Garden of Delights*." *Cine-Tracts* 4.2–3: 45–54.

Lara, Fernando. 1976. "Estructura y estilo en *La prima Angélica*." *La prima Angé-lica*, by Carlos Saura and Rafael Azcona. Madrid: Elías Querejeta Ediciones: 149–162.

———, and Diego Galán. 1973. "Los feroces lobos españoles (entrevista con Car-los Saura)." *Triunfo* 565 (July 28, 1973): 31–33.

Larraz, Emmanuel. 1973. *El cine español*. Paris: Masson et Cie.

Llinás, Francisco. 1987. *Cuatro años de cine español*. Madrid: Imagfic.

McCormick, John, and Mario Sevilla Macarenas. 1966. *The Complete Aficionado*. Cleveland: World Publishing Company.

Mangini, Shirley. 1987. *Rojos y rebeldes: la cultura de la disidencia durante el fran-quismo*. Barcelona: Anthropos.

Mérimée, Prosper. 1981. *Carmen y otros cuentos*. Madrid: Bruguera.

Metz, Christian. 1982. *The Imaginary Signifier: Psychoanalysis and Cinema*. Bloo-mington: Indiana University Press.

Miret Jorbá, Rafael. 1977. "El gran teatro de Carlos Saura." *Dirigido Por* 45 (June–July 1977): 20–21.

Monterde, José Enrique. 1978. "Crónica de la transición: cine político español: 1973–1978." *Dirigido Por* 58 (September 1978): 8–14.

Ortega y Gasset, José. 1961. "Teoría de Andalucía." *Obras completas*. 5a. edición Madrid: Revista de Occidente. VI: 111–20.

Plaza, José María. 1989 "Carlos Saura: Sin Berlín y Cannes yo no hubiese podido seguir haciendo cine." *Diario 16 Semanal* 387 (February 26, 1989): 11–17.

Pozo, Santiago. 1984. *La industria del cine en España* Barcelona: Publicacions i Edicions de la Universitat de Barcelona.

Rentero, Juan Carlos. 1976. "Entrevista con Carlos Saura." *Dirigido Por* 31 (March 1976): 12–17.

Sánchez Vidal, Agustín. 1988. *El cine de Carlos Saura* Zaragoza: Caja de Ahorros de la Inmaculada.

Saura Medrano, Antonio. 1989. "Entrevista con Carlos Saura: *La noche oscura.*" (Pressbook).

Saura, Carlos. 1986. *El amor brujo: "Guión de mi película y notas sobre El amor brujo."* Barcelona: Círculo de lectores.

———. 1960. "Declaración de Carlos Saura: Ante todo, *Los golfos* es cine revulsivo." *Temas de cine* 8–9 (October–November 1960): 7–8.

———. 1978. "Carlos Saura escribe sobre *Los ojos vendados.*" *Fotogramas* 1543 (May 12, 1978): 20.

———. 1977. "Carlos Saura escribe sobre su última película (*Elisa, vida mía*)." *El País Semanal.* (February 20, 1977): 4–5.

———. 1987. *El Dorado: Guión, fotogramas, documentos e historia de mi película.* Barcelona: Círculo de lectores.

———. 1984. "Historia de nuestra película." *Carmen: el sueño del amor absoluto* by Carlos Saura and Antonio Gades. Barcelona: Círculo de Lectores: 46–56.

———. 1989. "La noche de San Juan (*La noche oscura*)." *ABC* February 17, 1989: N. pag.

———. 1989. Personal interview, June 14, 1989.

———. 1962. "Por una mayor libertad de cámara: los nuevos sistemas de rodaje." *Nuestro Cine* 10 (April 1962): 29–32.

———. 1978. "Recuerdos de la guerra civil." *Penthouse* (Spanish ed.) 8 (November 1978): 109–11; 147; 156–57.

———. 1961. "Le Retour en Espagne." *Positif* 42 (November 1961): 26–30.

Silverman, Kaja. 1988. *The Acoustic Mirror.* Bloomington, Indiana: Indiana University Press.

Stephanson, Anders. 1988. "Regarding Postmodernism: An Interview with Fredric Jameson." in Ross 1988, 3–30.

Tubau, Iván. 1983. *Crítica cinematográfica española: Bazin contra Aristarco: la gran contraversia de los años 60.* Barcelona: Edicions Universitat de Barcelona.

Vázquez Montalbán, Manuel. 1987. *Los demonios familiares de Franco.* Barcelona: Planeta.

Vernon, Kathleen. 1986. "Re-viewing the Spanish Civil War: Franco's Film *Raza.*" *Film and History.* 16.2: 26–34.

Villegas, Marcelino. 1976. "Entrevista con Mario Camus." *Dirigido Por* 32 (April 1976): 12–16.

Selected Bibliography

Alameda, Sol. 1979. "Carlos Saura: El cine a su manera," *El País Semanal* 135 (November 11, 1979): 12–19.

Alcalá, Manuel. 1982. "Deprisa, deprisa." *Cine para leer: 1981* Bilbao: Editorial Mensajero: 131–35.

Alcover, Norberto. 1978. "Los ojos vendados." *Cine para leer: 1978.* Bilbao: Editorial Mensajero: 273–78.

———. 1975. "Carta abierta a Carlos Saura." *Hallazgos, falacias y mixtificaciones del cine de los '70.* Bilbao: Editorial Mensajero: 323–28.

———. 1977. "Elisa, vida mía." *Cine para leer: 1977.* Bilbao: Editorial Mensajero: 162–65.

Aude, Françoise. 1979. "Le Temps du Bunker (*La madriguera*)." *Positif* 219 (June 1979): 56–57.

Batlle, Joan. 1978. "El teatro de la tortura (*Los ojos vendados*)." *La mirada: textos sobre cine* 4 (October 1978): 67–69.

Benet, Juan. 1975. "Prólogo," *Cría cuervos* by Carlos Saura. Madrid: Elías Querejeta Ediciones: 9–16.

Besas, Peter. 1985. *Behind the Spanish Lens.* Denver: Arden Press.

Blanco Vega, José Luis. 1976. "*Cría cuervos.*" *Cine para leer: 1976.* Bilbao: Editorial Mensajero.

Blanco, Gabriel. 1977. "Cine y Psicología: *Elisa, vida mía.*" *Cinema 2002* 32 (October 1977): 34–40.

Calleja, Pedro. 1988. "Carlos Saura: La culminación de un sueño (*El Dorado*)." *Fotogramas* 1741 (May 1988): 54–58, 86.

Caparrós Lera, José María. 1978. *El cine político visto después del franquismo.* Barcelona: Dopesa.

———. 1976. *El cine de los años 70.* Pamplona: Eunsa.

Castellet, José María, et al. 1977. *La cultura bajo el franquismo.* Barcelona: Ediciones de Bosillo.

Caughie, John. 1981. *Theories of Authorship.* London: Routledge & Keegan Paul.

Clouzot, Claire. 1974. "Entretien avec Carlos Saura." *Ecran* 31 (December 1974): 75–76.

Declós, Tomás. 1983. "El cine español se defiende del triunfalismo." *El País: Artes* 189 (June 25, 1983): 1.

D'Lugo, Marvin. 1983. "Carlos Saura: Constructive Imagination in Post-Franco Cinema. *Quarterly Review of Film Studies* 8.2 (Spring 1983): 37–45.

———. 1986. "Historical Reflexivity: Saura's Anti-Carmen." *Wide-Angle* 9.3: 52–61.

Ferreira, Patricia. 1979. "Mamá cumple años." *Fotogramas* 1614 (October 5, 1979): 36.

Fernández-Santos, Angel. 1983. "Saura en la casa de los dioses." *El País: Artes* 189 (June 25, 1983): 4.

Frugone, Juan Carlos. 1987. *Rafael Azcona: atrapado por la vida.* Valladolidad: 32 Semana de Cine.

Galán, Diego. 1979. "Los americanos no quieren cine español." *Triunfo* 869 (September 22, 1979): 44–45.

García Escudero, José María. 1971. *Cine para el año 2000.* Madrid: Zero.

———. 1967. *Una política para el cine español.* Madrid: Editorial Nacional.

García Rayo, Antonio. 1980. "La década de los setenta en el cinematógrafo español." *Cinema 2002* 61–62 (March–April 1980): 24–28.

Gil de Muro, E.T. 1983. "Dulces horas." *Cine para leer: 1982.* Bilbao: Editorial Mensajero: 135–36.

Grant, Jacques. 1975. "Entretien Avec Carlos Saura." *Cinema 75* 201–2 (September–October 1975): 176–85.

Guerín, José Luis. 1980. "El cumpleaños de Carlos Saura." *Cinema 2002* 59 (January 1980): 56–63.

Haro Tecglen, Eduardo. 1975. "La huella de la memoria o el tiempo de nadie." *La prima Angélica* by Carlos Saura and Rafael Azcona. Madrid: Elías Querejeta Ediciones: 9–25.

Heredero, Carlos F. 1977. "Elisa, vida mía: reflexión sobre el transcurso del tiempo en clave de representacion." *Cinema 2002* 27 (May 1977): 46–48.

Hernández Les, Juan. 1981. "Carlos Saura: Se rueda *Dulces horas*." *Papeles de Casablanca* 9 (September 1981): 23–25.

Insdorf, Annette. 1980. "Spain Also Rises." *Film Comment* 16.4 (July–August 1980): 13–17.

———. 1983. "Soñar con tus ojos: Carlos Saura's Melodic Cinema." *Quarterly Review of Film Studies* 8.2 (Spring 1983): 49–53.

Kinder, Marsha. 1979. "Carlos Saura: The Political Development of Individual Consciousness." *Film Quarterly* 32.2 (Spring 1979): 14–25.

Lamet, Pedro Miguel. 1982. "Bodas de Sangre." *Cine para leer: 1981.* Bilbao: Editorial Mensajero: 102–5.

Lara, Fernando. 1975. *Siete trabajos de base sobre el cine español.* Valencia: Fernando Torres-Editor: 219–43.

Labré, Chantal. 1977. "Un rituel de la regression (*Elisa, vida mía*)." *Positif* 195–196 (July–August 1977): 105–8.

Maqua, Javier, and Carlos Pérez Merinero. 1976. *Cine español: ida y vuelta.* Valencia: Fernando Torres Editor.

Macía, Alberto. 1980. "Etica, estética e incapacidad guionística del cine español: aportaciones a una cultura." *Cinema 2002* 61–62 (March–April 1980): 51–53.

Marinot, Hélène and Michel Sineux. 1976. "Le Temps circulaire (*Cría Cuervos*)." *Positif* 85 (September 1976): 64–65.

Martínez Torres, Augusto and Vicente Molina-Foix. 1976. "Carlos Saura y las mujeres," *Cuadernos para la cultura* 163 (June 12, 1976): 58–60.

Méndez-Leite, Fernando. 1965. *Historia del cine español* I, II. Madrid: Ediciones Rialp.

Mermall, Thomas. 1973. "Aesthetics and Politics in Falangist Culture." *Bulletin of Hispanic Studies* 50.1 (January 1973): 45–55.

Miret Jorbá, Rafael. 1976. "Carlos Saura: Estudio." *Dirigido Por* 32 (April 1976): 1–11.

Molina-Foix, Vicente. 1975. "El cine de la distancia." *Cría cuervos* by Carlos Saura. Madrid: Elías Querejeta Ediciones: 133–37.

———. 1977. *New Cinema in Spain*. London: BFI.

Mortimore, Roger. 1978. "Carlos Saura." *International Film Guide: 1978*. London: Tantivy: 46–49.

Oms, Marcel. 1977. "Cinéma espagnol d'aujourd'hui." *Cinema '77*. 223 (July 1977): 8–16.

Paranagua, Paulo Antonio. 1978. "Le théâtre de la cruaté (*Los ojos vendados*)." *Positif* 208–209 (July–August 1978): 105–7.

———. 1981. "Cannes '81: 'Bodas de sangre.'" *Positif* 244–245 (July–August 1981): 92–93.

———. 1979. "Entretien avec Carlos Saura." *Positif* 224 (November 1979): 38–45.

———. 1979. "Les Loups et les Agneux." *Positif* 224 (November 1979): 36–37.

Pérez Gómez, Angel. 1983. "Antonieta." *Cine para leer: 1982*. Bilbao: Editorial Mensajero: 83–85.

———, and José L. Martínez Montalbán. 1978. *Cine español 1951–1978: Diccionario de directores*. Bilbao: Editorial Mensajero.

Pizzuti, Nadia. 1984. "D'une Carmen a l'autre: Entretien avec Antonio Gades." *Films: Ciné-Critiques* 15–16 (September 1983/January 1984): 13–14.

Rodero, José Angel. 1981. *Aquel nuevo cine español de los '60*. Valladolid: Semana Internacional del cine.

Ross, Andrew. 1988. *Universal Abandon: The Politics of Postmodernism*. Minneapolis: University of Minnesota Press.

San Miguel, Santiago. 1962. "Notas a *Los golfos*." *Nuestro Cine* 13 (October 1962): 5–9.

Saura, Carlos. 1962. "Para una autocrítica: notas a *Los golfos*." *Nuestro Cine* 13 (October 1962): 3–5.

Torres, Augusto et al. 1984. *Cine español: 1896–1983*. Madrid: Editorial Nacional, 1984.

———. 1973. *Cine español, años sesenta*. Barcelona: Anagrama.

Various Authors. 1984. *Le Cinéma de Carlos Saura: Actes du colloque sur le cinéma de Carlos Saura. 1 at 2 fevrier 1983*. Bordeaux: Presses Universitaires de Bordeaux.

Vizcaíno Casas, Fernando. 1976. *Historia y anecdotario del cine español*. Madrid: Ediciones Adra.

Index